Wagner

Lithographic portrait of Wagner, circa 1900, by Pierre Auguste
Renoir. The artist first painted Wagner following their brief meet-
ing in 1882, a year before the composer's death. Courtesy, the
Fogg Art Museum, Harvard University.

Wagner

John Chancellor

LITTLE, BROWN AND COMPANY • BOSTON • TORONTO

To my parents

T 10/78

FIRST AMERICAN EDITION

LIBRARY OF CONGRESS CATALOGING IN PUBLICATION DATA

Chancellor, John.
  Wagner.

  Bibliography: p.
  Includes index.
    1. Wagner, Richard, 1813–1883.   2. Composers—
Germany—Biography.
ML410.W1C43   782.1'0973   78–16490
ISBN 0–316–13622–0

Contents

Illustrations

Preface

I AM CONSTANTLY SURPRISED at people's ignorance about the life and works of Richard Wagner, despite the voluminous and ever-growing literature about that great man. Certain zealous Wagnerites, it is true, know irritatingly much about the life of their hero, arguing with each other about the ages of his pets and his favourite bath salts, whilst many non-Wagnerites know disgracefully little about him. It is not uncommon to come across educated persons who are unaware that Wagner was the son-in-law of Liszt; that he wrote the texts of his operas; that he spent many years in Switzerland as a political refugee; that Bayreuth is in Bavaria and not in the Middle East.

This book is written for those who have, perhaps inadvertently, in their intellectual and spiritual journeyings, passed Wagner by. Various factors have, in the last twenty years, led people to take an increasing interest in him. The brilliant success of Wagner's grandsons in 'denazifying' Bayreuth and their original interpretations of his operas revealed to the world many new psychological truths about Wagnerian music-drama. The hundredth anniversary in 1976 of the opening of the Bayreuth festival; its remarkable continuance as a family enterprise; the publication in 1976 and 1977 of Cosima Wagner's *Tagebücher* (Diaries), under lock and key and the subject of lawsuits as to their ownership for many years, have all contributed to the wish to know more about Wagner and his music.

Let us hope that this book will disabuse readers of the many prejudices which persist about Wagner and that they will read it invigorated, even enthralled, by the splendour of his achievement.

Let me also thank certain people who have provided hospitality and other exceptional kindnesses. I am thinking, in particular, of Nicholas and Susanna Johnston, Axel and Camilla von dem Bussche-Streithorst and Franz-Josef and Priscilla Waldburg-Zeil. In the tranquillity of their beautiful homes, enjoying incomparable views of the Berkshire Downs, the Lake of Geneva and the Bregenzer Wald, this book was written. It was then read by August Closs and Graham Storey, those illustrious names in German and English literary scholarship; the former is the author of *The Genius of the German Lyric* and the latter editor of the monumental edition of *The Letters of Charles Dickens*. Both were kind enough to read the manuscript carefully and to suggest certain changes whose implementation has undoubtedly been of beneficial effect.

Burg Glopper
Austria
September 1977

Wagner

CHAPTER ONE
Early Childhood
1813–22

ON 24 NOVEMBER 1813 Jean Paul,[1] the German poet and stylist, remarked that 'the Sun-god has, to this day, separately dispensed the gift of poetry with his right hand and the gift of music with his left; we are still earnestly awaiting the man who, uniting in himself these two arts, will both write the music and the words for his own operas'. These (for Wagnerites) historic words were written in the little Franconian town of Bayreuth in the very year that Richard Wagner was born. On 23 November, the day before Jean Paul's prophetic utterance, Wagner's father Friedrich Wagner was carried off in a typhus epidemic that was sweeping the streets of the Saxon city of Leipzig.

In October, the previous month, Leipzig was the scene of one of history's decisive battles, the *Völkerschlacht*, or Battle of the Nations, when Napoleon was defeated by the combined forces of Russia, Austria, Prussia and Sweden. The great battle raged from 16–19 October and its outcome spelt, at long last, the end of over twenty years of French revolutionary victories. The peaceful, legitimate order of Europe was soon to be re-established. In the early summer of 1812 Napoleon had strode across Germany, its undisputed master, en route for Russia. During the previous years he had, coolly and contemptuously, reorganized the plethora of petty German principalities; he abolished the Holy Roman Empire and declared himself to be Protector of the new *Rheinbund*, or Confederation of the Rhine, whose members – kings, grand-dukes and princes – offered him 'tribute' in the form of men, money and equipment for his campaigns. Over 100,000 of these

[1] Jean Paul, *Vorrede zu Fantasiestücken*, 1813.

men were to disappear in the Russian snow during the retreat of the *Grande Armée*.

On his way to Russia, in May 1812, Napoleon stayed at Dresden as the guest of his loyal friend and ally Friedrich August I, King of Saxony, of the ancient House of Wettin. In this beautiful rococo city on the Elbe Wagner was soon to spend his childhood and later, as *Kapellmeister* to Friedrich August II, to commit certain political indiscretions which would bring him into lasting disfavour with the Saxon royal house.

In Dresden Napoleon held the final international court of his reign; in the royal palace, with the Empress Marie-Louise at his side, he received the Austrian Emperor, the King of Prussia and his numerous royal German vassals. The festivities lasted several weeks at the end of which he left Dresden, with 600,000 men, to undertake the subjugation of Russia. After the disasters of that campaign, in which 20,000 Saxon soldiers perished, Saxony became the battleground for his desperate and brilliant efforts to reassert his authority.

Although other German rulers were impatient to avenge the ignominy of years of French oppression the King of Saxony never for a moment wavered in his support of Napoleon. He was to pay heavily for his obstinate and misguided loyalty. He sent what was left of his army to fight side by side with the French throughout the crucial months of the year 1813, helping Napoleon win the battles of Lützen and Bautzen in May, the month of Wagner's birth, and his final victorious skirmish at Dresden in August. Then came Leipzig. Half a million men took part in the great battle in which Napoleon's troops were outnumbered two to one. The King of Saxony was taken prisoner by the Allies; his last words to Napoleon were to apologize for the 'disloyalty' of his troops who deserted to the other side as soon as it became clear that the French were losing. No wonder that Napoleon said of him, 'J'ai conçu pour lui une grande estime'. Friedrich August, for his part, had seen in Napoleon a clear-sighted genius who would bring about some order in poor fragmented Germany whilst supporting the princes against their own occasionally restive subjects. He was punished for his steadfastness at the Congress of Vienna by being deprived of nearly half his territories and subjects which went to form the new province of Prussian Saxony.

The Battle of the Nations was the most dramatic single event in Leipzig's seven-hundred-year history. After two days of furious fighting in the neighbourhood Napoleon realized that his position was untenable and, as darkness fell, he moved his troops into the city. The streets were soon filled with dead and wounded; the hospitals were unable to accommodate them and thousands of citizens died in the ensuing plague. One of the victims was Friedrich Wagner, lawyer, *Polizeiaktuar* (police clerk) and amateur actor.

Leipzig in 1813, with a population of about fifty thousand, was Saxony's most important city and one of the half dozen largest in Germany. It lacked the architectural and aristocratic elegance of the capital, Dresden, sixty miles south-east, near the Bohemian hills; instead, it could boast of its long traditions in commerce, learning and the arts. The university, founded at the beginning of the fifteenth century, was almost as old as the famous Leipzig fairs, dating back to the end of the twelfth century which, every January, Easter and autumn, attracted thousands of visitors who came, above all, to trade in furs, textiles and porcelain. Goethe came from Frankfurt to study at the university; the boisterous student scene in *Faust* Part I is placed in Auerbach's Keller in Leipzig. As a student in the late 1760s he was struck by the absence of imposing pieces of architecture compared with those of his home town, Frankfurt. When, years later, he returned to Leipzig, he spoke of the huge buildings, looking like castles or half-cities, of the museums and spacious public gardens, which had sprung up since his youth. Leipzig was the birthplace of Leibnitz and Bach was cantor in the Thomas-Schule from 1724 to 1750; the Gewandhaus was famous for its concerts before Mendelssohn became its director in 1835. As a bookselling and publishing centre Leipzig ranked next to Paris and London. In its cultural and intellectual life Leipzig kept proudly aloof from the fashions of Dresden, the *Residenzstadt*, dependent on the tastes of the king and his courtiers. Members of the Saxon nobility did not, with a few exceptions, have residences in Leipzig; they kept to their estates and went to Dresden if their positions at court required it. Leipzig's artistic tastes were therefore fashioned by the members of the bourgeoisie of all classes from the patrician members of the mercantile community to the humbler educated members of the middle class. This was the class to which Friedrich Wagner belonged.

There is no indication that the Wagners occupied any important civil, academic or artistic posts in Leipzig or, for that matter, in other parts of Saxony over the centuries. Wagner himself said that his ancestry stopped short with his grandfather Gottlob Friedrich, a theological student turned customs and excise officer. Great men, however, require ancestors and now, thanks to the painstaking endeavours of several biographers, Wagner can lay claim to forbears and kinsmen as far back as the middle of the seventeenth century. They flourished in and about Leipzig and little villages in Saxony and Thuringia and they were generally *Kantoren* (cantors), parish schoolmasters and organists by profession. Wagner's earliest traceable ancestor is Samuel Wagner (1643–1705), a schoolmaster at Thammernhain near Leipzig, who was born in the midst of the devastation of the Thirty Years War.

Wilhelm Richard Wagner's birth took place on 22 May 1813, at daybreak, on the second floor of the House of the Red and White Lion in the Brühl in Leipzig.[1] His father, Friedrich, who died of typhus six months later at the age of forty-three, was a more interesting person than his pedestrian post of police clerk might suggest. The writer E. T. A. Hoffmann, who met him for the first time in Leipzig during this turbulent year and whose writings were later to fascinate young Richard, described him as an 'exotic character'. He spoke good French, a useful accomplishment, since Saxony was Napoleon's firm ally and the French occupied Leipzig. Friedrich was given the job of reorganizing both the city's legal system and police force. From all accounts he was a charming man and an admirable public servant. He was also a passionate devotee of the theatre, taking part himself in amateur theatricals. As Leipzig had no permanent theatre company – it went every winter to Dresden – these amateur performances filled a gap for the theatre-loving Leipzig public. Friedrich had a part in Goethe's *Die Mitschuldigen* (The Accomplices) and he gave his daughters the names of Goethe and Schiller heroines. Schiller was his real hero: the appearance of a new poem or play by the great man was for Friedrich an occasion of unparalleled excitement. He and his wife attended the first night of the *Jungfrau von Orleans* in the presence of Schiller himself. In Leipzig his plays, with their liberal and idealistic contents, were staged earlier than in Dresden,

[1] Not to be confused with the Brühl Terrace in Dresden, a promenade along the Elbe, laid out by Count Brühl in 1738.

as there the tastes of the king and the court determined the repertoire.

A result of Friedrich's interest in the theatre was his friendship with the attractive and versatile Ludwig Geyer, actor, portrait painter and poet, who married his widow nine months after his death. On several occasions Wagner raised the possibility that Geyer might have been his father. He found it difficult to understand why this handsome young actor, used to a Bohemian way of life, should have taken on the responsibilities of looking after an impecunious widow and her many children unless it were 'to atone for some guilt'. It is true that Geyer and Wagner's mother had a daughter, Cäcilie, six months after their marriage and one could infer that they had been lovers for some time. Wagner tells us that his mother often jokingly complained that his father dilly-dallied with actresses on his way home from work and that she found solace for his inconstancy in the company of their good friend and lodger Geyer.

It can be safely assumed, however, that Wagner was the ninth child of Friedrich Wagner. Like other Wagners he had a fine head and small body. He is himself largely responsible for later discussions about his paternity for he often spoke and wrote about 'my father Geyer'. Certainly the only father he knew was Geyer since Friedrich died when he was a few months old. He must have felt an affinity with his step-father, whose life of debts and vaga-bondage, music and drama resembled his own; his own occasional remarks and small untruths in his autobiography and careful omissions in early 'official' biographies led later writers to return to the subject of his paternity. For the last few years of his life Wagner was no longer the wandering composer, living from hand to mouth, besieged by creditors, with the easy morals of an artist. He was the Master, the founder of a new artistic religion, his wife, Cosima, to be its high priestess for the next forty odd years. This new religion had a philosophy of sorts. It was monarchical and undemocratic, cosy, high-minded and moral; his collected works were for many Wagnerites the Holy Writ of this new religion, and, ironically, respectability was one of its important elements. His many enemies, led by Nietzsche, jealous of his achievement, irritated by the pretensions of Bayreuth or repelled by his apparent 'conversion' to Christianity, seized upon his possible illegitimacy as a means of discrediting him. Added to the insinuation about Wagner's true parentage was the exciting possibility that Geyer might have been a Jew. Geyer, in fact, was not Jewish; he could claim the same sturdy descent as the Wagners. His pedigree also went back to the middle of the seventeenth century and his forefathers were also, for the most part, organists in small Thuringian towns and villages. His father was a lawyer and accountant in Leipzig who lost most of his money and then died when his son was simultaneously studying law and painting. Geyer found himself compelled to turn out portraits to support his family and it was at about this time that he turned to amateur theatricals and became the close friend of Friedrich and Johanna Wagner.

Johanna, Wagner's mother, was the daughter of Johann Gottlieb Pätz, a master baker from Weissenfels, not far from Leipzig. Her mother was the daughter of a tanner. Despite this modest parentage she claimed 'gentle birth' for herself and a mysterious nobleman, probably Prince Constantine of Saxe-Weimar, paid for her education at one of Leipzig's select schools. In spite of this advantage her family were agreed that she was not well educated; Friedrich pointed out Goethe and Schiller taking a walk along the Promenade at Lauchstädt one day, where they had gone for the opening performance of Schiller's *Braut von Messina*, rebuking her, at the same time, for her ignorance of their writings. What Johanna lacked in formal attainments, however, she made up with many other qualities. She was small, pretty, sensuous, placid and humorous, bore Friedrich four sons and five daughters and, later, a daughter to Geyer. Wagner loved her deeply; for him she was a creature of inexhaustible tenderness, wisdom and understanding, spiritually present at every moment of his life, inspiring his art and sustaining him in adversity. He made grateful tributes to her in Siegfried's invocation of a mother's love and Kundry's passionate lament in *Parsifal*. To others she was a more comic figure; she was so small that the maid generally carried her upstairs under one arm when she visited her daughter-in-law Minna; she suffered from 'head-gout' and wore nine caps, one over the other, to keep her head warm.

In August 1814, when Wagner was barely a year old, his mother and Geyer married and the family moved to Dresden where they lived in reasonable comfort. Geyer, apart from his frequent character parts at the court theatre, was in demand as a portrait painter; he was commissioned to paint portraits of members of both the Bavarian and Saxon royal families. He thought, or hoped, that he saw in the little five-year-old Wagner a talent for painting. This did not turn out to be the case although Wagner got as far as copying his step-father's portrait of Friedrich August 1 of Saxony. At a very early age, however, Wagner was captivated by the theatre. Geyer took his 'little Cossack', as he called him, along to rehearsals and Wagner used to watch his versatile step-father design costumes and paint the scenery. Geyer enjoyed the company of this responsive little boy with a large head and astonishingly blue eyes. It was inevitable that the theatre would exert a powerful hold over a boy of Wagner's imaginative sensibility; it had, after all, cast its spell over his father, step-father and most of his more prosaic brothers and sisters. His mother, on the other hand, who knew from experience the dangerous and dispiriting features of the life of the theatre, prayed that her youngest son would never become an actor.

When Wagner wandered amongst the stage properties and mixed with the actors behind the scenes he felt, in his own words, 'lifted from the dull reality of everyday life to the blissful regions of the spirit. Everything connected with a theatrical performance had a mysterious, intoxicating attraction for me.' In addition to the romantic delights of being transported into a make-believe world Wagner's erotic nature was strongly attracted by the *sans gêne* atmosphere of theatre life with its easy morality and spontaneous relationships. This compensated a bit for the fearful intensity of his imagination; there were times for example, at night, when the furniture and pictures came to life and he would wake up screaming. His brothers and sisters refused to sleep near him which only made his frenzy worse. Throughout his life Wagner disliked being alone; when not composing he craved for companionship. Perhaps he feared a recrudescence of those infantile nightmares?

A regular visitor to the Geyers' house at this time was Carl Maria von Weber who moved to Dresden at about the same time as the Geyers to take up the post of director of the court opera. Weber, founder of modern German romantic opera, was attracted by Geyer's light tenor voice and gave him one or two smallish parts in French and German operettas. With Weber's appointment Dresden now had two *Kapellmeisters*, a German and an

7

Italian named Morlacchi. It was still too early for the slumbering German musical giant to snap the silken threads of Italian domination which reigned in every German court, big or small. Weber's appointment, however, was a sign that interesting things would soon be happening in German musical life. Four years later, in 1821, he gave Germany something for which she had been longing – her first romantic opera: *Der Freischütz* (The Marksman). Transcendental influences for good and evil, magic bullets and charmed wreaths, mingled with scenes from medieval legend and German mythology.

Der Freischütz took Germany by storm, not least the nine-year-old Wagner. When his mother first introduced him to Weber at their home the composer asked whether he had ever thought of becoming a musician. Johanna answered that he was obsessed with *Der Freischütz* but had not, as yet, revealed much musical talent. Music had, in fact, been introduced into the Geyer home by two of Wagner's sisters, Rosalie and Clara, both of whom were taught the pianoforte. Wagner, oddly enough, was the only one of his brothers and sisters who did not have piano lessons. He attributed this to his mother's determination to keep him away from any activity which might, directly or indirectly, encourage his theatrical leanings. It was Clara who had originally brought Weber to their home; besides having a warm touch on the piano she also possessed, said her brother, a voice of exceptional sweetness which, to its lasting detriment, was prematurely developed. At the age of sixteen she appeared as primadonna at the Dresden Italian opera in Rossini's *La Cenerentola* (Cinderella).

In Dresden, therefore, the two worlds of German and Italian opera were juxtaposed. Wagner was able to compare them at close quarters and he was in no doubt which he preferred. Weber's visits sometimes alternated with those of Sassaroli, a huge male soprano. On these occasions the respective claims of German and Italian opera were discussed; the latter, still under the grip of Rossini, was favoured by all the courtiers and by Friedrich August I himself. Wagner admitted that the reason why he came down so heavily on the side of German opera was due to the repulsive habits and appearance of this vast, bloated eunuch, whose piping woman's voice, incredible volubility and permanent squawking laughter nauseated him. He compared this grotesque, repellent creature with the delicate, gentle, consumptive Weber, whose lively, yet often hooded eyes, and narrow, fine-featured face seemed sometimes to Wagner to glow with a kind of super-natural illumination. Wagner would sit at the window, trembling with excitement, as Weber limpingly (he had a congenital disease of the hip-joint) made his way towards the Geyers' house – generally at midday – after exhausting morning rehearsals.

It was Wagner's fierce longing to learn every detail of *Der Freischütz*, especially the overture, that made him start playing the piano. It wasn't enough for his sisters to play the passages to him; he had to master them himself. He later staged at home, assisted by schoolfriends, some performances of *Der Freischütz*, using his sisters' wardrobes and his own improvised paintings for decor and costumes. He put on these productions from memory. *Der Freischütz* is, it could be said, an opera in which musical beauty is less important than the emotions which the music arouses. There is nothing musically very memorable about its overture and it is interesting that Wagner should have felt compelled to learn the piano for its sake. The reason lay in its theatrical power; Wagner was a child of the theatre, whatever his mother could say or do, and at this stage of his life music came after poetry and drama in the order of his emotional and artistic needs and interests.

In September 1821 Geyer died. Wagner walked, aged eight, for three hours on foot from the village school at Possendorf, near Dresden, to be present at his step-father's deathbed. He was so exhausted when he arrived that he couldn't think why his mother was in tears. She asked him to play something for Geyer on the piano in the adjoining room. 'What if he has a talent for music?' said the dying man. Next morning, in the grey dawn, Johanna came into the night nursery and went up to each child in turn to say sobbingly that its step-father was dead. 'To each of us she had a special message, like a blessing, from him to impart. To me she said, "He hoped to make something of you".'

This was the end of frail, vital, delightful Geyer whose own verses provide the most endearing memories of him. He wrote line upon line of humorous, affectionate doggerel to his wife and step-children, upbraiding, comforting, encouraging them about one thing or another. Early in 1821 his comedy *Der Bethlehemitische Kindermord* (Massacre of the Innocents) had been produced in Dresden. Written in rhyming Alexandrine couplets it was even praised by Goethe. The theme is about the struggling artist being dragged down to earth from his visionary world by his material-istically-minded wife. This proved to be an accurate description of Wagner's later life with his first wife Minna. But the strain of painting, acting and playwrighting was too much for Geyer. Shortly before his death he went to rest at nearby Pillnitz where Augustus the Strong had built a ravishing summer palace on the Elbe and where Weber had a pretty house. It was in the nearby village of Grapau that Wagner, in an inn, later wrote part of the music for *Lohengrin*.

Geyer dead, Wagner returned, once again on foot, to his school at Possendorf, having lost two fathers by the age of eight. A month later he was removed from this school at which Pastor Wenzel had read him passages from a life of Mozart, Robinson Crusoe and reports about the Greek struggle for freedom from the Turks. This, Wagner claimed, was the beginning of his love for Greece. Equipped with these miscellaneous pieces of intel-lectual property he bade farewell to Pastor Wenzel and went and joined Geyer's younger brother Karl, a goldsmith at Eisleben where Luther was born and where he died.

Wagner's seventeen-year-old brother, Julius, was also living there as an apprentice goldsmith. What was happening to some of the other members of his family at this time? Albert, the eldest, was a twenty-two-year-old actor, living in Breslau; Rosalie, nineteen, was acting in Dresden; Luise, seventeen, followed Albert to Breslau where she went on the stage; Clara, thirteen, was being trained as an actress and singer; Ottilie, ten, and Cäcilie, six, were living at home.

Wagner returned home, after nearly a year at Eisleben, because Geyer's brother unexpectedly married. He does not appear to have said much about the private school to which he was sent in Eisleben other than it having made 'a serious and dignified impression' upon him. Johanna's household now consisted of Wagner and his sisters Rosalie, Clara, Ottilie and Cäcilie. The family lived from the sale of Geyer's pictures and Rosalie's theatre salary. It was in December 1822 that Wagner's education started in earnest with his admission, at the age of nine, to the Dresden Kreuzschule under the name of Richard Geyer.

For the next five years Wagner lived in the beautiful city of Dresden, so different from his birthplace Leipzig. The popular Friedrich August 1 was still on the throne; his subjects had blamed the Allies and not him for the dismemberment of Saxony. His great-grandfather had been Augustus the Strong, Elector of Saxony and King of Poland, that brave, able, sensuous and cultured ruler who established princely absolutism in Saxony and whose court at Dresden was, after Versailles, the most brilliant in Europe. Of his several hundred children the only one worthy of remembrance is the celebrated soldier Maurice of Saxony. His tastes ranged from military campaigning to immersion in the pleasures of the senses. After being forced out of Poland by Charles XII of Sweden he gave his finest regiment of Saxon dragoons to his dangerous neighbour, Frederick-William of Prussia, in return for a dozen porcelain vases. He became a Catholic to qualify for election to the throne of Poland thereby separating the ruling house of Wettin from its Protestant subjects and enabling Prussia later to become the standard-bearer of German Lutheran nationalism. The easy-going Protestant Saxons did not take their ruler's defection to Catholicism too much to heart. They disliked the Prussians and their grim flat-lands; what their rulers did they accepted with an uncritical admiration even when their judgment turned out to be deplorably wrong. They were proud of the beautification of Dresden with palaces, parks, museums and churches, largely the work of Augustus the Strong; it became known as the Florence of Germany, her finest *Residenzstadt*. Dresden no longer had a brilliant court and it had suffered much in August 1813 when Napoleon beat back the allied assault. It had, however, recovered some of its earlier poise and the establishment of a German opera under Weber was an indication that the court was alive to the stirrings of German cultural nationalism. Later, as *Kapellmeister* to the amiable Friedrich August II, Wagner was himself a court servant and his attempts to bring about theatrical and operatic reforms in the royal court theatre form the background to one of the most exciting periods in his life.

CHAPTER TWO

The Young Musician
1822–32

'IT WAS CLEAR to me – beyond any shadow of doubt whatsoever – that I was destined to become a poet.' It was poetry and drama, rather than music, that filled the thoughts of the frail little Dresden schoolboy with the high forehead and shining blue eyes.

During his years at the Kreuzschule (1822–7) intelligent instruction in the classics tempered his exuberant romanticism and his propensity for the 'fantastic'. He had by now fallen under the spell of the novels of his father's friend, E. T. A. Hoffmann, whose peculiar blend of realism and grotesque and gruesome fantasy left an abiding influence. 'I received from this romantic visionary a stimulus which gave me very peculiar ideas about the world.' Against this he began to receive a disciplined grounding in Greek and Latin philology. He was determined to read, in their own language, about the exploits of his heroes in Greek history and mythology. Encouraged by his teacher he was the only boy in the school who translated the first three strophes of the *Odyssey*. This teacher, who was called Sillig, was impressed by his mature translations, by his original poems and also by his efforts in recitation. When one of his schoolfellows suddenly fell dead Wagner's poem on the event was chosen to be read at the funeral. He tells us that it was printed and widely circulated and that his mother folded her hands in pious thankfulness that his vocation had been settled. From this triumph he went on to compose a grand epic in hexameters on the battle of Parnassus; this was interrupted and then replaced by another tragic epic poem on the death of Ulysses.

On 5 June 1826 Weber died in London where he had conducted

the première of his *Oberon* and twelve subsequent performances in the Covent Garden theatre. He had gone there knowing that he would not return to Germany alive. Exhausted by the *Oberon* performances and at an advanced stage of consumption he died peacefully, at the age of forty, in the house of his English host George Smart.

It was the news of Weber's death in June 1826 that turned Wagner's thoughts, from heroic literary themes, once again to music. Weber had arrived in Dresden in 1817, his aim being to found a genuine German opera; he composed during these Dresden years *Der Freischütz* and *Euryanthe* which were to exert over Wagner's mind a greater power than that of any other music except Beethoven's. Many years later, in 1844, when Wagner was *Kapellmeister* in Dresden he arranged, in spite of formidable difficulties, for the removal of Weber's bones from the Catholic church at Moorfields in London to Dresden. The difficulties were of a varied nature – it was feared that the little coffin containing Weber's bones or ashes might have gone astray or be no longer identifiable; the King of Saxony had scruples about disturbing the peace of the dead; Weber's widow regarded the death of her second son as God's judgment on this proposed act of sacrilege. Wagner relished such difficulties. They were all overcome; Weber's remains were fetched from London by his elder son and brought by boat down the Elbe to Dresden; a torchlight procession was formed; Wagner composed the funeral music out of themes from *Euryanthe* and delivered an eloquent funeral oration at the grave-side. At a certain moment during the oration he stopped and appeared to be unable to suppress his emotion. He later denied that this was either nervousness or absent-mindedness on his part but the result of having written out his speech and learned it by heart. 'I was so affected by the sound of my own words that I appeared objectively to myself and felt a different person from the man who was supposed to be standing and speaking there.'

In spite of his egoism and in spite of his belief in his mission to create a new musico-dramatic art form Wagner could and did, with delightful enthusiasm and humility, lavish praise on his great predecessors even if he was less appreciative about the merits of some of his contemporaries such as Schumann or Brahms. Weber always had a special place in his heart; perhaps, during the terrible pause at the internment ceremony, he remembered how he had, as a little boy, worshipped the ground upon which that gentle limping genius with the pale good looks had walked; how his passion for the overture to *Der Freischütz* had introduced him to the piano and how he was soon able to pick out the wonderful themes with his fingers instead of having to depend on the goodwill of his sisters to play them for him. 'My passion for *Der Freischütz* grew so strong that I remember taking a particular fancy for a young man called Spiess chiefly because he could play the overture which I asked him to do whenever I met him.'

It was Weber's death, or so Wagner thought, that rekindled his musical flame. His mother gave him some money to buy scored paper on which he copied out Weber's *Lützow's Jagd*, the first piece of music which he transcribed. He longed to hear the music of *Oberon*. This he could do by going along to the afternoon concerts in Dresden's Grosser Garten given by Zillmann's Town Band.

The mysterious joy I felt in hearing an orchestra play close to me still remains one of my most pleasant memories. The mere tuning up of the instruments put me in a state of mystic excitement; even the striking of fifths on the violin seemed to me like a greeting from the spirit world . . . the sound of these fifths was closely associated in my mind with ghosts and spirits . . . the long drawn A of the oboe, which seemed like a call from the dead to rouse the other instruments, never failed to raise all my nerves to a feverish pitch of tension and the swelling C in the overture to *Der Freischütz* told me that I had stepped, as it were, with both feet, into the magic realm of awe.

This is what Wagner dictated to his second wife, Cosima, forty years later; he was certainly a sensitive child even if he did not, like Mozart and Mendelssohn, stupefy his elders with his musical precocity. It is possible that the even balance of his youthful interests – theatre, poetry and music – held in check the premature eruption of his musical talent. He showed more musical sensibility than the average schoolboy and the harmonic genius, which he later revealed, was potentially present in the excitable little boy's reactions to the afternoon concerts in Dresden's public garden. Destiny was perhaps fashioning and controlling the development of his gifts, allowing them time to coalesce, in preparation for the *Gesamtkunstwerk*, that fusion of poetry, music, drama, dance and the decorative arts.

There was, it seems, thanks to Wagner's benevolent star, some quiet unifying force which allowed this imaginative little boy to dabble here and there and then later helped him piece together his new experiences. Years later another composer, Richard Strauss, described Wagner as a *Kombinationsgenie* (referring to certain passages in *Götterdämmerung*) where the motifs, which had steadily multiplied as the *Ring* operas unfolded, blended and dissolved in an exquisite pot-pourri of sounds. There was no dichotomy in Wagner's creative life, no set of interests unrelated to each other, which was the case with Goethe, for example. E. M. Forster said that in no country other than Germany would a great poet have written that long and boring essay 'Über den Granit'. Many people, it is true, regard Wagner's prose works as the 'granitic' side of his *oeuvre*; even if they are sometimes bombastic and convoluted in style their purpose was to inform his contemporaries of the nature of his much ridiculed and misunderstood new art form. That he was also a critic, and able to intellectualize, aroused the jealousy and suspicions of professional critics. A poet or a composer had no right, they said, to be capable of explaining in prose what he was trying to do. The more clearly he expressed himself the less 'spontaneous' he must surely be as an artist!

The thirteen-year-old schoolboy was doubtless unaware of the inspired eclecticism of his interests:

I was fond of life, merry with my companions, and always ready for a joke or adventure. Moreover, I was constantly forming friendships, almost passionate in their ardour, with one or the other of my comrades, and in choosing my associates I was mainly influenced by the extent to which my new acquaintance appealed to my eccentric imagination. At one time it would be poetising and versifying that decided my choice of a friend, at another theatrical enterprises, whilst now and then it would be a longing for rambling and mischief.

Unlike Mendelssohn and Liszt Wagner's childhood was not that of a *Wunderkind*. Liszt had given his first public recital in 1820 at the age of nine. Wagner, at the same age, was put at the bottom of the lowest class in the Kreuzschule at which the most that was expected of him was that he might learn to work. Even if he had been an only child of doting and ambitious parents, intent on furthering his career, instead of one of many children of a twice-widowed, impecunious mother, it is unlikely that his talents would have developed any faster. The reasons for this are already known; the emotional and metaphysical profundities of his later music dramas, set mostly in a timeless world of myth and legend, found their dramatic and musical expression in a new art form which defied any systematic preparation. The biographer of Wagner, therefore, who is obliged to devote a certain amount of space to his subject's youth, may select episodes from the life of this happy imaginative little boy which perhaps contain indications of his future greatness. We know, at least, that he was not an out-and-out conventional schoolboy. He responded, at times with an overheated imagination, to the heroic, strange, beautiful and grotesque; he loved Weber's operas, both for their musical beauty and for their world of medieval legends and sinister transcendental influences, a world of German mythology and magic bullets. This was properly balanced by the discipline of lessons and by some cheerful friendships.

Some of Wagner's stronger friendships were with dogs. In fact, his attachment to dumb animals was an expression of his general love of nature. He could not bear to see an animal maltreated; he had kissed and thanked the weary horses which had brought him part of the way to Eisleben; he knew every dog in the neighbourhood of his house in Dresden and he and his sister had an espionage system to rescue pups from drowning. Throughout his life he always needed something 'to bark around him'. He even thought of writing a 'History of My Dogs'.

At the end of 1826, when Wagner was thirteen, his elder sister Rosalie, who had been the family breadwinner since Geyer's death, accepted a well paid theatrical position in Prague. She was already one of the favourite actresses who visited that city where as Juliet in *Romeo and Juliet* she held audiences spellbound. Her mother and sisters (Luise, Clara, Ottilie and Cäcilie) followed her there. Their Dresden home was given up and Wagner was sent out to board with a Dr Böhme, whose son Rudolph was a schoolfriend. He found the atmosphere in the Böhme home turbulent after the gentle companionship of his mother and sisters. Wagner's stay with the Böhmes marked the 'beginning of my years of dissipation'. By 'dissipation' he appears to mean little more than boisterous high spirits. It was, however, with the Böhmes that he became aware of the attractiveness of the opposite sex. The grownup daughters of the household and their boyfriends seemed to fill up the small, narrow rooms. 'I recollect pretending to be too sleepy to move so that I might be carried to bed by the girls . . .

and I repeated this because I found, to my surprise, that their attention under these circumstances brought me into closer and more gratifying proximity with them.'

Early in 1827, in the middle of the winter, Wagner's mother collected him in Dresden and took him off with her to Prague for a week. Her methods of travel were, he tells us, unique: 'Until the end of her life she preferred the more dangerous mode of travelling in a hackney carriage to the quicker journey by mail coach so that we spent three whole days in the bitter cold on the road from Dresden to Prague.'

Wagner had no hesitation in setting out for Prague with his mother during that cold winter.

The thought of leaving Saxony on a visit to Bohemia, especially Prague, had a romantic attraction for me. The foreign nationality, the broken German of the people, the peculiar headgear of the women, the native wines, the harp-girls and musicians and, finally, the ever present signs of Catholicism, its numerous chapels and shrines – all this filled me with exhilarating impressions . . . above all the antique splendour and beauty of the incomparable city of Prague became indellibly stamped on my fancy.

A month or two later, in the spring of 1827, Wagner repeated the journey from Dresden to Prague – this time on foot – in the company of his rowdy friend Rudolph Böhme. Shortly before, on Palm Sunday, he was confirmed in the Lutheran Kreuzkirche in Dresden under the name of Geyer for the last time. It is amusing to compare two very different accounts of the impact of this solemn occasion on Wagner's mind. His devoted biographer Glasenapp tells us that the second half of the Grail-theme in *Parsifal* corresponds to the 'Amen' of the Saxon liturgy, both Catholic and Protestant: 'At what time and on what occasions could it have sounded more solemn to him than at this moment?' Wagner, on the other hand, recollects being repelled and embarrassed by the whole thing. His early religiosity, when he had 'yearned with ecstatic fervour to hang upon the Cross in the place of the Saviour', had given way to a spirit of levity. Now, like many other boys, he giggled during confirmation classes and spent on sweets the money which he was meant to give as fees to his religious instructor. 'I realised to my horror how things stood with me spiritually when, during the communion service, I walked in procession up to the altar to the sound of organ and choir. The shudder with which I partook of the bread and wine was so ineffaceably stamped on my memory that I never again went to Holy Communion.'

On their way to Prague Wagner and Böhme fell in one evening with a most strange man whom they met in an inn. He wore a black velvet skull-cap and carried a harp on his back. He sang, played and drank, lent the boys some money and finally, overcome with wine, fell slumped on some straw and was still sound asleep when they left the next morning. Wagner must have delighted in this 'Hoffmannesque' character.

The boys plodded on towards Prague, faint, hungry and penniless in the scorching heat. As they approached the outskirts a fine carriage drew up to them containing two aristocratic friends of his sister Rosalie, the beautiful daughters of Count Pachta. They recognized him despite his blistered face, blue linen blouse and bright red cotton cap. 'Overwhelmed with shame, unable to utter a word, I hurried off to my mother's to attend to the restoration of my sunburnt complexion. For two days I swathed my face in parsley poultices.' On the return journey, when he passed the scene of his discomfiture, he burst into tears, flung himself onto the ground and could not, for a long time, be induced by Böhme to continue the journey. What can be inferred from this episode? Throughout his life Wagner took a theatrical interest in clothes, particularly his own, and unfriendly biographers and critics have often written contemptuously about his dressiness. He obviously felt, on this occasion, that he had, with his urchin-like appearance, humiliated his elder sister of whose gifts and 'connections' he was very proud.

Shortly after this expedition to Prague, during the summer holidays, Wagner went to Leipzig with some other boys from the Kreuzschule. He hadn't been there since he was nine years old when he had spent a few days with his uncle, Adolph Wagner, who was now about to become an important figure in his life.

Adolph was a learned, uncreative and pedantic man; he had disapproved of his brother's theatrical interests and had carved out for himself a limited (but national) reputation as a theologian, philologist and literary scholar. His recognition was secure after Goethe had approved of his *Parnasso Italiano* (1826), a critical edition of Dante, Petrach, Ariosto and Tasso. In a fulsome dedication to Goethe, written in Italian *terza rima*, as 'principe dei poeti', Adolph has an imaginary conversation with the four poets in the Garden of Poetry; each in turn speaks of his admiration for the great Goethe in whose poetry he recognizes the essential features of his own art. It is not surprising that Goethe expressed a friendly interest in this work; he even gave the author a silver goblet.

Adolph Wagner was one of those outstandingly learned Germans of days gone by. Unambitious, he satisfied his modest worldly wants by writing articles on classical philology and by translating from the classics, particularly the Italian classics. Although Germans are tolerant of pedantry in the interests of scholarship Adolph was criticized for his obscure and cumbersome prose; it has been suggested that he passed this pretentious language onto his nephew.

Wagner's first visit to his uncle Adolph in the summer of 1822 had left him with strange, rather disturbing memories. Adolph Wagner had lived in the huge Thomä house in the marketplace where he shared a flat with two spinsters, his sister Friederike and Jeannette Thomä, the owner of the house which she had inherited from her father, a merchant. The King of Saxony stayed here on his visits to Leipzig. The strains of a household with two nagging women were the reason he gave for not being able to have his nephew to live with him after Geyer's death. Wagner remembered the two quarrelling women – Friederike, tall and thin and Jeannette, florid and stout. They put him into one of the royal state rooms with decorations and furniture dating from the days of Augustus the Strong. It overlooked the bustling marketplace where he saw the students in their striking, old-fashioned fraternity uniforms. Before long he was to take a near-obsessive interest in the Leipzig *Studententhum*, or student life.

The nights in his room in the Thomä house had terrified him. The portraits of high-born dames in hooped petticoats, with their youthful faces and powdered hair, turned into ghosts, which haunted him every night: 'To sleep alone in this distant chamber, in that old-fashioned state bed, beneath those unearthly pictures, was a constant terror to me.' Adolph occupied a dark room at the back of the house; there he sat surrounded by books and wearing a tall, pointed felt cap.

When Wagner returned to Leipzig six years later he found a certain change in his uncle's way of life. At the age of fifty Adolph had married Sophie, sister of his old friend Amadeus Wendt. He had left the Thomä house and moved to a quieter part of the town. Apart from that there had been no radical change. 'I am still the same old horse,' he said, '. . . but now belonging a little to my Sophie.'

Wagner and his school-fellows performed the final stage of their journey to Leipzig with great panache; they drove into the town in open carriages, their main purpose being to impress the university students. They had taken the precaution beforehand of removing all the spurious and extravagant student attire with which they had bedecked themselves on the way. Wagner's blood was tingling to see, once again, those glamorous, privileged, swaggering undergraduates. Six years before he had been much taken by the general effect of their long hair, quaint costumes, black velvet skull-caps and shirt collars turned back from their bare necks.

Towards the end of 1827 Wagner's mother moved from Prague to Leipzig; her daughter Luise, who later married the publisher Friedrich Brockhaus, had joined the cast of the Leipzig theatre. At Christmas Wagner also moved to Leipzig from Dresden, thus bringing his five years at· the Kreuzschule to a somewhat abrupt conclusion. We know from his earliest recorded letter to the publisher Schott in Mainz, dated 6 October 1830, that he and his family lived in the Pichhof outside the Halle Gate. It was the lure of Leipzig student life, rather than the prospect of rejoining his mother and sisters, that prompted him to leave Dresden.

How happy, ebullient and conformist was our schoolboy hero at this early stage of his marvellous life. We shall see over and over again, when reading his writings and listening to his operas, that Wagner was not an introverted or arrogant outsider, cultivating his art in an ivory tower. He took an immediate and passionate interest in any new, emergent fashion – not only in music but in more or less any area of thought and feeling. He was, in many ways, the incarnation of the nineteenth century; his quivering sensibility reacted compulsively and unpredictably to all the exciting and contradictory forces which characterized that century – socialism, nationalism, classicism, romanticism. He was, of course, as an artist, aware of the influences, literary, philosophical and musical, which were pervading Germany. To the eye and mind of the critic was added the genius of the creative artist. He was to feel that destiny had chosen him, through the expression of a new art form, to lead his countrymen and the world to the realization of their highest faculties as expressed, in this case, in the *Gesamtkunstwerk*. What later infuriated many insipid and querulous critics was that this composer-poet was also a hard-headed, hard-hitting man of action. He swore, rioted, drank, gambled, womanized; he was kind, gregarious and witty; he was 'normal'.

So young Wagner (he had dropped the surname 'Geyer'), cheerful, intelligent and excitable, came to Leipzig, his heart set on becoming a student. His first serious disappointment was that he was put in a lower form (upper third) in the Nikolai-Schule than that which he was in in the Kreuzschule in Dresden (second). This indignity hurt his pride and probably explains his defiant attitude to the school which was one of the two best in Leipzig, the other being the Thomas-Schule[1] where he later went. 'My disgust at having to lay aside my Homer, from which I had already made written translations of twelve songs, and take up the lighter Greek prose writers was indescribable. It hurt my feelings so deeply that I never made a friend of any teacher in the school.' He remained, however, at the Nikolai-Schule for over two years until Easter 1830. His recalcitrance at school forced him to find other outlets for his exuberant spirits. They took different forms.

Firstly, he sought the company of his uncle, Adolph. In his manner and conversation Adolph was very attractive; he had a rich and sonorous voice and could always be prevailed upon to display its qualities by reciting from the classics. Uncle and nephew went for long walks together: 'I called daily to accompany him on his constitutional walk . . . we provoked the smiles of those passers-by who overheard our profound and earnest dis-cussions.' These conversations and the use of Adolph's library started Wagner on his life-long habit of voracious and discursive reading. 'I tasted eagerly of all branches of literature without obtaining a real grounding in any of them.' He read the works of his uncle's famous friend Ludwig Tieck; also Friedrich Schlegel's erotic novel *Lucinde* and the Tannhäuser saga.

Secondly, he threw himself with passion into the completion

[1] Both these schools dated from the early sixteenth century.

of a colossal 'Shakespearian' tragedy he had been planning: *Leubald und Adelaïde*. It is a juvenile *Sturm und Drang* exercise, a verse phantasmagoria lifted from *Hamlet, Macbeth, King Lear, Götz von Berlichingen* and one or two other romantic tragedies. The wretched Leubald, more of a man of action than Hamlet, killed forty-two people during the play; Wagner was compelled to bring most of them back as ghosts in order to repeople the depleted stage. Nobody knew of this enterprise except his sister Ottilie; once, when he was reciting to her in secret some spine-chilling scene, a thunderstorm came on and she implored him to stop. *Leubald* can be seen as the first of Wagner's 'seminal works', to be followed during the next seven or eight years by several others – *Die Hochzeit, Die Feen, Das Liebesverbot* – all containing certain ideas, themes and phrases which are later recognizable in the master's mature works.

Wagner later spoke with a chuckle about this piece of 'Gothick' horror. He regretted the disappearance of the manuscript but remembered clearly the affected handwriting and the 'backward-sloping tall letters with which I tried to give it an air of distinction'. The manuscript of *Leubald* had not, as a matter of fact, disappeared; it was found after Wagner's death by his English admirer the Hon. Mrs Burrell in the possession of Natalie, Minna Wagner's illegitimate daughter, from whom she bought it. The handwriting is not as affected as Wagner claimed; in its neatness, its meticulous punctuation, and the careful presentation of the verses, Wagner set a standard from which he never departed. However disorderly were certain periods of his life everything he committed to paper – letters, essays, poems, scores – was exquisitely neat. He would no doubt have liked to include *Leubald* in his *Gesammelte Schriften* (Collected Works), just as Heine had had reprinted *Michael Ratcliff*, that quaintly gruesome product of his *Sturm und Drang* period, set in Scottish mists.

Leubald is a mixture of Hamlet and Hotspur; he faithfully obeys the injunction of his murdered father's ghost to liquidate every member of the house of Roderick, the murderer. He is driven mad by the importunities of his forty-two victims, who return as ghosts to torment him, and partly because he falls in love with Roderick's daughter, the only surviving member of the clan, whom Wagner calls Adelaïde after the heroine of Beethoven's song. Leubald, now raving mad, stabs her; she caresses him forgivingly, draws him to her bosom on which, demented by grief, he expires, her blood slowly enveloping his dying body. Is Adelaïde already showing the magnanimity of the true Wagnerian heroine? Has she redeemed the tormented Leubald by her expiatory act of love? Her faithful maid, Gündelchen, dies at her feet and Astolf, like King Mark in *Tristan und Isolde*, delivers a benign valedictory address over the body of Leubald in lines which might have been taken from that opera.

Wagner knew that the day was not far off when his mother would learn that he had been neglecting his lessons. He decided to produce his masterpiece as proof that he had not been idle. He sent it first to Adolph with a long, flattering letter, asking him to explain to his family that his time had been well spent in writing a work whose obvious merits owed so much to those long periods of literary intercourse enjoyed by uncle and nephew. Adolph reacted disconcertingly; he was horrified that this farrago of romantic nonsense was all that his nephew had to show from their elevated literary conversations and he visited Johanna Wagner to apologize for the deleterious influence which he had had over her son by corrupting him with conversations unsuited to his age. 'To this day I fail to understand why he showed so little sense of humour in judging my behaviour,' said Wagner.

Thirdly, another result of his failing to work at school was a sudden and dramatic quickening of his musical interests. The study of music was his chief interest from 1828 to 1832. The death of his beloved Weber had temporarily turned his thoughts towards music. The following year, on 26 March 1827, Beethoven died in Vienna. Wagner had shortly before heard the *Fidelio* overture in E major and been much impressed. He asked his sisters about Beethoven and they told him that he had just died. Beethoven now replaced Weber as his musical hero. Soon after arriving in Leipzig he flung himself into Beethoven's music. He could hear at the Gewandhaus[1] in Leipzig a lot of music which was not performed at Dresden. Every winter all Beethoven's symphonies were performed there without a conductor, but under the leadership of the *Konzertmeister* (First Violin). It was here that Wagner first heard a Beethoven symphony, the Seventh in A major. 'The effect on me was indescribable. . . . I conceived an image of him in my mind as a sublime and unique supernatural being. . . . This

[1] So called because originally a drapers' hall.

image was associated in my brain with that of Shakespeare; in ecstatic dreams I met them both and spoke to them and on awakening I found myself bathed in tears.'

He found on the piano his sister Luise's score of Beethoven's incidental music to Goethe's *Egmont*. This led to the inspired thought of setting *Leubald* to music. 'After everyone had deafened me with their laments over lost time and perverted talents I consoled myself with a wonderful secret – the work could only be properly judged when set to music and I resolved to start composing immediately.' His plan was that each of the many ghosts should be associated with a particular musical instrument. As Wagner had had no musical training of any kind he had difficulty in deciding how to begin. It was these very difficulties that started him on his musical career. The first thing he did was take out a copy of Logier's *Method of General-bass*[1] from Friedrich Wieck's lending library. Wagner tells us that Wieck was the first of the many creditors who pestered him throughout his life. 'I borrowed the book on the weekly payment system in the fond hope of being able to pay out of my weekly pocket-money. The weeks ran into months. . . . Wieck, whose daughter Clara afterwards married Robert Schumann, kept on sending me tiresome reminders of this debt; when the bill finally approximated the price of the book I had to make a clean breast of the matter to my family.' Thus another secret was out; he was engaged in clandestine musical studies.

Wagner's study of *General-bass* did not progress as quickly as he had hoped; he supplemented this with secret lessons from Gottlieb Müller, a member of the Gewandhaus orchestra and a passionate admirer of Beethoven. It was after he had been a pupil of Müller for at least a year that he started, in about the middle of 1829, to write his first musical pieces.

Wagner's decisive experience in April 1829 was hearing Wilhelmine Schröder-Devrient as Leonore in *Fidelio*. His decision to become a professional musician was made at that moment. 'When I look back upon my whole life I can find no event that made so profound an impression on me . . . after the performance I rushed into a friend's house and wrote a short note to the singer

[1] General-bass is synonymous with figured bass, thorough-bass and basso continuo, i.e. a bass which 'continues' or 'goes through' the whole composition, providing an unbroken background to the music.

in which I told her that my life had, from that moment, acquired its true significance and that if, in days to come, she should ever hear my name praised in the world of art she must remember that she had, that evening, made me what I had sworn it was my destiny to become.' He delivered the note at her hotel and rushed like someone possessed into the night. This famous singer was later to become his friend (and creditor) and to sing in *Rienzi, Der fliegende Holländer* and *Tannhäuser*.

Wagner professed to have learnt nothing from Müller; he found his lessons deadly boring and Müller, in his turn, complained that his pupil failed to pay his modest fees. For Wagner music was at this time 'a noble and mystic monster and any attempt to regulate it lowered it in my eyes'. Instead his brain was seething with some of the musical characters in Hoffmann's stories (*Phantasiestücke*) – Kreisler, Krespel and others. Nevertheless, he must have learned more from Müller than he admitted otherwise he could hardly have written the following impressive list of compositions up to the autumn of 1831:

1829 Piano sonata in D minor
      String quartet in D major
      Piano sonata in F minor

1830 Overture in B major
      Overture to Schiller's *Die Braut von Messina*
      Overture in C major

1831 Composition for Goethe's *Faust*
      Piano sonata for 4 hands in B major
      Overture in E flat major

All these works have disappeared.

Wagner left the prosaic Müller who must have wondered what to make of his pupil's exuberant musical mysticism. It was at this time that his reading of Hoffmann's stories reduced him to a state of musical dementia when he had visions similar to those experienced when first hearing *Der Freischütz*: 'I had day-dreams in which the keynote, third and dominant, seemed to take on living forms which revealed to me their mighty meaning; the notes I wrote down were raving mad.' In this mood it was difficult for him to find a conventional teacher. He carried on alone along the difficult path of self-education. He completely gave up his general studies, stayed away from the Nikolai-Schule and devoted himself to music. He spent hours copying out the scores of his favourite composers in that neat handwriting which has always been so much admired. Too much should not be made of Wagner's lack of formal musical education. He could, like many musically gifted children, read music like a natural language from an early age. Within a couple of years of Beethoven's death he was reading his quartets and symphonies whose subtleties had yet to be understood by professional musicians. Heinrich Dorn, who was *Kapellmeister* at the Leipzig theatre at this time doubted whether any young composer was more familiar with Beethoven's works than the eighteen-year-old Wagner. 'He copied the scores of almost all his overtures; he went to bed with the sonatas and rose with the quartets: the songs he sang and the quartets he whistled, for he made no progress with his playing. In short, it was a veritable *furor teutonicus.*'

Wagner's first technical, unaided tour-de-force was to write a piano arrangement of the full score of the Ninth Symphony. This had not previously been done; the public response to this symphony had been so indifferent that the publishers decided against commissioning a piano arrangement. When, therefore, on 6 October 1830 Wagner wrote to Schott in Mainz (his first recorded letter) enclosing his piano score for their consideration they declined to publish it. They kept his manuscript, however, and gave him one or two of Beethoven's published compositions in exchange. Years later, in 1872, Franz Schott returned the manuscript; as an expression of thanks Wagner wrote, for his wife Betty Schott, the *Albumblatt* (Album-leaf) in E flat major.

Beethoven's Ninth Symphony can, together with *Der Freischütz*, Hoffmann's tales, and Schröder-Devrient as Leonore, claim to have provided Wagner with one of those impassioned experiences, which he enjoyed so much describing:

It became the mystical goal of all my strange thoughts about music. I had heard that Beethoven wrote it when he was half mad. This was quite enough to arouse in me a passionate desire to study this strange work. At the very first glance at the score I felt irresistibly attracted by the long sustained pure fifths with which it opens . . . they seemed to form the spiritual keynote of my own life . . . the first thing to be done was to make this score, which surely contained the secret of all secrets, my own by laboriously copying it out ... once, when I was doing this, the sudden appearance of the dawn had such an effect upon my excited nerves that I jumped screaming into bed, thinking that I had seen a ghost.

Wagner's family gradually came to the conclusion that he was in earnest about wishing to become a musician. It was decided that a musician must be able to play some instrument with proficiency, preferably the piano. This Wagner refused, but he reluctantly agreed to have violin lessons with Robert Sipp, a member of the Leipzig orchestra. At the end of the century Sipp, aged ninety-three, said his illustrious pupil was 'lazy and would not practise'. He also agreed to receive instruction in harmony from the same wretched Müller whom he had never paid for the secret lessons which he had found so boring.

The fourth result of Wagner's disenchantment with the Nikolai-Schule, which he quitted officially at Easter in 1830, was what he called with relish his life of unbridled licentiousness and depravity, tempered, as it must have been, by his earnest musical studies, first as a schoolboy and later, in 1831, as a university student. 'After I got to Leipzig, I quite gave up my studies and regular school attendance.'

Wagner's biographer, Glasenapp, described the Leipzig of those days as 'sparkish'; the morals of polite society were notoriously easy-going. The Leipzig trade fairs had, throughout the centuries, engendered a certain cosmopolitanism; the town's geographical position had shown in 1813 and was about to show again in September 1831, with the arrival of large numbers of Polish freedom fighters fleeing from their Russian oppressors, that it lay unavoidably on the trans-European thoroughfare.

When Wagner returned to Leipzig from Dresden in 1827 he found, to his distaste, that the area around his old home on the Brühl had been taken over by Polish Jews who were doing a brisk trade in furs. Like Hoffmann's characters they amused and repelled him, in their shaggy pelisses and high fur caps, as they gesticulated wildly and bartered in broken German.

This, then, was the Leipzig where Wagner was about to sow his wild oats: 'I now entered into all the dissipations of raw manhood.' Maybe he wished to titillate the doting Cosima who sat there all agog, her pencil poised to take down the next sublime truth from her Husband, Friend and Master. His memoirs do not really leave one with the impression that his behaviour was all that depraved. The intensity of his musical experiences must anyhow have consumed quite a lot of his energy. His 'dissipation' was probably, as he suggested himself, a means of compensating for his inability or difficulty in having well-balanced friendships: 'In the midst of rowdyism and ragging of the most foolish kind I remained quite alone and it is possible that these frivolities formed a protective hedge around my inmost soul which needed time to grow to its natural strength and not to be weakened by reaching maturity too soon.'

Once again, as at the Kreuzschule, destiny saw to it that precocity would not cast a shadow over his future. It is touching to see how eagerly and poignantly the fearless, fiery Wagner entered into the students' life. Certain episodes stand out for their funniness or pathos; his clothes, first of all. After entering the Thomas-Schule in June 1830 he helped organize a club which masqueraded as a students' organization. He presided at the inaugural meeting wearing white leather breeches and great jack boots. At the beginning of the following year, although he never took the qualifying examination, he managed to realize his fervent aspiration to become a student; no sooner was he enrolled as a *studiosus musicae* than he rushed off to apply for election to the Saxonia Club, the smart university club. The term was about to end and new elections would not be held until the vacations were over. It was essential for him to be elected at once if he was to wear the gaudy club colours on which he had set his heart. He also acquired a splendid 'Saxon' cap, richly embroidered in silver, which belonged to a man called Müller, later a prominent police constable in Dresden. 'I was seized with such a violent craving for this cap that I managed to persuade him to part with it as he wanted money to go home.'

Gambling also cast its 'devilish snares' around him for a time. He got together with some of the smartest members of the Saxonia to start a gambling club. He wanted to make money quickly to pay off his debts but soon found that, as with the study of Logier's *General-bass*, things were not as simple as they looked. 'To win was not an easy matter and for three months I was such a victim of the rage for gambling that it drove every other interest out of my mind.' During this period he became indifferent to those things which had attracted him to the student life. 'I lost myself in the smaller gambling dens of Leipzig where the student scum congregated.' He climbed into the house at dawn; his family started to ignore him, his sister Rosalie casting the occasional contemptuous look at her little ashen-white, exhausted libertine brother. Then, one day, he decided to play for high stakes. He had a cheque for his mother's pension in his pocket. He would stake the lot; if he lost the money, which was more or less all the family had to live on, he would clear out of the country, never to return. If he won he would pay off his debts and never touch a card again. In fact, his luck turned; he won, kept on winning and broke the bank. He was delivered. He rushed back to his mother and confessed everything. 'Freed from the passion for gambling, which had earlier freed me from the usual student's vanities, I belonged now to an entirely new world. It was a world of real and serious musical study to which I now devoted myself heart and soul.'

In this new regenerative mood he found a perfect teacher, Theodor Weinlig, cantor at the Thomas-Schule, the same post as that held by Bach a century earlier. Wagner's previous attempts at composition had been floundering and discursive. A few months earlier, on Christmas Eve 1830, his Overture in B flat major ('New Overture'), a by-product of his efforts to write some incidental music 'à la *Egmont*' for *Leubald und Adelaïde*, was given a public performance in the Leipzig theatre. Wagner was present with his sister Ottilie; the experience for him was one of agonized embarrassment. The unusual feature of this overture was the interpolation of a fifth beat after every fourth bar, announced by a sharp blow on the kettle-drum. He wished to bring out what he called the 'mystic meaning' of the orchestra; this was, he thought, best achieved by 'a striking display of colour'. He therefore wrote the string part in red ink, the woodwind in green, and the brass in black. He took this strange, neat little score to Heinrich Dorn, *Kapellmeister* of the Leipzig theatre, who told him, to his astonishment, that he would play it at a Christmas concert for the poor. Wagner later suspected that Dorn's motives in agreeing to play it were mischievous; he thought it would be a good joke.

Wagner told nobody in his family, except his sister Ottilie, about the première of the 'New Overture'; the composer's name did not appear on the programme. They drove together to the theatre in the carriage of his brother-in-law, Friedrich Brockhaus, who had married his sister Luise. Ottilie went to the Brockhaus box and Wagner, suddenly finding that he had no ticket, had great difficulty in getting in. He heard the orchestra tuning up and thought he would miss the opening. It was only after he had revealed himself as the composer of the 'New Overture' that the doorman admitted him without a ticket. He slipped into one of the front rows in the pit just as the band struck up the opening bars. The fatal drum-beat (marked by Wagner 'fortissimo' throughout the piece), at the end of every fourth bar, at first perplexed the audience. Perplexity turned to merriment and merriment to hilarity. 'I suffered ten thousand torments and became almost unconscious ... not one of those phantoms in Hoffmann's tales could have had as devastating an effect on me as the sight of the audience when it was all over – the laughter had gone and they looked as if they had been through some terrible nightmare.'

It was Weinlig's task to impress upon Wagner the need to curtail, for a time, the exuberance of his musical fancy. Like Hans Sachs with Walter von Stolzing in *Die Meistersinger*, he persuaded him to take seriously the principles of harmony and counterpoint. As a successor of Bach Weinlig belonged to a distinguished tradition of organist-pedagogues. He saw, unlike Müller, that Wagner had plenty of creative, although undisciplined, musical ability. Wagner tells us that Weinlig had no particular teaching method but that he was clear-headed and practical.

He chose a piece, generally by Mozart, drew my attention to its construction, relative length and balance of section, the principal modulations, the number and quality of themes, and the general character of the movement. Then he set me my task; I had to write out a certain number of bars, divided into sections with modulations etc. Similarly, he set me contrapuntal exercises, canons and fugues. He analysed each example minutely and then gave me simple directions how I was to go to work. The real lesson consisted of the careful inspection of what I had written. With infinite patience and kindness he would put his finger on some defective bit and suggest what alterations he thought desirable.

Six months after the first lesson Weinlig told his pupil that there was nothing more he could teach him. He visited Wagner's mother to congratulate her on her son's musical progress and he refused to accept any fees, the pleasure of having taught him being, he said, sufficient reward. As a further sign of approval Weinlig persuaded Breitkopf & Härtel to publish two of Wagner's compositions for the piano – a Sonata in B major and a Polonaise (for four hands) in D major. They were published as Opus I and II, the only occasions when Wagner numbered his compositions.

The beneficent influence of Weinlig did not mean that Wagner's boisterous student days were over; his musical studies and undergraduate bonhomie went along, more or less, hand in hand. The bravado and swagger of the dashing clubman's life was given, however, a new and noble purpose by certain political events. In September 1830 Leipzig began to feel the effects of the July Revolution in Paris at which Charles X was driven from the throne and replaced by the Citizen King Louis-Philippe, son of the regicide, Philippe Egalité. The Catholic royal house of Saxony, even in Napoleonic days, had thought of France as their natural ally. Louis XVI and his brothers, Louis XVIII and Charles X were sons of the Dauphine, Maria Josepha of Saxony. Although the downfall of the Bourbons was a grievous blow to the King of Saxony, his distress was not shared by many of his subjects. Since 1815 Saxony had been incompetently governed; in Leipzig the corruption and brutality of the magistracy and police department were particularly resented. To earn some pocket-money Wagner had been doing some proof-reading for his brother-in-law Brockhaus. He was correcting the chapters dealing with the French Revolution in a revised edition of some 'Universal History' when the July Revolution broke out. 'History began for me at that very moment and my sympathies were naturally wholly on the side of the Revolution.' Suddenly Wagner found himself a revolutionary. It has often been said that he was a child of 1789, that he was throughout his life, under many disguises, a revolutionary, first aware of his revolutionary destiny in July 1830. On this occasion he did not hesitate to join his fellow Leipzig students when they marched to the prison and demanded the release of the prisoners. They went onto a brothel to flush out a few elderly 'guardians of law and order'. Next morning Wagner woke up to find on his bed a souvenir of the previous evening – a tattered piece of red curtain. Soon he and his fellow students found that they had themselves unwittingly become champions of law and order and protectors of private property as the police were too demoralized to deal with the marauding rabble. On a wider front King Anton, successor to Friedrich August I, had appointed his popular nephew, Friedrich (later King Friedrich August II) regent; he drew up the inevitable constitution in celebration of which Wagner wrote a political overture with the title *Friedrich und Freiheit* (Friedrich and Freedom). Friedrich Brockhaus offered the students his printing premises as their headquarters. This turned out to be a clever move; shortly afterwards they protected his modern printing machines against a mob of workers who wanted to destroy them in the cause of full employment.

Brockhaus was also president of a committee to help Polish refugees and exiles who poured into Leipzig after the Russians had savagely put down the Polish uprising. Wagner's passionate sympathies were aroused in the Polish cause. The autumn and winter of 1831 saw the last throes of the Polish rebellion, so hopefully begun. With tears in their eyes the bearded riders embraced their horses for the last time, flung themselves sobbing to the ground and broke the swords or sprung the muskets which they could no longer use in the service of their country. In January 1832 the first detachment of these noble men reached Leipzig. Wagner's excitement knew no bounds; he stood in the welcoming crowd, greeting as many as he could individually, clasping the hands of those who were 'so indomitable in their suffering and sorrow'.

The tragedy of the failure of the Polish uprising meant, for Wagner, bitter disillusionment with the values of his student companions. They laughed at him for taking this event so seriously. 'The terrible lack of fellow-feeling amongst the students struck me very forcibly. Any kind of enthusiasm had to be smothered or turned into romantic bravado which showed itself in the form of affectation or indifference. To get drunk with deliberate cold-bloodedness, without even a glimpse of humour, was reckoned to be as brave a feat as duelling.' Indeed duelling had been, with gambling, one of his chief enthusiasms. At one time he had four or five duels on his hands; however, his lucky star saw to it that none of them actually took place. One after the other something happened to prevent his adversaries from keeping the fearful appointment: one had the artery of his right arm severed in a previous affair; two others had to flee their creditors; another was involved in a fight in a brothel the night before and had to be taken off to hospital; finally, the most formidable student of all, the diabolical Degelow, feared and admired for his strength and wildness, a deadly duellist, was run through the body at Jena and fell dead on the spot.

Wagner's life was thus spared and his honour saved. He could meet those fearless Polish freedom-fighters at the Brockhaus premises knowing that he had also been in situations of mortal, or near mortal, danger. Here he got to know Count Vincent Tyskiewitsch, one of the heroes of the Battle of Ostrolenka. He had admired him from afar one night at the Gewandhaus, impressed by his powerful physique, aristocratic manner and air of quiet self-reliance. 'When I saw a man of such kingly bearing in a tight-fitting embroidered coat and red velvet cap, I realized my foolishness in ever having worshipped the ludicrously got-up little heroes of our student world.' Tyskiewitsch liked his young admirer whom he gradually made the repository of confidences, personal and political. To the former category belonged the calamitous ending of his first marriage: one night, in one of his many lonely castles, he suddenly beheld a ghostly apparition at his bedroom window. His name was called several times and he fired in self-defence only to find that he had shot his wife. It had been her idea of a good joke to frighten him by pretending to be a ghost.

Tyskiewitsch invited Wagner to a dinner for Polish refugees on 3 May 1832, the anniversary of the Polish constitution. The banquet turned into an orgy of drink and song; this memorable evening provided Wagner with the theme for his *Polonia* overture which was actually composed several years later (1836). A month or two later the Count offered him a lift as far as Brünn, the Moldavian capital, in his luxurious four-horse carriage. Wagner was now in his twentieth year. He longed to see Vienna, the home of Beethoven, the city of music. He had made a modest musical name for himself in his native city; three of his overtures had been publicly performed and well received by audience and critics during the previous months. He had just completed, in only six weeks, the Symphony in C major. With the three overtures and the symphony under his arm he set off on the first of many journeys to seek stimulus and recognition.

CHAPTER THREE

First Marriage and Early Operas
1832–9

'WHEREVER I WENT I heard *Zampa* – or Strauss's pot-pourris on *Zampa* – two things which were an abomination to me.' Wagner had expected to hear more edifying music; however, in the Vienna of 1832, Herold's *Zampa*, rather than the music of Beethoven, was the rage. The Count hummed the latest hits from *Zampa* as the capacious carriage trundled towards Brünn. Wagner's thoughts were more with his three overtures and Symphony in C major, which he hoped to get performed in the city of music. These compositions represented his absorption in the purely technical aspects of writing music. Anything smacking of poetry or 'feeling' had, under Weinlig's stern but friendly tutelage, been repressed. He was, perhaps, chafing at his contrapuntal bit and longing to burst into melody and therefore 'over-reacting' to the tuneful airs of *Zampa*.

In Brünn, after saying farewell to the Count, Wagner had one of those nightmarish experiences which sometimes visited him when he was alone. There had been, that year, a terrible cholera epidemic in various parts of Austria; Brünn and Vienna were badly hit. Wagner, on learning about the cholera, saw it as a demon bent on ensnaring him.

I didn't betray my terror to the people in my hotel but, when I found myself in a lonely wing of the house, I crept into bed with all my clothes on and relived those ghostly horrors of my childhood; the cholera stood in front of me, quite alive; I could see it and touch it; it got into my bed and embraced me. My limbs turned to ice . . . whether I was asleep or awake I never knew; I just remember waking up next morning and feeling exceptionally well and healthy.

This experience was not repeated during the month he spent in Vienna in the summer of 1832. He had a pleasant but unrewarding time; the hot summer air was too full of Strauss and *Zampa* for anyone to take much interest in his three overtures and his symphony. A professor at the Conservatory made a half-hearted attempt to get his pupils to play Wagner's Overture in D minor but it never came to anything. He put aside, for the time being, his own musical aspirations and decided to enjoy himself. 'I am afraid that I contracted a few debts which I paid off later when I was *Kapellmeister* at Dresden.' This was eleven years later in 1843; his Viennese creditors must have been startled to get their money back – if, indeed, they did. 'I visited the theatres, heard Strauss, went on excursions and had altogether a very good time.' When Strauss was playing his own waltzes, rather than airs from *Zampa*, Wagner's priggishness dissolved. He used to go along to a public-house, the Sträusslein, where Strauss, with his fiddle, made everyone frantic with delight. 'When he started to play a new waltz this demon of the Viennese musical spirit shook like a Pythian priestess on her tripod.' The audience responded with helpless groans of ecstasy which, assisted by drink, rose to bewildering heights of frenzy. The only piece of serious music which he heard in Vienna was a performance of Gluck's *Iphigenie in Aulis*, which bored him. He had not yet studied the score and his expectations had been raised by reading Hoffmann's story 'Ritter Gluck' in his *Fantasiestücke in Callots Manier*. Later, during his years in Zurich, Wagner was often to conduct works by Gluck whom he came to regard as the most important musical innovator of the eighteenth century and he wrote a concert version, as well as piano score, of his *Iphigenie in Aulis*.

Wagner left Vienna by stage-coach for Prague hoping that the Bohemian capital would show greater discernment and interest in his compositions. He had heard that Dionys Weber, the director of the Prague Conservatory, was a fanatical Mozartian who did not recognize anything by Beethoven after the Second Symphony; he thought the 'Eroica' to be 'an utter abortion' only partially redeemable by taking it at the quick tempo of a Mozart symphony. When Wagner met Weber he tactfully disclaimed any Beethovenian traces in his symphony and pointed out that its final fugue owed everything to his thorough assimilation of Mozartian principles. The delighted Weber, who had seen Mozart conduct several of his works in person, at once ordered his pupils to turn their attention to Wagner's compositions. They were compelled 'to practise with the greatest exactitude my new symphony under his dry and terribly noisy baton'. Wagner thus heard for the first time the last and most ambitious of his exercises in instrumental music. Shortly afterwards in January 1833 it was performed at a Gewandhaus concert in Leipzig; it was well received by public and critics and was given a good notice in the *Zeitung für die elegante Welt* which became, under the editorship of Heinrich Laube, the organ of the youthful, liberal movement *Das junge Deutschland*.

It was during this visit to Prague that Wagner fell in love for the first time – with black-eyed Jenny, one of the two elegant and illegitimate daughters of Count Pachta, who had discomfited him a few years earlier when she and her sister espied him from their carriage in his rags and patches, his face blistered by the sun. Count Pachta's estate at Pravonin was eight miles from Prague and he went straight there from Vienna. 'A youth of nineteen, as I then was, with a fast-growing beard, the close intimacy of such pretty girls could hardly fail to make a strong impression upon my imagination.' Jenny was tall, slim and dark; Augusta was a bit smaller and stouter, with fair hair and brown eyes. Both sisters flirted with him like mad. 'It amused them to see how embarrassed I got in my efforts to choose between them and, in consequence, they teased me tremendously.' Once again the girls made him conscious of his inferior social standing. Although illegitimate they belonged to an aristocratic house and he found them confronted with the dilemma of choosing husbands well-born and poor or middle-class and rich. Wagner soon realized that he was disqualified from the start. He therefore contented himself by giving them priggish, moralizing lectures about the futility of their way of life. He told them how contemptible were their chinless, impoverished, upper-class Austrian lovers, how untrained, shallow and unartistic their own minds. 'I recommended a complete change from the bad library novels (their only reading), from Italian operatic arias sung by Augusta, and last, but not least, from the noisy, insipid cavaliers who paid court to them in a coarse and offensive manner.' He warned them as a true son of the French Revolution, of the fate which had befallen many mindless well-born young ladies of the *ancien régime*. To Wagner's anger they made light of his warnings and continued to flirt with his social superiors. The final humiliation came when the Countess deliberately detained him one evening in an ante-room whilst the two girls, gorgeously dressed and perfumed, were chatting archly to those hateful young noblemen in the drawing-room. 'All I had ever read in Hoffmann's tales about certain demoniacal intrigues became hard facts.'

Wagner's letters at this time show all the signs of being in love with black-eyed Jenny. His first vocal composition, 'Abendglocken' or 'Glockentöne' (Evening Bells), was the result of his overpowering feelings when sitting next to her at the piano. The author of the poem on which it was based was his school-friend Theodor Apel, whose father, Johann August, had one of the grandest houses in Leipzig and was a friend of Adolph Wagner. Johann August wrote pseudo-classical tragedies and also a *Gespensterbuch* (Book of Ghosts) which provided Weber with most of his *Der Freischütz* material. To Theodor, Wagner wrote how his emotions flowed over as they sat at that piano. To conceal his tears he rushed out of the castle into the evening air, fastening his eyes upon the evening star; as it drank his tears he became calmer. He was unable to give a name to this sensation until the evening bells pealed out. Then everything became clear; Wagner rushed back to his room, found his friend's poem which he had fortunately kept in his pocket-book, improvised on it then and there at the piano and later wrote it out properly.

This earliest example of a vocal piece by Wagner has been lost. Nearly forty years later he remembered how it owed a lot to one of Beethoven's song-cycles, 'An die ferne Geliebte', and also how it was 'pervaded by a deliberate sentimentality which was brought into relief by the dreaminess of the accompaniment'. The dreamy sentimentality of 'Glockentöne' gave way to chillier, more horrific fantasies. He did not dare to declare his love. 'My dreams at night were disturbed; I often awoke after dreaming that I had avowed my love and I found nothing but the night that crushed me with painful foreboding . . . how paralysed was my glance back into the fiery stream of the past, into the icy vault of the future!'

Wagner decided that black-eyed Jenny was not worthy of his love ('Sie war meiner Liebe nicht wert'). He sat down at once to erect his first dramatic monument to an unrequited passion. Wagner described his operatic poem *Die Hochzeit* as a 'nocturnal drama in the darkest hue' ('ein Nachtstück von schwarzester Farbe'). He wrote the libretto furtively, in the house of Moritz, an actor friend of his family, where he generally spent the mornings. His own little hotel bedroom was too chilly for writing. Whenever he heard his host's footsteps he hurriedly hid the manuscript in the sofa.

Wagner wrote the entire libretto of *Die Hochzeit* during his remaining weeks in Prague. In December 1832 he returned to Leipzig, where he started on the composition of certain pieces. He showed Weinlig the introduction which he had composed for the first act; his old master praised its clearness and good vocal quality. He also composed an Adagio for a vocal sextet expressing the reconciliation of the hostile families whose enmity is the theme of Wagner's second tragico-dramatic work, written five years after *Leubald*. He had become, in the meantime, a promising young musician whose competent and conventional compositions had been publicly performed and reviewed. It was, however, a dramatic situation expressed in words, preferably written by himself, which stirred the musical ideas within him. Whether *Die Hochzeit* might have called forth music to match its many lurid and thrilling episodes we shall never know. His favourite sister, Rosalie, disapproved of the poem's spine-chilling romanticism. 'As my main object had been to win her approval . . . I made up my mind in an instant: I took the manuscript and without any suggestion of ill-temper destroyed it then and there.'

This is a touching example of Wagner's deference to the judgment of his sisters, Rosalie being the one that he most admired. He had invested his eldest sister with those admirable qualities of gentleness, unselfishness and conscientiousness, and she and his mother were the two people he most loved. Her disapproval of him during his feckless, gambling period had caused a rift between them which he was determined to repair. When she once again showed affection for him and interest in his work he was full of gratitude and happiness. 'She had no real talent for acting which many thought stagey and unnatural. Nevertheless, she was much appreciated on account of her charming appearance and her pure and dignified womanliness.' Despite her attractiveness she was slow in getting married. 'I remember, one evening, when she thought she was alone, hearing her sobbing and moaning. I stole away unnoticed but from that moment I vowed to bring some joy into her life principally by making a name for myself.' In 1836 Rosalie married the man of her choice, Professor Oswald Marbach of Leipzig University, only to die a year later giving birth to a daughter.

What was the piece for whose destruction we have the gentle Rosalie to thank? In his *Autobiographical Sketch*, Wagner has this to say about it:

When in Prague I wrote the poem for a tragic opera called *Die Hochzeit*. I no longer remember where the medieval material came from: a demented lover climbs up to the bedroom window of his friend's bride who is waiting for her husband. She wrestles with the maniac and flings him to the courtyard below where he is dashed to pieces. At the funeral the bride expires with a shriek on his corpse. On returning to Leipzig I composed the first number of this opera; it contained a large sextet which much appealed to Weinlig. My sister disliked the work; I destroyed it without trace.

He later elaborated on this succinct information. Details of its conception came back to him and he remembered that he had found the story in a book on chivalry by J. G. Büsching, *Ritterzeit und Ritterwesen* (Tales of Chivalry). 'Fascinated by the treatment of similar phenomena in Hoffmann's tales I sketched a novel in which musical mysticism, which I loved so deeply, played an important part.' He never finished the novel; but decided to use the subject for his new opera. All that remains of *Die Hochzeit* is the score of the first scene which had its première in Rostock in 1933, a hundred years after its composition.

Die Hochzeit contained more specifically 'Wagnerian' features than his three following operas; it was more personal, less conventionally operatic. He gave his characters fashionable Ossianic[1] names. Two kings, Hadmar and Morar, after years of enmity, settled that the wedding of the former's daughter Ada to a certain Arindal should symbolize their reconciliation. Morar, too old to go himself, sent his son Cadolt in his stead, accompanied by a loyal vassal Admund. They arrive as the bridal procession passes and Cadolt gives the bride a look of passionate, mysterious intensity. Ada sways before this Hoffmannesque look and asks her husband, 'Mein Gatte, sprich, wer ist der fremde Mann?'

[1] Ossian was the Gaelic 'poet' known to us by the remarkable forgeries of James Macpherson in the eighteenth century.

(Husband speak, who is the stranger?) Senta, in *Der fliegende Holländer* asks her father exactly the same question when transfixed by the Dutchman's glance, 'Mein Vater, sprich, wer ist der Fremde?' Later Ada sees Cadolt's frenzied eyes in her bedroom window and she pushes him to his death below. At the funeral she falls, Isolde-like, lifeless upon his body. We have, here, an early variation of the Tristan motif: 'Er sah mir in die Augen' (He looked into my eyes). Wagner, in abandoning *Die Hochzeit*, was probably following a correct instinct; he had had a glimpse of his future music-dramas and he realized that, at the age of nineteen, he was not yet musically equipped to write a tragic opera about love and death.

Once again, E. T. A. Hoffmann cast his strange spell over Wagner's new drama. This odd, versatile character infected his compatriots with delight and a certain uneasiness. Apart from the occasional wandering scholar or artist, Germans were expected to hold respectable positions and to perform their functions dutifully and unimaginatively. Here was E. T. A. Hoffmann, a successful lawyer and government official – and yet also a theatre manager, composer, conductor, novelist and poet. Wagner was not the only composer to be attracted by the paradox and whimsy of his *Phantasiestücke, Märchen* and *Romane*. Hoffmann was a powerful literary force behind the romantic movement in German music; he attracted Weber, Brahms and Schumann, whose 'Kreisleriana' were inspired by the Hoffmannesque character of that name. The hero of his opera *Undine*, Hildebrand, suffers a 'Liebestod' and may claim to be the ancestor of the Wagnerian hero who is redeemed by love. One of his stories, 'Die Bergwerke zu Falun', is full of prophetic dreams and subterranean caverns. The hero, a forerunner of Tannhäuser, is torn between the competing and differing attractions of a mysterious mountain queen and an earthly maid; once again, it is her love which redeems him. No other German writer, except Heine, could show such deftness of touch, could lead his readers in and out of intermingling worlds of appearance and dreams, reality and fantasy. Furthermore, Hoffmann's own life and character were in keeping with the unpredictable world of his novels and essays. His was a short life – he was born in Königsberg in 1776 and he died in 1822 – and an exceptionally active and industrious one; it was a life abounding with successes and failures, with happiness and suffering. His parents – his father was a provincial judge and his mother the daughter of a well-known lawyer – separated after a couple of years of marriage and young Hoffmann lived in the same house as his grandmother, mother, maiden aunt and uncle, a retired municipal councillor. This ménage had already the makings of a Hoffmannesque *Conte*; the grandmother was formidable in view of her age and physical bulk which contrasted with the exiguous outlines of the other four; the mother was sickly and melancholic and never left her room – one day he went in to say good morning and found her dead in bed; the aunt, on the other hand, was good and gay and very attached to her nephew; the uncle was like many councillors to be found in Hoffmann's stories – he did his utmost to bend his nephew to his will and to fit him into the methodical way of life which he had fashioned for himself. Although Hoffmann disliked being thus manipulated he was fond of this uncle who gave him his first lessons in reading and in music.

Like Wagner, Hoffmann showed no exceptional precocity during his early years at school. When he was fourteen his talents for music and for painting began to burgeon and in no time he was improvising his compositions on the clavicord and drawing with an accuracy that aroused the jealousy of his teacher. Later, at the university, he studied jurisprudence in order to qualify for a secure post in the public service and the arts for his own pleasure. He didn't bother to attend the historic lectures of Kant at the university of Königsberg; he couldn't, he said, understand a word of his teachings. Hoffmann duly passed the Prussian 'examen rigoureux' and was about to be awarded the post of assessor at Posen when some scurrilous sketches he had done of certain scandalous features of Königsberg society were shown to the minister who, as a punishment, exiled him to a far away place called Plozk. He married a Polish girl who followed him into exile. In Plozk his gifts unfolded: he wrote many things – newspaper articles and plays; he composed some masses and a sonata in accordance with the rules of double counterpoint; he drew portraits and caricatures and copied Etruscan vases. His friends soon managed to get him transferred to Warsaw as *conseiller de régence*, some kind of legal position. In no time he became the general factotum of a newly established musical society; at the end of a day of consultation and writing legal opinions he would rush off to decorate the theatre, often followed there by clients who found him perched on the scaffolding in a canvas overall, surrounded by pots of paint, with a glass of wine in one hand. He would come down, take the clients into a corner and start several hours of most complex consultations.

Hoffmann's head and heart were with Mozart and Haydn, rather than with Napoleon; he preferred reading scores to newspapers and had not reflected on what might happen to him should the French take Warsaw. This is just what happened; he lost his job and lived as the happiest of men until his money ran out. Then he fell on hard times; he moved from Warsaw to Berlin, from Berlin to Bamberg, where he lived by giving music lessons. Then he remembered his pen and he wrote to Rochlitz, editor of the *Musical Gazette* in Leipzig. Rochlitz asked him to write for his journal a story about a musician who had gone mad. This was the origin of the biography of Johann Kreisler and of the *Phantasiestücke* and of Hoffmann's place in German literature. Although talented as both musician and painter he was a writer of genius. He developed a style of singular originality, Rabelaisian in its reckless gaiety and reminiscent of Sterne or Max Beerbohm in its capriciousness and whimsicality. Above all, it is permeated with German fantasy, sometimes reaching delirious heights of superstition and terror, sometimes indulging in wild complicated arabesques. His tremendous imaginative and stylish powers were sometimes employed in vaporous regions uncomfortably far removed from 'reality'. This was the man whose writings meant so much to the youthful Wagner.

'In January 1833, my symphony (in C major) was performed in the Gewandhaus and was enthusiastically applauded. At this time I met Laube.' With these words Wagner introduces Heinrich Laube who had recently arrived in Leipzig from Silesia. He had been dazzled by Rosalie's performance as Gretchen in *Faust*. Once she had admitted him into her circle of friends he spent much time at the Wagner's home in the Pichhof. Wagner tells us that his family thought Laube a genius: 'His curt and biting manner of speaking made him appear both original and daring; his sense of justice, his sincerity and fearless bluntness made one respect his character, hardened as it had been in youth by great adversity.' What the nature of this adversity was we do not know. Laube came from Silesia and he hoped to make a name for himself in

Leipzig, as a progressive publisher and writer, before proceeding to Paris.

Thanks to his spirited writings he soon became the acknowledged intellectual leader of the Leipzig youth. The first part of his novel, *Das junge Europa*, had just appeared and it was devoured by Wagner and his friends. Joyous, libertine, carefree, iconoclastic, permissive – these are the words to describe the writings of Heinrich Laube. The ideals of *Das junge Europa* became the ideals of the youth movement, *Das junge Deutschland*, whose philosophy of living for the moment and freedom from all restraints was at the heart of Wagner's early writings and stage works.

Shortly after his appointment as editor of the well-known Leipzig journal *Die Zeitung für die elegante Welt*, Laube wrote the most flattering review of the first performance of Wagner's Symphony in C major. Whether this was partly to please Rosalie we do not know. Maybe not, because on the strength of his opinions on Wagner's symphony he asked him to write the music of the libretto for an opera which he had just written about the Polish hero, Kosciuszko, which he had intended for Meyerbeer. Wagner had already made up his mind not to write music to other people's words. Not wishing to hurt Laube's feelings by refusing too peremptorily and also to avoid military service in Saxony he left Leipzig for Würzburg to take up the badly-paid post of chorus trainer at the local theatre where his brother Albert was stage-manager and leading tenor.

Before leaving for Würzburg in January 1833 Wagner, encouraged this time by his sister Rosalie, wrote the poem of his first complete opera *Die Feen*. The inspirers of his work were the Venetian dramatist Carlo Gozzi and E. T. A. Hoffmann. Wagner took the story from Gozzi's *La Donna Serpente* which he had read in the house of his uncle Adolph who had translated the writings of Gozzi. Laube was not at all pleased to hear later that Wagner had preferred to base his opera upon some fanciful Venetian fairy-tale rather than upon his own heroic political poem.

The different phases in the musical composition of *Die Feen* were carried out during the year he spent at Würzburg in 1833.[1]

---

[1] Wagner's technique of composition comprised there different phases. After the prose draft and poem there are three clear musical stages: firstly, the compositional sketch (*Kompositionskizze*). This is the musical sketch or draft, which already contains all the essential motifs. Secondly, the orchestral

Extracts from the opera were played in Würzburg at concert performances. The full score was finished in January 1834. *Die Feen* marks another clear step along the road to Wagnerian music-drama.

The story of *Die Feen* is, briefly, as follows. (Wagner gave all its characters Ossianic names some of which he lifted from *Die Hochzeit*.) The hero is a prince called Arindal and he is loved by a fairy called Ada who has held him under a spell and kept him for the last eight years or so in fairyland far away from his kingdom. He is found by some faithful friends who implore him to return to his country which is going to wrack and ruin. The king has died of grief and the capital has fallen into the hands of the enemy. Ada longs to leave the immortal land of fairies and share the faith of Arindal as his earthly wife. This she can only do if he carries out a formidable number of terrible tasks. He must be steadfast and loyal to Ada, even when she is perpetrating the most poisonous and horrible deeds against him, if he is to rescue her from her fairy state. Unfortunately, he is tormented beyond endurance and, when cursing her, turns her into stone. Arindal then goes mad with grief. He finds a helpful magician, Groma, who equips him with various magic weapons and charms with whose help he descends into the underworld in search of Ada. When he sees his lifeless fairy-wife he brings out a lyre to the sounds of which he expresses his remorse for failing her. The stone is moved by the magic of his lyre and Ada comes to life again. She does not come to human life – that is denied her because of Arindal's former inconstancy. He is allowed however to become a fairy and together they are united and live happily ever after in fairyland.

Certain dramatic musical ideas can be seen in *Die Feen* which were later to be developed in Wagner's operas, for example, the painful reaction of the worlds of spirits and of humans upon each other, redemption through love, the first glimmerings of Wagner's tonal language and the use of musical motifs to characterize certain recurring situations. The redemption of the fairy Ada through the love of Arindal, her mortal husband – is turned by Wagner into a motif of inner development whereas Gozzi used

sketch (*Orchesterskizze*), which is the systematic arrangement of the thematic material, and its division into voices arranged along a system of staves. Thirdly, the full score, which means the complete instrumentation.

it as an external trick for releasing the wife from her enchantment. Wagner's efforts to get his opera performed in Leipzig, and later in Prague, were not successful. *Die Feen* was not performed during his lifetime. The first performance of it took place in Munich in 1888 under Hermann Levi, the first *Parsifal* conductor. The Munich Hoftheater was given the sole rights for performing *Die Feen*, in return for its orchestra and choir taking part in performances of *Parsifal* in Bayreuth.

In *Die Feen* Wagner had tried to do exactly what E. T. A. Hoffmann had recommended. He blended the fantastic world with that of real life. There had been a vogue in Germany ever since *Der Freischütz* for operas full of fairies and spirits and otherworldly creatures. All too often they were simply employed to titillate the uneducated audience. Wagner had, in *Die Feen*, made the first of his many bold efforts to relate the unfathomable world to the world in which we live although he still lacked the dramatic and musical ability to realize his conception satisfactorily.

Albert Wagner, leading tenor and stage manager of the Würzburg theatre, was quite an important personality in that small, beautiful baroque city when his younger brother arrived to take up his duties as chorus trainer. Wagner experienced for the first time what it was like to work in a small badly-equipped provincial theatre. The reportoire of the average German theatre in those days was very large. The audience was unexacting in its standards, people travelled little and were unable to make comparisons with other theatres. Each small town either had its own permanent company or relied upon visits from travelling companies. As the resources were not available for good singing, good playing, good décor and such matters, it was really of very little importance how often the programme was changed.

It was some consolation and diversion both for audience and singers to have as much variety as possible. During the first few months of Wagner's stay at Würzburg operas were put on by Weber, Auber, Rossini, Bellini, Beethoven, Herold and several others. The climax of the season was Meyerbeer's *Robert le Diable* which had been first produced in Paris only two years earlier. Another notable production was Marschner's *Der Vampyr* which, with *Der Freischütz*, could claim to be the godfather of *Die Feen*. Wagner's first job in Würzburg was to train the fifteen-member chorus for *Der Vampyr* and *Robert le Diable*; Albert took the tenor part of Aubry in *Der Vampyr* and had to sing a long important aria with a feeble ending. Wagner therefore composed for him a new ending, an animated Allegro of 142 bars. It was quite in order for a theatre, once it had acquired the right to perform a composer's opera, to make any changes which might be thought desirable. Wagner noted that the decline in his taste for classical music dates from this period. He found himself judging third-rate melodies not on their intrinsic merits or demerits but simply by whether they were popular or not with the audience. Albert, who had his brother's future musical career at heart, encouraged this lowering of Wagner's musical standards.

In January 1834 Wagner returned to Leipzig, the score of *Die Feen* finished, and happy in the knowledge that his latest opera had met with his sister's approval. At the end of the third act he had written: 'Finis, laudemus Deum, Richard Wagner.' 'It was exactly midday,' he wrote to Rosalie, 'and the bells pealed from all the towers as I wrote "Finis" beneath my composition.' His year in Würzburg had provided him with his first practical responsibilities in the theatre; he displayed for the first time his enormous appetite for work and also his resentment at the narrow confines of the music and dramatic world within which he had to operate and from which he would, in the future, be constantly breaking out. In Würzburg he had a couple of enjoyable love affairs[1] and he succeeded in inducing one of the young ladies to jilt her betrothed, an oboist, on his account.

Wagner was confident that, with his sister's help, *Die Feen* would be accepted by the Leipzig theatre. His main anxiety was that the singers would lack the necessary vocal and acting ability to do justice to his opera. At the age of twenty he was, already, the uncompromising artist, unwilling to make the smallest concession to the exigencies of theatre directors and singers or to the tastes and habits of the theatre-going public. In *Die Feen* anticipatory harmonies of *Der fliegender Holländer* and *Lohengrin* can be heard as well as experiments with chromaticism and the orchestral hinting of motifs before the scenes are realized on the stage. Where they came from nobody knows. They did not, at any rate,

---

[1] One was a grave-digger's daughter, Thérèse Ringelmann, who sang in the chorus trained by Wagner and the other, Friederike Galvani – a mechanic's daughter – small, dark and vivacious, with a pretty voice, had been taken up by Albert.

appeal to the bass singer and theatre manager, Franz Hauser, who rejected the opera. Wagner wrote to him in March 1834, 'You dislike my opera; worse than that – you dislike the whole direction of my art.' For the conservative Hauser opera had stopped with Gluck; his chief musical regret was that Bach had never written an opera. Many years later Wagner wrote to his patron, King Ludwig of Bavaria, with whom he was in disagreement about the staging of *Das Rheingold*, 'Do you want my work performed as I want it – or don't you?' Although often accused of ingratitude and high-handedness towards Ludwig and others Wagner was always, in his recalcitrance, expressing the artist's striving for independence; his career, culminating in the opening of his theatre at Bayreuth, was, amongst other things, a successful struggle for the emancipation of the nineteenth-century artist. Although prepared to write the occasional eulogistic piece for the Kings of Saxony and Bavaria and for the German Emperor he never became the humble, socially inferior court musician, turning out compositions to glorify his princely Maecenas. Through his personality and insistence that his operas be shown the respect befitting a work of art Wagner raised immeasurably the social and intellectual status of the artist in the eyes of the bourgeoisie.

Wagner soon got over his disappointment at the rejection of *Die Feen*; as if deliberately, he turned away from this eerie world of redemptive gloom and threw himself, with renewed vigour, into the musical, political and intellectual life of the moment. He once again read Heinrich Laube's *Das junge Europa* and Wilhelm Heinze's *Ardinghello*, first published in 1785, one of the by-products of the *Sturm und Drang* movement, which announced a new endemonic principle of life based upon unbridled sensuality and the religion of the 'here and now' (*Diesseits-Religion*). 'The art of applying life to the maximization of well being,' was how Jeremy Bentham defined this endemonic system of ethics which Wagner would certainly have endorsed. This 'religion' was soon to find expression in his new opera, *Das Liebesverbot* (Forbidden Love), conceived in June 1834 when he and Theodor Apel took a fortnight's holiday together to go to Teplitz in Bohemia, a part of the world which had for him such happy, romantic memories. A few days before setting off he wrote an article, 'Die deutsche Oper', for Laube's *Zeitung für die elegante Welt*. He was inspired to write it after seeing Schröder-Devrient as Romeo at a performance in Leipzig of Bellini's *Montecchi e Capuletti*. The text was ludicrous and the music pathetically threadbare – and yet the opera made a great impression on him. Why? He tried to answer this question in his article. Bellini, he said, knew how to write a *song*; whatever the other weaknesses of his operas he could make his characters sing thereby filling them with the warmth of life, with passion and with feeling. The German composers – Spohr, Marschner and even, at times, his beloved Weber – could not do this with their 'learned' operas. So Bellini joined Heinze and Laube as one of Wagner's new endemonic heroes. He remained grateful to Bellini, throughout his life, for opening his eyes to the importance of song; many years later, when he was in Italy in 1880, in search of health and writing the music for *Parsifal*, he met at the Naples Conservatory the old musicologist Francesco Florimo who had been a great friend of Bellini. Wagner embraced him with the words, 'Bellini! Bellini!' Before leaving he turned to him again, 'Long live the great Bellini!'

It was as a tribute to Bellini, a Sicilian, that Wagner shifted the action of *Das Liebesverbot*, based on Shakespeare's *Measure for Measure* from Vienna to sixteenth-century Palermo. One summer morning he climbed the Schlackenburg hill near Teplitz and there, his view ranging over the Bohemian hills and valleys, wrote a quick draft of his new opera. The main liberty which he took with Shakespeare's play, to which he otherwise adhered, was to leave out the figure of the Duke and, with him, the underlying Shakespearean question of the proper exercise of justice by authority. The central theme of the opera became the conflict between restrained and unrestrained sensuality; a condemnation of hypocrisy and of austere morality; the glorification of the endemonic principle of 'free sensuality' which found expression in the riotous revelry of the carnival scene in the finale. *Das Liebesverbot* has, ever since Wagner presented the score to Ludwig in 1866 describing it, in a dedicatory poem, as a 'sin of my youth' (*Jugend-sünde*), been dismissed by Wagnerites as an unfortunate relapse, after the promising tendencies of *Die Feen*, into the meretricious ways of light French and Italian opera. It is, in fact, a delightfully melodious opera as those who saw the performances, in University College, London, in 1965 and in Bayreuth by members of the Internationales Jugendfestspieltreffen in 1972, will testify. It pullulates with charming melodies and vivid pieces of orchestration;

it embodies what Wagner took to be the precepts of Bellini and, in its Italianate style, recalls Rossini and anticipates Verdi. Thickening gloom and pedantic hypocrisy is represented by Friedrich (Shakespeare's Angelo), the German governor of the island, who is painted by Wagner in sombre musical colours thus expressing his dislike of the cultural values of contemporary Germany. Wagner never became reconciled to this 'wild' work of his youth. The only good thing he could find in it, he told Cosima at the end of his life, were the melody and harmonies of 'Salve regina coeli' in the convent scene with Isabella and Mariana, note for note the same as the redemption motif in *Tannhäuser*. Isabella, the sister of Claudio, sentenced to death by Friedrich for 'loving' (*'ich liebte nur'*), is a shadowy early version of Elisabeth in *Tannhäuser*. Apart from that Wagner had nothing good to say about his opera – it was 'horrifying, repulsive, disgusting . . . the instrumentation was good; I learned that on my mother's knee'. He played Cosima the overture and she was impressed by the theme of forbidden love (*Verbot-Thema*) – 'soulless, authoritarian, stern and dramatic' – which has the function of a leitmotiv throughout the opera. She preferred the overture of *Die Feen*, although Wagner was of the opinion that the *Das Liebesverbot* overture showed 'more genius'. He concluded, nevertheless, by expressing his astonishment at how bad the opera was: 'what phases one goes through! It is difficult to believe that one was the same person.' When he said this he was in the middle of writing the *Parsifal* music and not in the mood to feel charitable about his 'youthful' (*'kindisch'*) aberration. During the next few years Wagner tried, engagingly and heroically, to achieve a synthesis of certain fundamental and disparate intellectual experiences – his love of Beethoven and Shakespeare, the 'young German' endemonism and his enthusiasm for the various freedom movements of the day. It must be remembered that, throughout his life, he took up and absorbed in his music, writings and conversations ideas which were 'in the air'. It is a mistake to attach all that much importance to his 'politico-cultural' views, unless expressed in his music or in his writings about music, whether about socialism, German nationalism or Jews. Although he spoke about Jews, in general, in a venomous and splenetic way he correctly and perceptively analysed the reasons for their failure to make, up to that time, any significant contribution to western musical culture.

Although Wagner made no further operatic use of Shakespearean plots he never lost his early admiration for Shakespeare.
At the end of his life he read aloud Shakespeare's history plays, in
their German translation, to the faithful members of his circle.
He told them that he was 'disturbed' that Shakespeare's had been
possible in the English tongue, English being a 'mixed language'
and therefore of no cultural value. Cosima recorded in her diaries
these magisterial observations.

When, at the end of June 1834, Wagner returned to Leipzig
from Teplitz he found awaiting him an invitation to become
musical manager (*Musikdirektor*) of a Magdeburg theatre troupe
during their summer season in Bad Lauchstädt. There he met the
actress Minna Planer who was four years older than he. Wagner
gives, in his autobiography, an unforgettable description of this
seedy troupe, of the drunken manager Bethmann who, despite an
allowance from the King of Prussia's treasury for services
rendered by his wife to the monarch in the past, was permanently
bankrupt, and of the wife who now spent all day reclining on a
sofa exchanging amorous pleasantries with an elderly bass singer.

Minna Planer, Wagner's first wife, is sometimes thought to
have been badly treated in Wagner's autobiography, dictated to
Cosima, his second wife, and in later Wagner biographies written
in the stern shadow of the Haus Wahnfried in Bayreuth. The stage
was not her calling; she became an actress to support herself and
her parents. At the age of fifteen she was seduced by a certain
Captain Ernst Rudolph von Einsiedel, by whom she had a
daughter, Natalie, who was always known as her sister. Wagner's
lodgings in Bad Lauchstädt were in the same house as Minna's.
'The young actress was agreeable and fresh in her appearance,'
he dictated to Cosima, 'and her movements and behaviour
were characterized by a remarkable grace and composure which,
added to a very pleasant expression, gave her a captivating
dignity. ... I was introduced to her in the passage as the new
musical manager and she was astonished that one so young should
have this post. ...' In no time he fell in love with her and she
soon accepted him, without much enthusiasm, as her lover.
Although Minna was dignified she was of fairly easygoing
morality, regarding it as her duty to bestow the occasional favour
on theatre managers and patrons. She did not love Wagner and
discouraged his passionate protestations. Why did he fall in love,

it has been often asked, with this unremarkable woman who neither understood him nor believed in him? The answer seems to be that her combined erotic and motherly appeal defeated all considerations.

By January 1836 Wagner, who was now musical manager in Magdeburg, had finished the score of *Das Liebesverbot* and on 29 March, after only ten days of rehearsals, the première took place under his direction. At the insistence of the police, who regarded the title *Das Liebesverbot* as conducive to immorality, it was changed to *Die Novize von Palermo* (The Novice of Palermo). As the troupe was about to be disbanded none of the cast had bothered to learn their parts. Two days later there was to be a second performance; when the time came, the theatre was almost empty – according to Wagner the audience consisted of one Polish Jew – and the singers settled lovers' quarrels behind the stage. The performance had to be cancelled. Thus ended Wagner's career as music manager in Magdeburg. On the day he left he witnessed the execution of a delinquent who was broken on the wheel. This was his last impression of Magdeburg; from there he proceeded to Berlin where he hoped to arrange a performance of *Das Liebesverbot* in the Königstädter theatre and then on to Königsberg in pursuit of Minna who had got a theatre engagement there and whom he had good reason to believe was carrying on with a Jewish salesman. On 24 November 1836 they were married at Trägheim near Königsberg.

Both before and after his marriage Wagner started accumulating debts. The proceeds of the ill-starred second performance of *Das Liebesverbot* were to have been for his personal benefit. On 1 April he became musical manager of the Königsberg theatre; a few weeks later the theatre went bankrupt and the debts which he had incurred in expectation of his salary could not be paid. At the end of May Minna disappeared with a business man called Dietrich; Wagner tracked her down to Dresden where she was staying with her parents. She was not disposed to return to him unless he could get a secure job. This was the first dramatic crisis of his marriage. In June he was offered the post of music manager at the theatre in Riga; he hoped thereby, with a regular income and a settled existence, to save his marriage. Königsberg, Riga, Paris and Dresden – these were the places of the leanest periods in the married life of Wagner and Minna. After her unsteady start she accepted the fate of being the wife of a wayward, unpractical, visionary and intellectual musician. Wherever they set up house she made him a comfortable home and showed, within her limitations, a considerable degree of patience and unselfishness which Wagner always recognized. In Riga Wagner and Minna were reunited; they were out of reach of their creditors in Magdeburg and Königsberg. His Riga appointment was not destined, however, to last long. He antagonized Karl von Holter, the director of the theatre, by including his own compositions in the programmes. Holter resigned suddenly to avoid damaging disclosures about his behaviour; before doing so he engaged Heinrich Dorn from Leipzig as *Kapellmeister* for the coming season. His successor was bound by this decision and Wagner found himself out of a job. His Riga creditors were at his heels and he decided that now was the moment to escape from the petty confines of provincial German music and make for Paris, the musical capital of the world.

CHAPTER FOUR
Poverty in Paris
1839–42

ON 9 JULY 1839 Wagner fled from Riga to escape his creditors. This was the first, and most sensational, of his getaways, the other being ten years later, in May 1849, when he made for Zurich from Dresden as a political fugitive. The flight across the Russian border, followed by a stormy sea journey from Pillau to London, was one of the most adventurous episodes in his life. It was almost as dangerous then to leave Russia without a passport as it is today. The frontier was very carefully guarded; every few yards a Cossack kept watch at a sentry-box. Wagner, Minna and his large Newfoundland dog, Robber, were taken by friends first to a smuggler's den near the frontier where they spent the evening with some 'hideous, evil-smelling Polish Jews'; then, as night fell, they took refuge in an unoccupied sentry-box; at a certain moment they made a dash for the frontier ditch and scrambled up into Prussian territory. Had they been seen by any of the patrolling sentries they would have been shot. The details of their flight had been planned and executed by a certain Abraham Möller, a wealthy Königsberg patron of the arts. Möller, who had been waiting for the fugitives in Prussia, now accompanied them to Pillau; on the way, near Königsberg, the rude cart in which they were travelling overturned in some farmyard and Minna was so shaken that she had to spend the night in a peasant's hovel. Her subsequent childlessness was a possible consequence of this misadventure; she may have suffered certain internal injuries during the harrowing journey.

Poor Minna was certainly paying for her past infidelities with the Jewish salesman from Königsberg in 1836 and with that other

Königsberg salesman, Dietrich. Wagner was affected by his wife's physical and mental misery during this long ordeal. 'I could not,' he said, 'find words to convey to my utterly exhausted wife my regret for it all.'

At Pillau the Wagners and Robber boarded the *Thetis*, a small merchant boat with a crew of seven men, bound for London. The journey should have taken about a week; on this occasion it took about three and a half weeks. There were two reasons why Wagner chose this circuitous way of reaching Paris rather than travel there by land. Firstly, Robber would have felt too cooped up in a coach (railways were hardly known) and, secondly, the journey was much cheaper by sea.

A prolonged calm prevented the boat from leaving Pillau and Wagner made use of the time to improve his French by reading a novel by George Sand.[1] After a week of sailing in calm water the boat ran into a storm at Skagerrak and they were forced to seek shelter on the Norwegian coast. As the boat sailed into the quiet waters of a fiord, the encircling rocks breaking the crashes of the storm, their enormous granite walls echoing the sturdy shouts of the seamen as they cast anchor and furled the sails, Wagner's genius got to work. 'The sharp rhythm of this call shaped itself into the theme of the seamen's song in *Der fliegende Holländer*. The idea of this opera was, even then, ever present in my mind and it now assumed a precise poetic and musical colour.' He had, a month earlier, finished scoring the second of the five acts of *Rienzi*; the story was taken from Bulwer Lytton's novel. A remarkable feature of Wagner's creativity was the sudden appearance in his mind of characters and musical themes for a work quite different from the one on which he was actually working.

The *Thetis* had to endure two more terrible storms before they sighted the English coast. 'I felt new life in me when I saw, in the distance, the English pilots racing for our ship. As competition is free amongst pilots on the English coast they come out as far as possible to meet incoming vessels even when the risk is very great.'

On 12 August the Wagners arrived in London. The ground still felt unsteady under their feet; their huge double bed at the King's Arms in Old Compton Street, Soho, rocked unbearably. 'Every time we shut our eyes we sank into frightful abysses and,

[1] He had been taking French lessons in Riga, up to the very day of his departure, in preparation for his musical assault on Paris.

springing up again, cried out for help.' After recovering his balance Wagner set about exploring London. Robber did the same and went off on his own as far as Oxford Street; however, he found his way back to the King's Arms. In March 1837, when he had been at Königsberg, Wagner had written the overture 'Rule Britannia' which he sent to Sir George Smart, conductor of the Philharmonic Society. It was a tribute to British liberal, civic virtues, as compared with those of the Holy Alliance. Smart, in whose house in Great Portland Street Weber had died in 1826, never answered and Wagner now tried to find him, only to learn that he was out of town. The Philharmonic Society in March 1840 finally returned the score to Wagner when he was living in penury in Paris; he could not afford the seven francs carriage and the packet was sent back to London, where it disappeared from view, to be rediscovered in strange circumstances at the beginning of this century.

Bulwer Lytton was the next person on Wagner's list. During that distressing spring and summer of 1837, after the bankruptcy of the Königsberg theatre and during Minna's infidelities with Dietrich, he had been much comforted by the kindness and hospitality of his sister Ottilie who had married the oriental philologist Hermann Brockhaus. He paid daily visits to their villa in Dresden's famous Grosser Garten from the lodgings which he had taken in the little village of Blasewitz on the Elbe. 'During my convalescence in the bosom of my sympathetic family I worked out a scheme for a grand opera under the inspiration of Bulwer Lytton's *Rienzi*.' There followed his prose draft of the story, the libretto, the orchestral sketch and score of Act I and the orchestral sketch of Act II.

This was as far as he had gone in the composition of *Rienzi* when he reached London. Wagner now wanted to meet Bulwer Lytton and discuss with him the operatic possibilities of his novel. Someone had told him on the Continent that Lytton was a Member of Parliament – so off he went to the Palace of Westminster in search of the author of *Rienzi*, undeterred by the fact that he did not speak a single word of English. He had realized the inadequacy of his English when endeavouring to converse with the landlady of the King's Arms – although he remembered translating a monologue from *Romeo and Juliet* at the age of twelve. 'The good dame's social position led her to think she could talk French to me and her attempt made me wonder which of us knew least of that language.' At the Houses of Parliament his ignorance of English proved an unexpected benefit; each official who couldn't understand what he wanted referred him to a higher dignitary until he found himself being asked in polished French by a distinguished-looking man what it was that he wanted. 'He seemed favourably impressed when I enquired for the celebrated author.' Lytton was indeed a 'celebrated author' at this time; he had published thirteen novels and two plays and had acquired a baronetcy the previous year, changing his name from Bulwer to Bulwer-Lytton. He had sat in the House of Commons as a Liberal M.P. since 1831. Wagner learned from his courteous interlocutor that the novelist was not in town. To compensate for this disappointment he was allowed to sit in the Strangers' Gallery at the House of Lords whilst a debate was in progress. The Prime Minister, Melbourne, was moving the second reading of the Slave Trade Suppression Bill. The Duke of Wellington also spoke. 'He looked so comfortable in his grey beaver hat with his hands thrust deep into his trouser pockets and he made his speech in so conversational a tone that I lost my feeling of excessive awe.'

The other noteworthy episodes of Wagner's first visit to London were a trip by train (his very first) to Gravesend Park with Minna and the captain of the *Thetis*; experiencing 'a ghastly London Sunday'; a visit to Westminster Abbey to pay his respects to the statue of Shakespeare, and to the Royal Hospital, Chelsea, where a snuff-taking pensioner addressed him in Saxon. On 20 August Wagner, Minna and Robber crossed to France by steamer, arriving the same evening at Boulogne.

Both Wagner and Minna had premonitions that the 'conquest of Paris' would not be as easy as they had supposed, particularly in the holiday month of August, and they decided to tarry a few weeks in or near Boulogne-sur-Mer. They moved into two un-furnished rooms in the shabby little house of a country wine merchant on the main road to Paris, about half-an-hour's journey from Boulogne. With extraordinary ingenuity they managed to find a bed, two chairs and a table which they took it in turns to use – Minna laid the meals and Wagner scored *Rienzi*, Act ii.

By a funny coincidence Meyerbeer happened to be staying in Boulogne at this time. Wagner decided to call on him. 'I had often read in the newspapers of his proverbial amiability and I bore him no ill-will for not answering my letter.' The letter in question had been written by Wagner in February 1837 in Königsberg. In it he told Meyerbeer that his (Meyerbeer's) works had shown him the new direction that dramatic music should take; before that his passionate veneration for Beethoven had led to a one-sided development of his productive energy. 'In you the task of the German composer has found fulfilment; he may now take the best features of the Italian and French Schools in order to *universalize* the creations of his own genius.' The present deplorable state of composition in Germany had led him to the conclusion that German composers must go to Paris and from there export their works to Germany. He was obviously thinking of Meyerbeer's operas *Robert le Diable* (1831) and *Les Huguenots* (1836) which were composed and first performed in Paris before causing such a sensation in Germany. He had, he wrote, hit upon an excellent subject for a French opera in a recent German novel, Heinrich König's *Die neue Braut*, of which he had sent a prose sketch to Scribe[1] in Paris which he had followed up with the score of *Das Liebesverbot*. He told Meyerbeer, untruthfully, that he had deliberately refrained from trying to get *Das Liebesverbot* performed in Germany because 'its free and somewhat frivolous tunes as well as its entire musical colour' had persuaded him that it was a more appropriate piece for France. Would Meyerbeer, therefore, obtain the score form Scribe and, if he liked it, have the text turned into French and offered to the Opéra Comique? To encourage the famous composer to do something on his behalf Wagner indulged in some flattery. 'Your reputation is that of a noble, munificent man . . . further artistic fame is for you now impossible as you have attained the unimaginable; wherever people sing, your melodies are heard; you have become a small God on this earth. . . .' It will be remembered how disappointed Wagner was with Meyerbeer's *Robert le Diable* when he rehearsed it at Würzburg in 1833. 'I found neither originality nor novelty in this transparent work . . . the only thing which impressed me was the unearthly sound of the trumpet which represented the voice of the mother's ghost'.

Giacomo Meyerbeer (alias Jakob Liebmann Beer), a rich Jew

---

[1] Eugène Scribe (1791–1861), the prolific and popular French playwright and librettist.

from Berlin who had settled in Paris was, after Rossini and Weber, Europe's most popular operatic composer. His fame was at its height at the time of the Bourgeois Monarchy. During the nine years that had elapsed since the July Revolution in 1830 the French bourgeoisie had attained a position of great financial power; a thrusting, vulgar society was replacing the more tired and disillusioned one of the Bourbon Restoration. It had a vague sense of operatic values and Meyerbeer was the composer to meet the hour. His music exploited the bourgeoisie's craving for forsaken grandeur; it was flashy and rhetorical with no real sense of purpose or humour. It expressed, however, the showy needs of a new rich, philistine public. Heine, who was living in Paris at the time, said, 'Only when the great choruses of *Robert le Diable* or *Les Huguenots* roared harmonically, rejoiced harmonically, sobbed harmonically, did men's hearts hearten and sob and rejoice and roar in inspired accord.'

It is not therefore surprising that Wagner should have written a letter to this important man. From his arrival at Boulogne on 20 August 1839 to his departure from Paris on 7 April 1842 Meyerbeer was to play an important part in Wagner's Paris years. Their relationship became increasingly complicated and ambiguous; Wagner began, it seems, by having a genuine admiration for the amiable and influential composer which slowly turned into distrust and contempt. When they met in Boulogne Wagner was impressed by Meyerbeer's musical achievements; he had earlier written an article comparing him with Handel, Gluck, Mozart and Beethoven, each having, he said, brought to its zenith an epoch in the development of dramatic music. 'Time in its restless, renewing creative power will find a new hero for a new epoch. He [Meyerbeer] is still with us in the plenitude of his powers . . . we need not therefore look ahead but simply await the next flowering of his genius.'

Meyerbeer received Wagner kindly. 'The years had not given his features that flabby look which, sooner or later, mars most Jewish faces.' He encouraged him to try his luck in Paris as a composer of operas. He listened attentively as Wagner read him the first three acts of the libretto of *Rienzi* and he kept the completed scores of the first two acts. He irritated Wagner by repeatedly praising his minute handwriting, 'an accomplishment he considered especially Saxonian'. No explanation was forthcoming as to why he had not answered Wagner's letter from Königsberg appealing for help.

Wagner, Minna and Robber left Boulogne in a stage-coach on 16 September and they arrived in Paris the following day. His brother-in-law, Eduard Avenarius, who had just married his half-sister Cäcilie and ran a bookshop in Paris, found some lodgings for him in 3 rue de la Tonnellerie near Les Halles. Wagner was horrified by the squalor of the locality although mildly consoled to see on the front of the house a bust of Molière with an inscription, 'Maison où nacquit Molière'.

Now began two-and-a-half nightmarish years of penury and humiliation for Wagner and Minna which severely tested their vivacity, courage and confidence. They knew what it was to starve; he spent a night behind bars in a debtor's prison; he fell, needless to say, into the hands of moneylenders.

Meyerbeer had given Wagner a letter of introduction to Duponchel, director of the Paris Opéra. He had succeeded Veron, a repulsive-looking little man – 'scrofulous, paunchy, thick-lipped and sycophantic'[1] – who had managed to turn the opera into a profitable concern for himself; in 1835, he retired, after four years of incumbency, with a profit of about a million francs. Until his day the Opéra, despite its privileged position – it received both a state subsidy and a share of the takings of all theatres and concert-halls in Paris – was always in debt. Veron reversed this trend in two or three ways; he gave the public just what they wanted – magnificent settings, costumes and ballets; at that moment *Robert le Diable* fell from the skies and multiplied the box-office receipts; he threw open the wings to the rich dandies who were sometimes permitted, dressed up in bearskins, to mingle with the female dancers on the stage. Heine, who was living in Paris at the time, had this to say about Veron: 'He has adorned the temple of the goddess of music but shown the goddess herself the door. Nothing can surpass the luxury that obtains at the opera which is now the paradise of the hard of hearing.' 'It was this institution,' says Ernest Newman, 'heavy with iniquities, cynical with long experience of human cupidity and folly, towards which the young green German provincial named Richard Wagner had bent his hopeful steps from the other end of Europe.'

[1] Ernest Newman, *The Life of Richard Wagner*, 1933–49, 4 vols.

Duponchel's main virtue was that he kept no mistresses in the Opéra. During his period of office the fashionable, aristocratic habitués had tended to desert the opera, their place being taken by the bourgeoisie. His one success was *Les Huguenots* in September 1836. He resigned in 1841, during Wagner's stay in Paris, and was succeeded by Léon Pillet, a journalist.

Duponchel agreed to receive Wagner. 'Fixing a monocle in his right eye he read through Meyerbeer's letter without betraying the slightest emotion having doubtless received many similar communications from the composer. I went away and never heard another word from him.'

Meyerbeer's introduction to the elderly Habeneck, conductor at the Opéra and at the Conservatoire concerts, was more promising. Habeneck said he was prepared to play something by Wagner at one of the orchestral practices at the Conservatoire. The only short orchestral piece which he could offer was the *Columbus* overture to the play of Theodor Apel which had been performed in Magdeburg in February 1835. Its success on that occasion had been largely due to the spirited playing of the trumpeters from the Prussian garrison. Habeneck duly rehearsed the overture but warned Wagner that it was unlikely to be performed. In fact it was the only one of his works ever to be given a public performance during his two-and-a-half years in Paris. This was in February 1841; by that time Wagner had made something of a name for himself not as a musician but as a writer for Maurice Schlesinger's *Gazette Musicale de Paris*. Another of Meyerbeer's introductions, Schlesinger was a German Jew and, according to Wagner, 'a monstrous person', who made the most of an author's unprotected position in those days.

The Wagners had arrived in Paris in the golden days of the July Monarchy. The three-day uprising in Paris in July 1830, known as 'Les Trois Glorieuses', had resulted in the deposition of the Bourbon Charles x and the accession of Louis-Philippe, the Citizen King. Wagner had, in far-away Leipzig, rejoiced at this event. In France deep depression soon set in about the character of the new regime and the classes which flourished under it, described by Balzac in *Eugénie Grandet* (1833) and in his other novels. Society had become grossly vulgar and materialistic, dominated by the 'nouveaux riches'; no doubt they frequented the Opéra and were admirers of Meyerbeer. Money had become the most coveted of all commodities; this was the period of the ruthless 'arriviste', like Julien Sorel in Stendhal's *Le Rouge et le Noir*. Paris was, at the same time, the most dazzling city of Europe. Rich Parisians, even if vulgar, dressed and entertained lavishly and were anxious to cultivate their artistic sensibilities. The July Revolution had, it seemed, encouraged the development of an individualistic and sentimental romanticism in literature. Between 1830-40 masterpieces of this genre by de Musset, Victor Hugo, Stendhal, Dumas and Balzac appeared. It may appear strange, at first sight, to find Stendhal, with his classicism of form and his horror of sentimentality, treated as a romantic writer, but Julien Sorel is one of the most brilliant creations of individual romanticism.

Liszt and Berlioz were both in Paris at this time. Schlesinger introduced Wagner to Liszt at the end of 1840 when Wagner's fortunes were at their very lowest ebb; he wrote piteous letters to his friends and family; he went around Paris begging a few francs to enable his wife and himself to eat; 'more hideous days,' he wrote to Laube, 'it would be impossible to imagine'. He mostly existed on small sums given him by Schlesinger for correcting musical manuscripts and doing piano arrangements.

Liszt was, on the other hand, at the height of his fame as a virtuoso pianist. Three years older than Wagner he had succeeded, thanks to his looks, his culture and his prowess on the pianoforte, in being accepted almost as an equal by French high society. He was not fully accepted – artists who took money for their performances were socially not all that far removed from servants, even in the 'democratic' days of the Citizen King. Musicians were treated with similar condescension in England and Germany. In London, at aristocratic soirées, they were expected to arrive at the tradesmen's entrance and were separated by a cord from the other guests in the drawing-room. Mendelssohn, when he came to England, was perhaps the first musician to be treated as an equal by London society – and this was because he was known to be rich and not dependent on his fees for a livelihood. (Many years later, in 1861, Hans von Bülow, Liszt's son-in-law and Cosima's husband, was not permitted to play at a court concert in Stuttgart because the King of Württemberg found it disagreeable to see an aristocrat by birth appearing as an artist.) The two most lionized musicians of the last century were Liszt and Chopin. 'Musical patronage,' wrote Ernest Newman, 'was mostly in the hands of women who are much more susceptible to piano playing or fiddling or singing than to creative intellectual work.'

In 1835 Liszt had run off to Geneva with the Comtesse d'Agoult – it was said that he stowed her away in his piano – causing a 'frisson' in Parisian society. She was animated less by love than by a wish to show her disapproval of the condescending attitude of her class to the artist. Liszt was touchy about the inferior social status attached to the artist. Nevertheless, his success in personally breaking through these social barriers led him to indulge in elaborate displays of fine manners and elegant breeding which made him appear ridiculous both to contemporaries and to posterity. It was Wagner, the rough unpolished Saxon, who was to free the nineteenth-century artist from his social shackles.

He did not share Liszt's snobbish susceptibility and, through his genius and personality, he later compelled governments, princes, aristocrats and *Kapellmeisters* to bend to his will; Wagner thus brought about a revolution in German life which was not only social but also artistic and political. He met Liszt twice during his time in Paris; neither meeting was particularly successful. Wagner was impecunious and nearly starving; Liszt was basking in the adoration of beautiful society women and the rich concert-going public, delighting them with dazzlingly intricate piano arrangements of tunes from their favourite operas. Wagner's shortcomings precluded this sort of success. 'He played no instrument that could give him the entry to fashionable circles. He inspired no romantic attachments in excitable high-born women. His speech, his clothes, his manners, and his accent were those of the Saxon bourgeoisie.'[1] He went to a couple of Liszt's recitals and was irritated by the atmosphere of opulence and feminine adoration in which he appeared to luxuriate. Liszt pandered to his ignorant audience by playing his fantasia on *Robert le Diable*. Wagner wrote satirical reports to the Dresden newspaper, *Die Abendzeitung*, about these recitals. During these unhappy days he was haunted by the thought of the monstrously successful Liszt making a fortune with his piano playing. In April 1840 the Wagners moved into a larger apartment in the rue de Helder, off the Boulevard des Italiens. They did this on the strength of a promise that the Théâtre de la Renaissance would

[1] Ernest Newman, *The Life of Richard Wagner*, 1933–49, 4 vols.

take *Das Liebesverbot*. In fact the theatre went bankrupt a few days later and Wagner was later to lend a willing ear to the theory that Meyerbeer, who had effected the introduction to Antenor Joly, director of the Théâtre de la Renaissance, knew all along of the impending bankruptcy, his scheme being to divert Wagner from the Opéra towards this moribund theatre.

The bankruptcy of the Théâtre de la Renaissance was a hideous blow for Wagner. He was now forced to accept any kind of hack work, if only to pay his rent. Schlesinger asked him to do a series of complicated arrangements of Donizetti's *La Favorita*, then the rage in Paris. Wagner got down to this tedious work philosophically; he treated it as a penance in expiation of past sins. 'To save fuel we only used the bedroom, making it serve as drawing-room, dining-room and study as well as dormitory. It was only a step from my bed to my work-table; to be seated at the dining-table all I had to do was to turn my chair round and I only left my seat late at night when I wanted to go to bed. Every fourth day I took a short constitutional.' Wagner regarded this regime as marking the beginnings of the gastric disorders from which he suffered on and off for the rest of his life. To emphasize his renunciation of the world he stopped shaving and grew quite a long beard to his wife's annoyance. 'I tried to bear everything patiently, and the only thing that threatened to drive me to despair was a young piano teacher in the adjoining room who practised Liszt's fantasy on *Lucia di Lammermoor* all day.' By way of retaliation Wagner moved his out-of-tune piano up to the party wall. His lodger Brix, an amiable German commercial traveller, then played on his piccolo-flute Wagner's arrangement for piano and violin (or flute) of the *Favorita* overture, with Wagner accompanying him loudly on the piano. This stopped for a time his neighbour's strumming of *Lucia*.

Wagner's life in Paris could not be described as gregarious or smart. Because of his poverty and his indifferent French he preferred the company of his fellow countrymen. He found three who were as poor and badly connected as he was himself. The first was a musicologist, introduced to Wagner by his brother-in-law Avenarius, who went under the name of 'Anders' – he wished to conceal his real name, it being associated with too many misfortunes. Anders was an ailing, learned, paranoid bachelor in his fifties who had a miserably paid job in the music department of the Bibliothèque Royale. He spoke mysteriously of his noble birth and extensive estates in the Rhineland from which he had been driven by the machinations of his enemies. Wagner chose this rather pathetic creature to be his chief adviser in his musical conquest of Paris. Anders called in, to help in these discussions, his friend Samuel Lehrs, a philologist from Königsberg. He worked for the publisher Didot, who also underpaid him, as an assistant editor of an edition of the Greek classics. Wagner tells us that his acquaintance with Lehrs was to develop into one of the most beautiful friendships of his life. Anders and Lehrs lived in the same 'hotel garni' in the rue de Seine where the rapacious landlady took most of their incomes. The third friend was Ernst Benedikt Kietz from Dresden, introduced to Wagner by his sister, Luise Brockhaus, on her way through Paris. 'He had a curious and childlike disposition and his lack of all serious education combined with a certain weakness of character had made him choose a career in which he was destined, in spite of all his talent, to fail hopelessly.' The career was that of a portrait painter. He spent most of the day mixing colours and cleaning his brushes and never actually finished a picture, complaining that his sitters died before he could complete their portraits. Needless to say Kietz had very little money and was always in debt. We have him to thank, however, for the only portrait of Wagner at this period.

Wagner infected this curious trio with some of his own vivacity and energy and before long they were inseparable. They were soon joined by another German painter, Friedrich Pecht, whom Wagner met one day in the Louvre. In his memoirs Pecht described Wagner as being of striking appearance, the large head and expressive face making up for the shortness of leg. His dress was 'particularly elegant'. He appeared to speak very little French. Wagner was described at this time by an employee of Schlesinger as being 'morose, unsociable, murdering the French language and abusing everybody'. He was not cut out for gracing cosmopolitan circles. Twenty years later, when he was famous and back in Paris, one of his French friends described him as 'having neither grace nor elegance, ignorant of social ways, and, like all great minds, much more preoccupied with what he had to say than with the effect he was producing'.

On the other hand Wagner delighted his friends and acquaintances with his wit, pluck and ebullience during those grim days in Paris. Heinrich Laube came to Paris with a rich young widow, whom he had recently married. Although she did not know him, she had learned of his arrest and sentence to a year's imprisonment and, filled with compassion, resolved to marry him at the beginning of his term, so as to be useful to him in prison. This, together with the fact, that he managed to get himself imprisoned in Silesia, near the estates of his influential friend Prince Pückler-Muskau, did much to mitigate the rigours of his sentence. Now the Laubes were celebrating his freedom by enjoying themselves in Paris. Wagner was pleased to see his old Leipzig friend again and hoped, naturally, that he would give him some money. 'Laube was the first to approve, in his kindly and humorous way, of our folly in moving to Paris.'

Through Laube, Wagner met Heinrich Heine, who was also living as an expatriate in Paris. From all accounts, Heine was, in spite of his brilliant poetic and journalistic gifts, an odious person – venomous and sarcastic – who used his pen as a blackmailing instrument to extract money and other favours from the rich and influential. Wagner did not, understandably, take to him; on top of this, he could not quite forgive him for being a Jew. Nevertheless, Heine left his mark on *Der fliegende Holländer* and on *Tannhäuser*; In Riga Wagner had read his *Memoiren des Herrn Schnabelewopski*, from which he may possibly have taken the story of his *Der fliegende Holländer*. Unlike Liszt and Meyerbeer he was too unimportant to suffer the stings of Heine's malice in Paris. On the contrary: 'Heine joked good-humouredly over my extraordinary situation, making even me laugh.' Wagner delighted him and his friends with his boisterous account of the sea journey to London and with his disarming expectations of musical successes in Paris. Words poured out of him, according to Pecht, covering his listeners like a 'snow-storm'.

Wagner's privations in Paris and his need to take on any kind of pot-boiling hack work to keep alive brought about changes in him as a human being and as an artist. His friends noticed his elasticity of temperament – how he was able, in the midst of appalling practical pressures, to rise to spiritual and intellectual heights; the strength and clarity of his views on all branches of aesthetics; the alertness of his humour. His artistic consciousness was deepening, despite the triviality of much of the work he was compelled to do. The first unmistakable sign, in Wagner's view, of these artistic changes in him were Habeneck's rehearsals at the Conservatoire of Beethoven's Ninth Symphony. 'Where formerly I had only seen mystic constellations and weird shapes without meaning, I now found, flowing from innumerable sources, a stream of the most touching and heavenly melodies which delighted my heart.'

As a boy he had been in ecstasies over the score of the Ninth Symphony; this later turned to bewilderment when he heard it 'slaughtered under Pohlenz's baton' in the Leipzig Gewandhaus. Now these French musicians, trained in the Italian lyrical school, had grasped that melody and song were the secret of all music. 'That glorious orchestra actually *sang* this symphony.' In this mood Wagner also wished to compose something, despite the wretchedness of his Paris existence, which would give him artistic satisfaction. So he sketched, on 12 January 1840, an overture to Goethe's *Faust*. This was to have been the first movement of a Faust Symphony; he already carried the second movement, *Gretchen*, in his head. This overture, in the D minor key, looking both backwards to the Ninth and forwards to *Der fliegende Holländer* was reconstructed by Wagner, at Liszt's advice, fifteen years later.

Wagner gave literary expression to his reborn enthusiasm for Beethoven by writing a short story for the *Gazette Musicale*, 'Une visite à Beethoven'. This was one of several articles for Schlesinger's journal. In this and other essays Wagner showed that he was an excellent literary journalist, his style poised somewhere between that of Heine and Hoffmann. He found himself a journalist in a characteristic manner. Schlesinger had earlier refused to publish any of the songs which Wagner had written for the French public. His 'advisory board' – Lehrs, Anders and Kietz – had advised him to write some short simple songs, which could be offered to popular singers for concert purposes. They even provided the words for some of them. 'I have no reason to be ashamed of these small pieces,' Wagner later tells us. One of them, 'Dors, mon enfant', reminiscent of the spinning song in *Der fliegende Holländer*, written by a young friend of Anders, Minna found heavenly for sending her to sleep when Wagner strummed it softly on the piano. He took this song and others round to influential singers, in the hope that they would agree to sing them. This approach led to disappointment. None of his songs were accepted and he never forgot the humiliating treatment meted out to him by these self-satisfied French singers. One of the rejected songs, a setting to a French version of Heine's 'The Two Grenadiers', Wagner decided to publish at his own expense. As he was later unable to pay Schlesinger his fee for engraving the song, he agreed to work off the debt by writing articles for the *Gazette Musicale*. This commission led to a flow of intelligent, charmingly written and imaginative stories and articles – very different from his turgid writings of later years when his thoughts sometimes appeared to be too weighty for his pen to handle.

Another tribute to Beethoven was to have been a biography of him, written by Wagner assisted by Anders who had plenty of facts and documents but who lacked the ability to express himself on paper. Wagner, in a letter to Laube about this project, said it was not to be a dry-as-dust biography, crammed with chronological data, but rather the life of the artist written in the form of a novel (*Künstlerroman*). Alas, no German publisher could be found to take an interest in the work.

In his new found earnestness he was anxious to hear more of Berlioz's music. Berlioz had listened patiently to the playing of Wagner's *Columbus* overture in the Conservatoire and had praised his story, 'Un musicien étranger à Paris', in which he described with grim humour his treatment by the rapacious Schlesinger and others. Heine went as far as saying that Hoffmann would have been incapable of writing such a piece. Wagner went to a performance of Berlioz's new symphony *Romeo and Juliet*, with Berlioz conducting. He was overwhelmed by the grandeur and intricacy of the orchestration. 'It was beyond anything I could have conceived. The fantastic daring, the sharp precision with which the boldest combinations – almost tangible in their clearness – impressed me, drive back my own ideas of the poetry of music with brutal violence into the very depths of my soul.' Wagner was also much impressed by the *Sinfonie Fantastique* and *Harold en Italie*. What he admired most of all was Berlioz's *Grande Symphonie Funebre et Triomphale*, composed in 1840 in honour of those heroes who had died during the July Revolution. Berlioz conducted the massed military bands in person at the foot of the column of the Place de la Bastille.

In Paris Wagner met Eugène Scribe. He had sent that

indefatigable writer of libretti the score of *Das Liebesverbot* from Riga. Although Scribe never acknowledged it Wagner was certain that he had received it and that the great librettist knew of his existence. This was a factor that had encouraged him to set out for Paris from the Baltic. After the collapse of the Théâtre de la Renaissance, Wagner persuaded the director of the Opéra to arrange an audition for *Das Liebesverbot*. Scribe attended the audition and said he would be happy to write a libretto as soon as Wagner had been commissioned to write an opera. He made some polite noises about *Das Liebesverbot* but did not betray any wish to translate the libretto. Wagner saw, quickly enough, that he could not expect any help from the genial Scribe.

In April 1841 the Wagners moved into a cheap summer residence at Meudon on the outskirts of Paris. Their financial position was getting steadily worse. A few weeks later he heard that *Rienzi* had been accepted for performance in Dresden. (It was in Blasewitz, near Dresden, exactly four years earlier, that he had come across Bulwer Lytton's novel and written the prose sketch of his *Rienzi*. By November 1840 he had completed the score of the five-act opera, 'this most voluminous of all my operas'.) Before he sent off a petition to the King of Saxony for the acceptance of *Rienzi* and the score to the director of the court theatre, August von Lüttichau, Wagner borrowed a metronome – he did not possess one – in order to mark the correct 'tempi' on the opera score. One morning he went out to return the metronome to its owner, carrying the instrument under his thin overcoat. Apart from delivering the metronome he needed to borrow some money for their next meal, to get the holders of bills that had fallen due to agree to their renewal and to raise some money from Schlesinger to pay for posting the score of *Rienzi* to Dresden. The bill holders were living all over Paris.

That day I had to propitiate a cheesemonger who occupied a fifth floor apartment in the Cité . . . as I had to deliver the metronome I left Minna early in the morning after a sad goodbye. She knew from experience that, as I was on a money-raising expedition, she would not see me again until late at night. The streets were enveloped in a thick fog and the first thing I saw on leaving the house was my dog Robber who had been stolen a year before. At first I thought it was a ghost but I called him sharply in a shrill voice. The animal seemed to recognize me and approached me cautiously; my sudden movement towards him with outstretched hands seemed to revive memories of one or two thrashings I had foolishly given him. He drew timidly away from me . . . I followed him through a labyrinth of streets, hardly distinguishable in the thick mist, until I lost sight of him altogether, never to see him again. . . . For a while I stood motionless, glaring into the mist, wondering what the ghostly reappearance of the companion of my travelling adventures might portend. The fact that he had fled from his old master with the terror of a wild beast filled my heart with a strange bitterness and seemed to me a horrible omen. Sadly shaken, I set out again, with trembling limbs, upon my weary errand.

Wagner said his opera had come into the world after the most atrocious birth-pangs. He had hoped, of course, that *Rienzi* would be accepted by the Opera. It was, after all, a *grosse tragische Oper,* with five splendid finales, hymns, massed choirs, processions and tempestuous orchestration. 'Meyerbeer's best opera', as von Bülow later called it, would have taken Paris by storm had it been written by Meyerbeer. But it wasn't – it was written by a brash, provincial young German, languishing perhaps in prison at the time of its completion. This is, at any rate, what Minna wrote in October 1840 to Theodor Apel in her desperate entreaty for money:

> This morning Richard had to leave me to go to the debtor's prison . . . a fortnight hence the overture to his *Rienzi*, which he has just finished and which everyone believes will be a great success, is to be played; but without his personal presence at the rehearsal this will not be possible . . . of what avail are my tears? Is this to be the end of us? Will you allow him to be lost to us because a greater sacrifice than usual is needed?

The playing of the *Rienzi* overture never took place and the opera was lost to Paris. Several years later when the Opéra asked Wagner's permission to stage *Rienzi* he refused. Even today *Rienzi* is very seldom, if ever, performed, both because of its length and its unevenness of musical quality. Wagner himself soon turned against the opera: 'I cannot bear the din.' He called it his *Schreihals* (bawler or bellower). The music of *Rienzi* reflects, to a certain extent, the contradictions inherent in it as both a drama and a spectacle. Exquisite, truly Wagnerian melodic passages in, for example, Rienzi's 'Prayer' and 'Santo Spirito, cavalieri', change suddenly into commonplace melodies à la Meyerbeer.

Rienzi is enjoyable if treated as an example of the 'grand opera' so fashionable in the middle of the last century. Its weaknesses may be accepted as weaknesses of that particular genre and we may enjoy, above all, the youthful exuberance which informs the whole opera – even its length!

The last three acts of *Rienzi* were written, then, in harsh and difficult circumstances with Wagner eking out a living as best he could. A generation later he could not talk about this painful Paris period without tears coming to his eyes. He remained, throughout his life, profoundly grateful to Minna for having stood by him so bravely and so philosophically. His disappointments had touched her heart. The sight of him working day and night, churning out arrangements of inferior operas for Schlesinger, filled her with pride and pity. (She became less understanding during their Zurich period, ten years later, when he, so she thought, wasted his time writing unreadable theoretical works instead of building on the reputation he had gained at Dresden as the composer of three successful operas.) In Paris, however, whether in the rue de la Tonnellerie, the rue de Helder, in Meudon or in the rue Jacob, where they moved in October 1841, she accepted any sacrifice, pawning first her few jewels and then the pawn tickets themselves. In Paris Wagner developed, even perfected, what Pecht called his 'inborn gift for debt-making' – he had never seen in any other man such skill and versatility of technique when it came to borrowing money. Wagner did not think that his family, the Avenarius's, or Brockhaus's, or friends like Apel, Laube and others, had helped him as much as they could or should have done. In most cases he already owed them money from his Leipzig, Magdeburg, Königsberg or Riga days. He had not had any musical successes worth mentioning and they were disinclined to throw good money after bad. But with the acceptance of *Rienzi* by the court theatre at Dresden his arguments gained credibility and so he moved into his next borrowing phase.

During those weary Paris months of musical pot-boiling and journalistic scribbling, Wagner went for long walks with Minna and spoke to her wistfully about life in what he called the 'South American Free States', where music and opera were unknown and where a sensible livelihood could be obtained by honest work. He had been reading a book about the founding of Maryland, which he may have thought was in South America, and in it he had found 'a very seductive account of the sensation of relief experienced by European settlers after their former sufferings and persecutions'. Minna persuaded him that it would be more sensible to stay in Paris than to leave for South America, but the idea of emigrating to America returned to him on several occasions in future years when he felt incapable of struggling further against German obstinacy and stupidity.

Another thought which haunted him, whether engaged on his hack-work or on the more creative and edifying *Rienzi*, was the memory of the storm off the Norwegian coast, the whistling of the wind in the rigging of the *Thetis* and the sailors' shouts as they echoed along the granite cliffs. As he worked on *Rienzi*, on board ship, the sailors had told him the tale of The Flying Dutchman; during the storm it had assumed a strange but definite shape in his mind. The noise of the wind in the rigging had, on him, such a demonic effect that he suddenly saw another ship loom up and disappear with equal suddenness into the darkness. He believed that he had seen the Flying Dutchman and the music gradually took shape in his mind. Most people had, of course, heard of the tale of the Flying Dutchman. In Riga Wagner had read Heine's version of it in his *Memoiren des Herrn von Schnabelowopski*, the novel element in it being that only a woman's redeeming love could save the soul of the doomed captain. He fastened onto the idea of redemption and in Paris the poetical and musical elements in his opera slowly ripened. Wagner also hoped that he might, with a short, single-act opera, make a better musical début in Paris if *Rienzi* was turned down by the Opéra. He thought that it might, as a curtain-raiser to a ballet, have a better chance of being accepted. In the summer of 1840 Meyerbeer introduced him to Léon Pillet, the new director, to whom Wagner gave a sketch of his proposed opera. Pillet was much taken by this sketch but he did not wish Wagner to set it to music. Instead he proposed that he sell him the plot for 500 francs, advising him strongly to accept this offer, as there was no likelihood of his being asked to compose anything for the Opéra for at least seven years. Wagner took this advice. His sketch formed the basis of the opera *Le Vaisseau Fantôme*, the libretto by Paul Foucher, a brother-in-law of Victor Hugo, and the music by Pierre-Louis Dietsch, an indifferent composer who later, in 1861, conducted, in notorious circumstances, the Paris version of *Tannhäuser*. *Le Vaisseau Fantôme* was staged at the opera in November 1842 and ran for ten performances, to be thereafter forgotten.

Wagner had earlier, in July 1840, sent Meyerbeer three numbers from the as yet incomplete opera – 'Senta's Ballad', the chorus of the Norwegian sailors and the song of the crew (*Spukgesang*). This step turned out to be of the greatest significance not only for *Der fliegende Holländer* but also for his future technique of composition. 'Senta's Ballad' contains the theme of the whole opera. This embryonic theme was able to develop slowly and when, in Meudon in the summer of 1841, he sketched out the musical composition of *Der fliegende Holländer* he involuntarily let the thematic material in 'Senta's Ballad' spread like a web over the whole opera. Within four months the whole score was finished and at the end of 1841 he sent it to Wilhelm von Redern, the intendant of the Berlin opera. He had previously sent the poem, the earlier prose sketch of which described the action as set off the Scottish coast, to the directors of the Leipzig and Munich operas; both refused it, the former considering it too gloomy and the latter as unsuited to prevailing German taste.

In *Der fliegende Holländer* Wagner revealed, for the first time, his particular ability to develop, out of embryonic motifs from an original melody, the themes for the entire work. His technique was not yet sufficiently developed for this new thematic principle to be worked out in full; with this opera, however, he turns away from the facile temptation to become a conventional opera composer and sets out on the lonely, noble road to music-drama. In Paris, the scene of his dashed hopes, he realized Jean Paul's prophecy that a man would appear to blend the arts of poetry and music.

Wagner now saw himself as a dramatic poet, intuitively possessed of the musical expression of his poems. He gave one of the best definitions of his aesthetics in a letter written a couple of years later to Carl Gaillard, a young Berlin admirer who, after seeing the Berlin production of *Der fliegende Holländer* in January 1844, thought he understood Wagner's new operatic values and wished to further the Wagnerian cause in his journal, the *Berliner Musikalische Zeitung*: 'Before I wrote any lines of verse; before I even lay out a scene, I am already inhaling the musical fragrance of my composition; all the characteristic musical motifs are alive in my mind so that, once the verse is written and the scenes arranged, the opera is more or less complete.'

With the completion of *Der fliegende Holländer* Wagner became aware of his revolutionary vocation: 'I trod a new road – that of a revolution against the contemporary public.' His failure to achieve any kind of success in Paris, the musical capital of Europe, turned him into a revolutionary idealist. It also turned him into a nationalist; he now longed to return to his native Germany. The production of *Der Freischütz* at the Opéra in June 1841 brought back those youthful memories. 'How happy I am to be a German', he wrote to the Dresden newspaper, *Dresdener Abendzeitung*. In Germany conditions were, he thought, favourable for the transformation of musical taste which he hoped to bring about. In his first article for Schlesinger's *Gazette Musicale* he had written lovingly of the honest and simple musical culture in every small German town, where amateurs were often better than professionals, where the local orchestra could play the most difficult symphonies and where a simple bandsman played several instruments. His friend Anders, on reading the article, said that, if all this was true, Germany must be a paradise for musicians.

The hour soon struck for Wagner's deliverance: 'The day came on which, as I devoutly hoped, I might turn my back on Paris forever.'[1] It was 7 April 1842. His emotion on parting from his dear friends, Anders, Lehrs and Kietz was almost overwhelming. He was sure that the first two were destined for early deaths and that he would never see them again, and, as for Kietz, he was worried about his childlike good nature. 'Thinking that I mightn't have enough money for the journey he forced upon me another five-franc piece which was all that he possessed at that moment; he also stuffed a packet of good French snuff in the pocket of the coach in which we rumbled along the boulevards towards the barrier of the city which we could not see as our eyes were blinded by tears.'

[1] The acceptance of *Rienzi* by the Dresden court theatre and Berlin's favourable response to *Der fliegende Holländer* were the immediate reasons which prompted him to return to Germany.

75

CHAPTER FIVE

Hofkapellmeister and Revolutionary
1843–9

'FOR THE FIRST TIME I beheld the Rhine; my eyes filled with tears and I swore that I would, although only a poor artist, devote my life to the service of my German fatherland.' This was one of two bright and memorable moments in an otherwise dreadful journey back to Leipzig via Dresden. Dreadful because the perfect spring weather in Paris turned into wind and snow the deeper they got into Germany and because, after Frankfurt, they were swept into the stream of pilgrims heading for the Leipzig Easter Fair. The second memorable moment was, during the only sunlit part of the journey, the sight of the Wartburg outside Eisenach, that mountain fortress which sent his thoughts back to the legend of Tannhäuser. As they drove along the valley Wagner pictured to himself the scenery for the third act of *Tannhäuser*.[1] The scene remained so vividly in his mind that he was able, three years later, to give Despléchin, the French scene-designer, exact details of what he wanted for the Dresden première of *Tannhäuser*. The view of the Wartburg 'so warmed my heart against wind and weather, Jews and the Leipzig Fair, that in the end I arrived, on 12 April 1842, safe and sound, with my poor, battered, half-frozen wife, in the self-same city of Dresden which I had last seen on the occasion of my sad separation from my Minna [July 1837], and my departure for my northern place of exile.'

Wagner's oath of eternal loyalty to his fatherland after seeing the Rhine was his own way of saying goodbye to Paris. He had not in the past made many favourable references to patriotism

[1] A valley in front of the Wartburg with the Hörselberg hill on the left.

and nationalism except to the Polish freedom fighters. As a student at Leipzig he had abhorred the stuffiness of German culture and had thrown himself into international and liberal literary and political causes. Those awful years in Paris had made him look on Germany with a more friendly eye. On top of this he had, towards the end of his Paris period, been reading some German *Volksbücher* or sagas[1] procured for him by Lehrs. Earlier, he had been influenced by Raumer's *History of the Hohenstaufen*. He was captivated by the personality of the Emperor Frederick II, *Stupor Mundi*, and sketched the plan of a five-act opera about Frederick's son, Manfred, and Fatima, who happened to be the love child of Frederick and a noble Saracen lady. The opera was to be called *Die Saraʒenin* (The Saracen Woman). Wagner never reached the stage of writing the music as his attention was diverted to those pamphlets which Lehrs had brought him about the Tannhäuser and Lohengrin legends. 'Everything that I regarded as essentially German I suddenly found presented to me in the simple outline of a legend, based upon the old and well-known ballad of "Tannhaüser".' Lehrs had brought him the tales of the 'Venusberg' and the 'Sängerkrieg auf der Wartburg' (Song Contest on the Wartburg) and also a copy of a yearbook of the Königsberg German Society which contained an essay on the Wartburg song contest and a sketch of the Lohengrin epic. 'A new world opened up for me,' said Wagner. This brought his mind back to Tieck's *Phantasus* from which he had first learned of Danheuser, a fallen *Minnesänger* (love poet) who squandered money on women and took two baths a week. Worse than that, he had called on Venus at her grotto in the Hörselberg, near Eisenach,[2] where he spent at least a year with her, gratifying his senses.

He also remembered reading E. T. A. Hoffmann's account, in his *Kampf der Sänger*, of the song contests held at the Wartburg, the court of the thirteenth-century Landgrave Hermann of Thuringia. Within a framework of very strict rules the courtly *Minnesänger*

---

[1] Wagner was a voracious reader; throughout his life he read on average eighty pages a day and he put together several libraries during his tempestuous career. He must have been the most widely-read musician who has ever lived – at any rate in non-musical subjects.

[2] There is today a splendid collection of Wagneriana in the Fritz Reuter Villa in Eisenach.

composed and declaimed their verses on the nature of love, in which the sentiments were pure and the love object unattainable, on Christianity, the German fatherland and the Holy Roman Empire. There were six *Minnesänger* in all; the singer who invariably carried off the prizes was Heinrich von Ofterdingen, the two other famous ones being Walther von der Vogelweide and Wolfram von Eschenbach. Although the Wartburg and the Hörselberg were both in the immediate vicinity of Eisenach the story of the song contest was not in any way connected with the errant Danheuser, or Tannhäuser, and the Venusberg. The author of the essay on the Wartburg song contest, C. T. L. Lucas, had, however, diffidently suggested that Heinrich von Ofterdingen and Tannhäuser were one and the same person. This suggestion was all that was needed to blend the two stories in Wagner's imagination; all of a sudden the essential features of a drama occupied his mind, thus causing *Die Sarazenin* to be permanently shelved.

In the German saga Danheuser repented of his self-indulgent life in due course and went off to Rome for absolution which the Pope refused to give him owing to the heinousness of his offence. Danheuser, thereupon, rushed back to Venusberg as fast as his legs could carry him. The Pope, who had intended to forgive him – but not in front of the other pilgrims – sent a messenger after him, post-haste; but it was too late and Danheuser never again left the Venusberg.

Wagner's discovery of the world of German medieval legend had the expected effect. 'A tender, nostalgic patriotism entered my being, of which I had not, until now, any glimmering. This patriotism had no political coloration; I was, in those days, so enlightened that political Germany, like political France, possessed no attraction for me.'

It was not long before these sentiments gave way to more savage ones. 'Dresden, in which such momentous years of my childhood had been spent, seemed cold and dead in the wild, gloomy weather. No hospitable house received us; my parents-in-law lived in cramped and dingy lodgings. . . .' The many friends of his past had since disappeared. The officials of the opera house made it clear that they found him impatient and importunate; the shining exceptions were the chorus master, Wilhelm Fischer, and the costume designer, Ferdinand Heine, who had been a friend of Ludwig Geyer. These two men became very fond of Wagner; they shared his high artistic ideals and did all they could to meet his wishes, however exacting, relating to the première of *Rienzi*. These two friends apart, he was soon disillusioned with Dresden, Saxony and Germany. He wrote to Lehrs saying that, if he had to fail, he would rather it be in Paris than in Dresden. 'I have no geographical preference and my fatherland, in spite of its chains of hills, woods and valleys, repels me. These Saxons are an accursed lot – slimy, temporizing, oafish, slothful and coarse – why should I have anything to do with them?' (He himself, although deserving of none of these epithets, never lost his thick Saxon accent.)

Wagner was delighted to see his mother (now housed in a comfortable flat), and other members of the family again after six years. He then went on to Berlin to discuss with the intendant, Redern, the production of *Der fliegende Holländer*; Redern had agreed to take the work at the beginning of 1842, when Wagner was still in Paris. His acceptance was due, above all, to Meyerbeer's intervention. Wagner's attitude to Meyerbeer has caused his apologists a certain amount of uneasiness. From his arrival in Boulogne in August 1839 he wrote Meyerbeer innumerable letters, often couched in terms of extravagant servility, always requesting a favour of some sort – either money or that Meyerbeer put in a good word for him with the director or intendant of the opera houses in Paris, Berlin, or Dresden. Meyerbeer undoubtedly admired Wagner's intelligence, musicality, and general culture; he admired also his energy and his pluck in the frustrating situation in which he found himself. Although he went to reasonable lengths to help him, Wagner and his friends became convinced that, not only could he have done very much more, but his apparent help was, more often than not, a deceitful front, behind which he schemed to thwart the career of the potential younger rival. Up to the end of his Paris period Wagner had only the nicest things to say to, and about, Meyerbeer and at the end of 1839 he wrote to Schumann, 'Stop disparaging Meyerbeer; I owe this man everything – especially my imminent fame.' Yet at the beginning of 1842, in another letter to Schumann from Paris, he described Meyerbeer as a 'deliberate, cunning double-crosser'. From then on the discrepancy becomes more and more grotesque. As Wagner's artistic consciousness developed he saw Meyerbeer's meretriciousness as symbolizing all that was wrong in contemporary music. Nevertheless, in 1842, Meyerbeer was a powerful person – he had just been appointed general musical director of the Berlin opera – and his goodwill was essential for Wagner. Being forced to flatter him he found compensation by running him down in private.

After arriving in Berlin Wagner learned that Redern was about to retire; his successor was Küstner who had, in Munich, rejected *Der fliegende Holländer* as being 'unsuited' to German taste. He could not repudiate his predecessor's decision; instead, he procrastinated.[1] Needless to say Wagner called on Meyerbeer to ask his help in overcoming these delays. 'He said he was on the point of going away – a state in which I always found him whenever I visited Berlin.'

After the disappointment about *Der fliegende Holländer* Wagner's spirits sank and he turned against Berlin. 'After my acquaintance with London, and still more with Paris, this city, with its sordid spaces and pretensions to greatness, depressed me deeply and I breathed a hope that, should no luck crown my life, it might at least be spent in Paris rather than in Berlin.' He persisted, however, in trying to secure a footing for himself in Berlin; a success there meant much more than a success in Dresden which ranked as a provincial stage. Furthermore, Berlin paid royalties for each production whereas Dresden only paid a flat fee. He set high hopes on the patronage of the King of Prussia, Friedrich Wilhelm IV, who had admired *Rienzi* and who wanted Berlin to become the leading city for all the arts in Germany. He even dreamed that the music-loving king might become the instrument for the realization of his artistic ideals but, from first to last, his hopes of Berlin were dashed and none of his opera premières were held there.

On this visit to Berlin in April 1842 Wagner sought out Mendelssohn who had given up the post of conductor in the Leipzig Gewandhaus to become one of the general musical directors to the King of Prussia. This was part of Friedrich Wilhelm's ambitious plan to make his capital the centre of German music. It was not a great success. The conceited Spontini, who had been *Kapellmeister* in Berlin, later told Wagner when he came

[1] In the end, the première took place in Dresden on 2 January 1843 and in Berlin on 7 January 1844.

to Dresden in October 1844, 'There was some hope for Germany when I was the Emperor of music at Berlin; but since the King of Prussia has abandoned his music to the disorder created by those two wandering Jews [Mendelssohn and Meyerbeer] all hope for it has been lost.' Mendelssohn told Wagner that he disliked his assignment and wished to return to Leipzig. He made no reference to the great C major Symphony which Wagner had sent him in May 1835 and which he had never acknowledged. (Mendelssohn is another figure regarded by Wagner partisans as not having sufficiently pulled his weight to help Wagner in the early stages of his career.) Like Schumann he took a priggish, superior attitude to Wagner's music, criticizing it on tedious, technical points. The only thing in *Tannhäuser* which Mendelssohn found to his liking was a piece of canonic imitation in the second finale. When he conducted the *Tannhäuser* overture at the Leipzig Gewandhaus in February 1846 he did so with ostentatious ill-humour, taking the tempo so quickly that the piece was unintelligible. Young Hans von Bülow was there and described it as an 'execution', in every sense of the word. Mendelssohn did not particularly admire Wagner and did not use his great influence to help him. Wagner, on the other hand, made many disinterested approaches to Mendelssohn, whose music he admired, but never got much response.

Wagner left Berlin to return to Dresden for the preparations for *Rienzi*. On the way he stayed with his sister Ottilie and her husband Hermann Brockhaus, now Professor of Oriental Languages at Leipzig University. They had arranged, with other members of the family, to give him 35 thalers (about £5) a month for six months until *Rienzi* had brought him in some money. One evening he broke into a violent fit of weeping; the atmosphere of domestic contentment and quiet intellectual activity in the Brockhaus household moved his 'homeless and vagabond soul'. Once again, Ottilie comforted him as she had done in the summer of 1837 during his crisis with Minna.

Before the *Rienzi* rehearsals started in earnest Wagner, Minna and his mother, the two women meeting for the first time, went for a holiday to Teplitz, the watering-place where he had gone with Apel in 1834. Wagner, as had been his habit in the past, left them to go on a ramble lasting several days in the Bohemian mountains. He wanted to work out his plan for the *Venusberg* which was the title he then intended for his next opera (later called *Tannhäuser*). He took a simple room in Aussig on the romantic Schreckenstein, at night sleeping on straw. Just for the fun of it he spent the whole of one moonlight night, wrapped only in a blanket, clambering amongst the ruins of the Schreckenstein and hoping to terrify some unsuspecting wayfarer. Here he wrote in a small red note-book[1] the complete plan of his three-act opera. One day, when he was climbing the Wostrai, the highest peak in the neighbourhood, he saw, on a crag, a goatherd piping a merry tune: 'All at once I was standing amongst the chorus of pilgrims as they filed past the goatherd in the valley.' (*Tannhäuser*, Act 1)

In the church in Aussig Wagner admired a picture of the Madonna by Carlo Dolci. He wrote to Kietz saying that, if Tannhäuser had seen it, he would have had a very good reason for turning from Venus to Mary without having any particularly pious convictions. 'At any rate, I now pictured my Saint Elizabeth.' After the song contest and the Venusberg Elizabeth was the most important feature of *Tannhäuser*; she was, more or less, Wagner's invention. In the opera she becomes the counterpart of Venus; in modern productions the parts of Elizabeth and Venus are often taken by the same singer – a parallel to the theory that Danheuser and Heinrich von Ofterdingen were one and the same person.

Wagner returned to Teplitz in excellent spirits and there he completed the second prose sketch of the opera. The other phases followed during the next three years. The score was finished in April 1845 and the première took place in Dresden in October of that year.

With *Tannhäuser* Wagner first became clearly aware of the nature of his artistic genius. His interesting letter to Carl Gaillard was written just after he had finished the orchestral sketch of Act 1 in January 1844. In it he said that all the musical themes and motifs were in his mind before a single word had been written; all that then needed doing were the versifying and ordering of the scenes. He now realized that only by uniting the poet and musician in a single person could anything of significance be achieved in opera. In his own case he hardly knew when he was functioning as a poet or as a musician. *Der fliegende Holländer* had been his first clear move in the direction of the 'total artistic

[1] This note-book is now in the Burrell Collection in Philadelphia.

experience' (*Gesamtkunstwerk*), where the arts of poetry, music and drama are combined.

Wagner's sufferings in Paris had two important results which greatly influenced his future operas, particularly *Tannhäuser*, the first 'autobiographical' opera in which his own psychic and emotional problems were presented in poetry and music. Firstly, because he felt rejected in Paris, he thought indulgently and nostalgically about Germany, about the Saxon and Thuringian countryside, about the medieval Germany of courtliness and song, myths and legends – so different from that febrile, decadent French culture. He had started to read German *Volksbücher* and sagas. As well as his rediscovery of the German mythical traditions, his Paris sufferings had also got him thinking about the problem of the artist in society. They had convinced him that middle class, capitalistic society spelt death for the creative artist. In addition to that he had his own personal problems – a youth dominated by his mother and a premature marriage. He was looking therefore for two apparently incompatible forms of musical sublimation: the romantic world of German medieval musicians, as expressed in simple musical forms, and the decadent tortured world of Venus – a world which produced more interesting music. The lower emotions, such as envy, lust, contempt, offer greater opportunities for rhythmic and melodic subtlety.

The use of leitmotivs, or the single embryonic idea, as in *Der fliegende Holländer*, was now becoming an essential part of Wagner's musical language. Wagner himself never used this expression, which was coined many years later by Hans von Wolzogen[1] when referring to Weber's *Euryanthe*. The Wagnerian definition of a 'leitmotiv' would perhaps be that it is a musical phrase being constantly modified, harmonically, rhythmically and melodically, to express the various facets of a musical and poetical idea. In Wagner's music dramas after 1850 the leitmotivs enter fully into the symphonic texture of his operas; since his characters, especially Siegfried, tended to repeat themselves a good deal in their thoughts and actions, and as each thought and action had its own appropriate musical phrase, the leitmotiv became quickly recognizable. In the *Ring* operas, with the continuous introduction of new ideas and situations and the retention of the old ones, there is a constantly expanding texture which blends to form

[1] Editor of *Die Bayreuther Blätter*, the Wagnerian journal.

exquisite patterns of sound. Because of his effortless ability to combine different sounds, Wagner was called a *Kombinationsgenie* by Richard Strauss. In *Tannhäuser*, as in *Der fliegende Holländer*, these leitmotivs tend to be rather isolated melodies, but they are beginning to play their appointed parts as 'emotional signposts' (*Gefühlswegweiser*), to recapitulate, to emphasize, to remind us of developments. Sometimes, as in *Tannhäuser*, the leitmotivs may be compressed in the overture, thus giving a kind of 'digest' of the opera – perhaps, some of its critics might say, making the rest of the opera superfluous.

On 18 July 1842 Wagner had to break off his holiday at Teplitz and return to Dresden. The singers, Tichatschek and Schröder-Devrient, had arrived and Reissiger, the *Kapellmeister*, was about to start the rehearsals for *Rienzi*. The rehearsals took place in an elated atmosphere; Tichatschek, the *Heldentenor*, loved the part of Rienzi and his suits of silver armour and Schröder-Devrient, although prejudiced against her part as Adriano, as it was not that of the heroine, was moved to tears by the beauty of the opera. Wagner discussed, in a jocular way, possible cuts with his friends, Fischer and Heine, with whom he spent many happy evenings eating potatoes and herrings. 'I believe,' he said, 'that the whole theatrical body, down to its humblest officials, loved me as though I were a real prodigy. I think this arose from sympathy and fellow-feeling for a young man whose exceptional difficulties were not unknown to them and who was now stepping out of complete obscurity into splendour.' The singers clapped their favourite moments in the opera; Tichatschek, a good-hearted simpleton with a glorious voice, declared the B minor ensemble in the third finale to be so beautiful that every member of the cast should pay the composer a silver penny each time it was rehearsed. 'No one suspected that these gratuities, given me as a joke, actually helped defray the cost of our daily food.' Certainly his artistic ardour, his pinched face and emaciated frame won him a lot of sympathy from well-wishers before and after the production of *Rienzi*.

The première of *Rienzi* on 20 October 1842 was a success surpassing all expectations – one of the most successful premières in Wagner's career.

When I try to recall my condition that evening I can only picture it with all the paraphernalia of a dream. Of real pleasure or agitation I felt none at all. I seemed to stand quite aloof from my work; whereas the sight of the crowded auditorium agitated me so much that I was unable to glance at the audience whose presence affected me like some natural phenomenon – something like a continuous downpour of rain – from which I sought shelter in the furthest corner of my box. I was quite unconscious of applause and when, at the end of each act, I was tempestuously called for I had to be driven on to the stage.

The public clearly realized that there was something new and adventurous about this opera for which Wagner was paid a flat fee of 300 thalers.[1] This went a small way towards satisfying some of his Paris creditors.

On 2 February 1843 Wagner was awarded the life appointment of Royal Saxon *Kapellmeister* at a salary of 1500 thalers. He accepted this appointment with considerable misgivings, already suspecting that the operas he wished to compose were beyond the capacities of a provincial opera house. He saw the danger of a conflict between his profession and his vocation. Minna had pressed him to accept the post. 'In Germany the greatest value is laid on these court appointments, which are tenable for life, and the dazzling respectability pertaining to them is held out to German musicians as the acme of earthly happiness.' He had to buy a court uniform costing a hundred thalers which he called a 'ludicrous outgoing'. The uniform was a reminder that he was simply a court servant – not that he often saw the monarch who had made this historic appointment. A few days later King Friedrich August II summoned him to an audience. 'This kindly, courteous and homely monarch expressed his satisfaction with my two operas which had been performed in Dresden [the other being *Der fliegende Holländer*].' The only mild criticism which the king ventured to put forward was that there could perhaps have been a clearer definition of the characters who were overpowered by the elemental forces controlling them: in *Rienzi* the mob, in *Der fliegende Holländer* the sea. The king had a passion for Gluck's operas and, a few days after the interview, Wagner conducted the Dresden première of Gluck's *Armide* which gained him a reputation as an interpreter of Gluck. In December 1846 he was to interrupt his work on *Lohengrin* to carry out a textual and musical revision of Gluck's *Iphigenie in Aulis*.

Der fliegende Holländer had had its première in Dresden on 2

[1] A thaler was worth three marks.

January 1843. Coming so soon after *Rienzi*, with its brilliance and pageantry and with Tichatschek so blissfully at home in his part and in his suit of silver armour, it was thought by the public to be, in Laube's words, 'ghostly pallid'. It is difficult to see how the splendid songs in the opera could have failed to have pleased the public. As it was, 'the audience fell to wondering how I could have produced this meagre, crude and gloomy work after *Rienzi*, in every act of which movement abounded, and Tichatschek shone in an endless variety of costumes'. The trouble lay in the fact that the public and the singers had to acquire a new sense of drama in opera. This was, after all, the struggle in which Wagner was engaged. During his years at Dresden he came to have faith in the public ultimately understanding his art but bitter disillusionment with almost everyone in the professional world of music.

Schröder-Devrient's magnificent performance as Senta turned, at any rate, *Der fliegende Holländer* into a 'succès d'estime'. Wagner might well have felt satisfied at the turn events had taken since his return from Paris less than a year before. Despite his new-found success this did not mean, unfortunately for him, that there was any demand for the two scores from other opera houses; the word had got around that his operas were difficult to stage. They were, in fact, very seldom staged in any German opera house and it was only during his exile in Switzerland, when Liszt actively took up his cause and arranged the première of *Lohengrin* in Weimar in August 1850, that they slowly entered the repertoire of German provincial opera.

Dresden in 1843 was a town with about 70,000 inhabitants (Berlin had 400,000 and Vienna half a million). Its links with Italy were strong, partly because the royal house was Catholic (although the population Protestant) and it had had a flourishing Italian opera since the middle of the seventeenth century. A German opera had been founded in 1817 to run side by side with the Italian. Since Weber's day there had not been any striking musical changes; Friedrich August II, who came to the throne in 1836, favoured Gluck.[1] A fine new theatre had been built in 1841

---

[1] Christoph Willibald Gluck (1714–87), was an Austrian composer and reformer of Baroque opera. Wagner's conservative and classical interpretations and adaptations of his operas *Armide* and *Iphigenie in Aulis* won him golden opinions not only from the King of Saxony but also from his arch-enemy the Viennese critic Eduard Hanslick.

by the architect Gottfried Semper who was later to play, for him, an unrewarding part in Wagner's grandiose operatic schemes. *Rienzi, Der fliegende Holländer* and *Tannhäuser* were all produced in this building which had excellent acoustics; it was burnt down in a couple of hours in 1869.

The Dresden opera ranked as one of the good second-class European opera houses. It employed two of the leading German singers of the day – Schröder-Devrient and Tichatschek, now only remembered for their Wagnerian parts. Wagner's niece Johanna, the daughter of his brother Albert, was later to join the Dresden opera and become the first Elizabeth in *Tannhäuser*; she later became a leading German singer. The orchestra was reasonably good but needed improving. Berlioz, when in Dresden, had complained that a contrabassist was too old to support the weight of his instrument. One of the violinists was Theodor Uhlig, later Wagner's devoted friend and admirer. Despite its general competence the Dresden orchestra was unfit to play Wagner's operas. Not only were there too few instruments but the leading player in each section lacked the technical skill to follow his instructions. It is remarkable how, in spite of these shortcomings, a few discerning members of the public grasped the essentials of Wagnerian music-drama and kept the flame alive until the right conditions had been created for its proper performance.

Although Wagner had serious reservations about accepting the post of *Kapellmeister* once he had taken it on he threw himself into his duties with passionate ardour. He tried in the Dresden theatre, with his uncompromising integrity, to give, if possible, perfect performances of works by great artists. He forced the pace and made enemies for himself.

Meanwhile he continued working on *Tannhäuser*; he took a month's leave in July 1843 and returned with Minna to Teplitz. This time he took grander rooms, as befitting his new station, and he had a piano moved into his room. Although he broke all the strings in his efforts, no satisfactory music emerged. He had been suffering from gastric disorders and rushes of blood to the brain. He tried a water cure; with Grimm's *Deutsche Mythologie* and a bottle of mineral water he sought out remote places. The cure did not work and his excitability increased as often happened when new music was taking shape in his brain. He spent whole days in bed reading Grimm and sketching the music for the

Venusberg scene in *Tannhäuser*. To escape from this doleful condition he drove to Prague in an open carriage with Minna and looked up some of his old friends. He was gratified to learn that the two Pachta girls had both married members of the 'highest aristocracy'.

Back in Dresden he continued composing the music for the first act of *Tannhäuser* which was completed by January 1844. In October 1843 the Wagners moved into a spacious apartment in the Ostra-Allee facing the Zwinger. He spent more than he could afford on furnishing it: 'Everything was good and substantial, as is only right for a man of thirty who is settling down at last for the whole of his life.' The sensation of being in possession of a respectable salary and the prospect of a flow of fees from German theatres for his operas justified this extravagance. In his new home, adorned with a concert grand piano from Breitkopf & Härtel, for which he paid eight years later by giving them the publishing rights of *Lohengrin*, he settled down with his lapdog Peps, Papo, a parrot and, of course, his wife Minna who taught Papo to whistle selections from *Rienzi*. His pride and joy was his library, carefully composed of books representing his future reading on classical, old German and historical subjects. This was the library taken by Heinrich Brockhaus, brother of Friedrich and Hermann, after Wagner's flight from Dresden, in liquidation of a debt of 500 thalers.

Der fliegende Holländer had its première in Berlin on 7 January 1844 with Wagner conducting. The audience, which included the King of Prussia, responded to the first act with total silence and then burst into applause at the end of the remaining two acts. Mendelssohn and Meyerbeer were present and the former congratulated Wagner wearily with the words, 'Well, you should be satisfied now.' A second performance, two days later, was less well received because of the damaging reviews after the first night. 'A terrible spasm cut my heart as I realized the contemptible tone and unparalleled shamelessness of their raging ignorance regarding my own name and work.' In March Wagner went to Hamburg to conduct *Rienzi*. It was a wretched experience. He had a perilous crossing over the Elbe, full of floating ice; the town was more or less in ruins after a fire and the opera house represented all that was worst in a badly managed, badly equipped provincial theatre. The Rienzi was an elderly, flabby, voiceless tenor: 'He was so dreadful that I had the idea of making the capitol tumble down in the second act so as to bury him earlier in the ruins.'

Wagner came to the fateful conclusion that his works would become better known to the theatrical world and to the public if piano arrangements existed. He accordingly decided to go into business on his own account and commissioned the court music dealer, C. F. Meser, to print the scores. Meser had never before, said Wagner, published anything more ambitious than a waltz. Under an agreement made in June 1844 Meser was to be the nominal publisher and receive ten per cent commission on the sales of the operas whilst Wagner would provide the necessary capital! Schröder-Devrient offered to finance the project by selling her Polish bonds. By the time Wagner needed the first instalment she had handed over all her money to her latest lover, a treacherous young Guards officer. The engraving and printing of the operas were already in progress and there was no possibility of Wagner withdrawing from this commitment. In addition to the piano arrangements Wagner had twenty-five copies of the full scores of *Rienzi* and *Der fliegende Holländer* lithographed. In the case of *Tannhäuser*, in April 1845, he copied out the score himself on special lithographic paper which was then transferred to the stone. The only hope of recovering his expenses was to sell the scores to the theatres in return for performing rights; they were all returned, and, in the case of the Munich theatre, unopened. Wagner now 'plunged into a series of entanglements and troubles which henceforth dominated my life, and plunged me into sorrows which left their dismal mark on all my subsequent enterprises'. As catastrophe approached he was forced to admit his financial plight to Lüttichau, the intendant of the opera, and ask for a loan of 5000 thalers which represented three-and-a-half-years' salary. His request was granted and he received a loan, at five per cent interest, from the Theatre Pension Fund.

In July 1845 Wagner and Minna, with their dog and parrot, went on a five-week holiday to Marienbad. His spirits were good. Through working very hard and getting up early, even in winter, he had written the score of *Tannhäuser* on special lithographic paper and had a hundred copies printed. Meser, his associate in that ill-fated publishing enterprise, advised him against the title of *Der Venusberg*. 'As I did not mix with the public, he said, I had no idea what horrible jokes were made about this title. The medical students would be sure to make fun of it as they had a predilection for obscene jokes. I was sufficiently disgusted by these details to consent to a change.' Lüttichau, the intendant, agreed that no expense should be spared on the costume and the scenery; he and his colleagues were confident of success. For the first time Wagner read a favourable reference to himself in the Dresden evening newspaper which spoke of the *Tannhäuser* poem as having been written 'with undoubted poetic feeling'.

Wagner intended to take it easy during his cure in Marienbad before returning to Dresden to prepare for the production of *Tannhäuser*. He had carefully chosen a few books from his new, well-stocked library – the Carl Simrock edition of the poems of Wolfram von Eschenbach (*Parzifal*), the anonymous old epic of *Lohengrin*, with a long introduction by Joseph Görres, and Gervinus' *History of German Literature*. He had resolved, after completing *Tannhäuser*, to spend a year dawdling and dipping into his library. There was no question of his starting work on some new drama immediately – at least a year would be needed for the poetic and musical idea to take shape within him. He did not realize that this process had already started.

The marvellous summer weather in Marienbad put him in high spirits. Every morning he wandered into the woods with Wolfram's *Titurel* and *Parzifal* and the *Lohengrin* epic under his arm. By the shady stream he conversed with the strange characters in the saga. Once again the 'volcanic soil' of Bohemia, as with *Das Liebesverbot* and *Tannhäuser*, cast its spell over his poetic imagination – *Lohengrin*, the story of the Knight of the Grail, stood clearly before him, complete in every detail of its dramatic construction. He had been warned by his doctor to avoid any kind of creative excitement and he struggled hard against his urge to put his ideas on paper. He did this in an unusual and typically Wagnerian way; reading Gervinus brought his mind back to Hans Sach and a street brawl he had witnessed in Nuremberg many years earlier in July 1835. On one of his walks he thought out the scene when the cobbler teaches the marker a lesson by hammering hard on his last during the marker's song. This was followed by the scene with the people running excitedly along the crooked little Nuremberg streets and culminating in the great brawl. 'Then, suddenly, the whole of my *Meistersinger* comedy assumed such vivid shape that, as it was a cheerful subject and unlikely to tax my nerves, I felt I had to defy doctor's orders and write it out.' Wagner wrote, then and there, a prose sketch of all three acts of *Die Meistersinger* right up to the moment

'Zerging das heil'ge römische Reich in Dunst,
Uns bliebe doch die heil'ge deutsche Kunst.'[1]

He had hoped that the *Meistersinger* therapy would free him from the grip that *Lohengrin* was acquiring over his mind. But not at all – 'No sooner had I got into my medical bath at noon than I felt an overpowering desire to write out *Lohengrin*; after a few minutes I jumped out and, barely giving myself time to dress, rushed home to write out what was in my mind.' By 3 August the whole sketch of *Lohengrin* was on paper. After this Wagner was advised by his doctor to give up water cures. 'My excitement at this time had grown to such an extent that my efforts to sleep generally ended in nocturnal adventures.'

When Wagner had read the middle-high German poem of *Lohengrin* in Paris the figure of Lohengrin made little impression on him. On finishing the prose sketch of *Lohengrin* in Marienbad he wrote to his brother Albert, now resigned to a badly paid job in a small theatre in Halle, saying that he had previously found the old German poem 'most meagre and skimpy'. The mythical archetypal concept, however, of the fatal love of a god for an earthly woman had entered the realm of his subconscious and there it lingered for the next three years.

Wagner repeatedly emphasized to those later responsible for the costumes and decor of his *Lohengrin* that the drama was set in the early Middle Ages, as opposed to the High Gothic period of *Tannhäuser*. He believed that he had, with *Lohengrin*, given a complete picture of the Middle Ages at a period when simplicity and intimacy characterized relationships – even those between the Emperor and his humblest vassal.[2] He was anxious that producers of *Lohengrin* should dispense with an elaborate ceremonial which was not suited to the naïve and noble simplicity of the time.

[1] 'The Holy Roman Empire may fade away,
But Holy German Art is here to stay.'
(Original Marienbad version, 1845)
[2] Cosima later went further; *Lohengrin*, she said, summarized perfectly the whole of the Middle Ages and made further study of them unnecessary.

We have before us, in its most attractive, ideal form, the old *German* idea of kingship. Here nothing is done as a routine matter or as part of a courtly ceremonial; rather everyone has a feeling of personal, direct commitment to his allotted task; there is no trace of despotic pageantry with its bodyguards (oh! oh!), which push the people back to form a lane for the high and mighty personages.

Into this simple earthly world stepped Lohengrin: a supernatural being had entered the world of reality. Lohengrin's tragic nature lies in his loneliness. He is a miracle in a world which, in the form of the heroine Elsa, longs for the miraculous but which insists, at the same time, in secularizing it, in forcing it to conform to wretched human standards. In *Lohengrin*, as in *Der fliegende Holländer*, indeed as in Wagner's earliest opera, *Die Feen*, there is a union between the human and spiritual world. Lohengrin was the artist in the modern world; he was Wagner, the miracle, the genius who appears in our daily lives. Tannhäuser had looked for more artistic joys and sorrows than had his friend Wolfram and the courtly singers; he went to Venusberg in his search for a new artistic kingdom. Lohengrin is the new artist; he is what Tannhäuser would have become. He is Richard Wagner or, at any rate, a Wagnerite. Genius, like that of Lohengrin or Wagner, demands a 'suspension of disbelief', as symbolized in Lohengrin's stipulation (*Fragverbot*) to Elsa that she ask him no questions about himself. Genius demands total fidelity and highest trust; daily life demands information: our name, date and place of birth, our family tree; the miracle must be analysed and rationalized. Lohengrin could not be simultaneously the Knight of the Grail, husband of Elsa and ruler of Brabant. Lohengrin's confrontation with the 'real' world had, therefore, to end tragically. The tragic ending was not, as it happened, a foregone conclusion. Since the conflict between Elsa and Lohengrin was essentially an intellectual one – it was not, unlike *Tannhäuser*, a tragedy of passions – Wagner was strongly tempted to give the opera a 'happy ending'. To put a stop to any further equivocation he worked backwards, starting with the orchestral sketch of the third and last act in September 1846; he finished it in March 1847.

The more Wagner absorbed himself in the subject of Lohengrin the more out of touch he felt with the world around him. The horrid little critics were barking at his heels; like vultures with carrion they seized upon the slightest weaknesses in the production of his operas. They showed themselves to be contemptibly mean-minded and unimaginative and it was left to a few intelligent members of the public to give him moral and practical support. It was at about this time that Wagner realized that the most thoughtful friends of his art were those people who, as a rule, rarely visited the theatre, least of all the opera. To them he clung, emotionally and artistically, during the years of anxiety and incomprehension that lay ahead.[1] The professional musicians seemed incapable of understanding his new ideal of the relations of drama and music in opera. This led him to read his poems and explain the nature of his art to friends in small gatherings and to embark on long-winded critical works like *Oper und Drama* written in 1851. The more his art developed, the more it was misunderstood. *Tannhäuser*, after a hesitant start, became popular in Dresden, but was not in demand anywhere else. Wagner had wanted to dedicate *Tannhäuser* to the King of Prussia and was told that the King only accepted the dedication of works known to him. A way of bringing *Tannhäuser* to his notice would be for Wagner to make an arrangement of airs from it to be played by a military band at the changing of the guard. He knew that *Lohengrin*, which represented a further step along the road to music-drama, would widen the gulf even more between himself and the rest of the musical world. So, his operas were not performed outside Dresden; he received no fees and his debts piled up; even his eminently thoughtful and practical suggestions, as expressed in his reports *Die Königliche Kapelle betreffend* (Concerning the Royal Orchestra) of March 1846 and his *Entwurf zur Organisation eines deutschen Nationaltheaters für das Königreich Sachsen* (Plan for the Organization of a German National Theatre for the Kingdom of Saxony), written in May 1848, were rejected.

Wagner was at this time generally tense, irritable and unwell. His friend Ferdinand Heine wrote this about him to Ernst Benedikt Kietz in Paris:

> On the one hand he overstrains his spirit; on the other, his enemies and enviers strew so many thorns amongst his scanty but well-deserved laurels that he feels wounded in body as well as mind. I am afraid that the same fate will overtake him as many another great genius; he will not live to see his triumph . . . everything cuts too deeply with him and swiftly eats away at his vital spirits . . . the papers tear him to pieces;

[1] Until his death he gratefully accepted offers of help from any quarter.

other theatres take their cue from these papers so that his works are not given elsewhere – and will not be until he is dead when people will fight to have them! I am convinced he will not live to be old.

He and Wagner drank beer together before the important second performance of *Tannhäuser*: 'After looking at my head for some-time, he swore that it was impossible to destroy me . . . he spoke about the peculiar heat of my temperament. Although it might consume others I was at my best when it glowed most fiercely; he had, several times, seen me positively ablaze. I laughed and did not know what to make of this nonsense.' The good Heine also started a system, with another of Wagner's friends, August Röckel, the socialist musical manager, to counteract the smear campaign in the Dresden newspapers. Wagner noticed, to his surprise, that malicious little pieces about him were regularly rebutted by witty and forceful corrections which turned out to be the work of Heine and Röckel.

In November 1845 Wagner read the poem of 'Lohengrin' at one of the regular meetings of the Engelklub; this was a circle of artists and writers who met once a week at Engel's restaurant in Dresden. Wagner had been introduced to it by Ferdinand Hiller, an indifferent conductor and composer. Amongst those present on this particular occasion were Schumann, Semper, Pecht and the popular painter Julius Schnorr von Carolsfeld. The general verdict on the poem was that it was 'effective' (*effektvoll*); none could see how it could possibly be set to music. Schumann, to his consternation, found no arias written for individual singers; Wagner then 'had some fun in reading him different parts in the form of arias and cavatinas after which he laughingly declared himself satisfied'. Semper was the one member of the Engelklub whose company he enjoyed. He was at first antagonistic to Wagner, treating him as a protagonist of Catholicism; the news-papers had suggested that he had been bribed by the Catholic political party to write *Tannhäuser* to counter Meyerbeer's *Hugue-nots* with its glorification of Protestantism. Semper was relieved to learn that there was nothing pietistic about Wagner's preoccupa-tion with German antiquity and early Teutonic myths.

In May 1846 Wagner obtained three months' leave from the management of the Dresden opera to improve his health in rustic retirement. With Minna, Peps and parrot he took a peasant's cottage in Gross-Graupa, in 'Saxon Switzerland', near Pillnitz.

He had, the previous month, conducted a brilliantly successful performance of Beethoven's Ninth Symphony, the receipts going to the Theatre Pension Fund. The management and staff had been bitterly opposed to this choice as it had, in the past, always failed miserably in Dresden; Reissiger and the other conductors were incapable of interpreting the score. Wagner imposed his wishes and it became for him a point of honour that his stand be vindicated. He edited a special concert programme with 'helpful' passages from Goethe's *Faust*; he inserted, at his own expense, enthusiastic anonymous notices about the Ninth Symphony; he had twelve rehearsals alone for the phrasing of the recitation of the cellos and basses; he coached the solo singers and immersed himself in this symphony which had been the delight of his boyhood and whose magic he had rediscovered in Paris. Amongst the spectators were the sixteen-year-old Hans von Bülow and Ludwig Schnorr von Carolsfeld, who later became the great Wagnerian singer.

In Gross-Graupa Wagner sketched out the musical composition for all three acts of *Lohengrin*. His work was made more difficult by his inability to get out of his head various arias from Rossini's *William Tell*, the last opera he had conducted in Dresden. He managed to expel them at last by singing very loudly, during his walks, the first theme from the Ninth Symphony. On one of these walks he heard a bather whistle the tune of the pilgrim's chorus from *Tannhäuser*. 'The first sign of the possibility of popularizing this work made an impression on me which no subsequent similar experience has ever been able to surpass. . . .'

Whilst Wagner proceeded with the composition of *Lohengrin* from May 1846 until 28 April 1848, the date of the completion of the score, his thoughts, during these two years, were grappling simultaneously with other subjects – German mythology, Greek tragedy and revolutionary socialism. Lohengrin and Tannhäuser were both, like Richard Wagner, artists unable to find satisfaction for their aspirations in a corrupt, conventional, materialistic society. The artist, Wagner believed, had the true vision of reality which no longer corresponded, as it had perhaps in some distant primeval past, to the false, so-called 'reality' of our own hateful society. Elsa failed because she loved Lohengrin in too 'earthly' a way; Lohengrin was also to blame for thinking that he could reconcile his mission with a marriage and the responsibilities of a ruler. The real antagonists in the opera are Lohengrin and Ortrud, a political woman, who does not know love, a dabbler in witch-craft, hating the present, obsessed with her ancestry – a reactionary. 'A political man is unattractive,' said Wagner. 'A political woman is repulsive. A woman has to love something and in Ortrud's case her obsession with her ancestry and the past turns into a murderous fanaticism. . . .' She embodies our odious, aristocratically domi-nated world into which the isolated, incompatible artist, Lohengrin, has strayed. Lohengrin, or the 'Grail', was forced to leave this everyday world of hate and greed where proper love seemed to have disappeared.

In *Lohengrin* Wagner had, he thought, presented an accurate picture of the Middle Ages. He now had the urge to reach further back into Germany's mythological past, into a world free of those elements which distorted modern society, into a world where justice obtained and where the creative artist had an im-mediate rapport with the people (*Volk*). With this purpose in mind he not only, once again, took up Grimm's *Deutsche Mythologie* but started investigating the Nordic sources of this work which had inspired him to write the *Tannhäuser* music in 1843. In April 1847 Wagner and Minna moved into a cheaper establishment in the Marcolini Palace in the Dresden suburb of Friedrichstadt; during the hot summer afternoons, the mornings having been spent working on the music of *Lohengrin*, he reclined under the old trees in the French garden behind the house and immersed himself in Aeschylus, Aristophanes, Plato and the Nordic myths. He read the 'Edda', the 'Wilkina', the 'Niflung-Saga', the 'Heimskringla', the 'Völsung-Saga' and the 'Völuspa'. Goethe, in his autobiography, *Dichtung und Wahrheit*, admitted that, whilst he had enjoyed hearing about the 'Edda' myths as a child, they had not become part of his poetic equipment as they could never take sensuous, plastic shape in his mind, unlike the figures from Greek mythology. Wagner, on the other hand, approached the German myths from his reading of the Greek tragedians, Aeschylus in particular. At this time his friends com-mented that he preferred to discuss German myths and Greek drama than music. In his mind's eye he saw the mighty tragedies of Aeschylus being re-enacted; he saw the giant amphitheatre at the foot of the Acropolis filled with twenty thousand people; he saw the choirs and the orchestra. Later, through his *Ring* music, he invoked the spirit of Attic drama. 'There is,' wrote Nietzsche, 'such nearness and affinity between Aeschylus and Wagner that we are forcibly reminded of the relative concepts of time.' How Wagner managed to breathe life into the misty figures of German mythology and to turn them into beings of universal significance is a permanent subject for discussion. His Greek studies may have helped him humanize the world of Nordic mythology and to create a work which, in its poetic treatment of certain universal human subjects – fear, love, youth, age, eros and the Mother – combines mythical primordialism with modern psychoanalysis. In October 1848 Wagner wrote his first prose study of the *Ring,* which was published under the title of *Der Nibelungen-Mythus.* A few weeks later he finished the prose draft of 'Siegfrieds Tod' (later to become *Götterdämmerung*). He wrote, 'The purpose of the gods will have been attained if they destroy themselves with this human creation; they must sacrifice their own influence in the interests of the freedom of the human will.' The sense of this conforms to the final ending of *Götterdämmerung* in 1874.

In November 1847 Wagner and Minna returned in low spirits to Dresden from Berlin. The Berlin première of *Rienzi* had not been a success; apart from not getting any fee for conducting the première and two subsequent performances, because he was doing so at his 'request' rather than by 'invitation', he had allowed himself to agree to a number of deplorable changes in the interests of the success of the production. 'It was never clearer to me than now what hideous pressures, resulting from the artistic and social conditions of our time, oppress, embitter and corrupt the free heart.' As 1848, the year of revolutions, drew near, Wagner was in a dangerously dissatisfied state of mind. As *Kapellmeister* he had achieved much. In arranging the theatrical programmes he had observed and improved upon the best traditions of German operatic art; as a conductor and composer he was proud to be the successor of Carl Maria von Weber whose remains he had had brought over from London in 1844; his Palm Sunday performance of Beethoven's Ninth Symphony in April 1846 was a personal triumph as was also his own adaptation of Gluck's *Iphigenia in Aulis* which he directed and conducted in February 1847.

Wagner, nevertheless, became a revolutionary, for which he paid the price of many years of exile. After the last performance of the Ninth Symphony he was warmly congratulated by the Russian anarchist and nobleman Michail Bakunin who went up to the orchestra and shouted to Wagner that 'should all music disappear in the coming world conflagration we shall all join together and risk our lives for the retention of this symphony'. Born in 1814, a year after Wagner, he had left his fortune and title behind in Russia in order to further the cause of revolution in Western and Central Europe. Bernard Shaw saw him as the model for Siegfried. Wagner and Bakunin were brought together by August Röckel. Wagner was much attracted by Bakunin's mind and personality. This colossal, bearded, immensely energetic Slav could be found in any part of Europe where social trouble was brewing between 1840 and 1849. 'This wild distinguished fellow,' Wagner told Cosima towards the end of his life, 'was the personification of the future of Russia.' Until his meeting with Bakunin his knowledge of extreme political and social movements had mostly come from Ludwig Feuerbach, Max Stirner[1] and Pierre Joseph Proudhon whose *De la propriété* was published when Wagner was in Paris in 1840. Proudhon's theory that all property is robbery left its mark on *Das Rheingold*. Feuerbach's *Das Wesen des Christentums* (The Essence of Christianity) appeared the following year; whether he actually read these two books or merely discussed them with his friend, Lehrs, we do not know. In any event, Feuerbach's teachings were to bring him very close to atheism and to influence the basic idea of the *Ring* – the end of the gods. His friendship with Laube and his espousal of the beliefs of *Das junge Deutschland* had made him an adherent of the earthly religion (*Diesseits-Religion*) of human love. Although Wagner, in his autobiography, played down the importance Bakunin's effect had on him, calling him a 'confused hothead', he admitted to being fascinated by the power and terrifying import of his revolutionary arguments. 'It was impossible to counter any of his arguments which stretched far beyond the most extreme limits of radicalism.' Wagner realized that his own ideas about the extent and purpose of a revolution differed from those of Bakunin. Nevertheless, for a few giddy months, Wagner was the close associate of this famous international anarchist who, after masterminding the Dresden uprising, was sentenced to death,

[1] Author of *Der Einzige und sein Eigentum* (The Individual and His Property), 1845.

delivered to the Russians, fled from Siberia, went to London, broke with Karl Marx and died in Italy in 1876. The other member of this revolutionary circle was August Röckel, shortly to spend twelve years in gaol for his activities.

It was not merely the indifferent reception to *Rienzi* in Berlin that had cast down Wagner's spirits. The King of Prussia had failed to attend the première and, on his return to Dresden, the King of Saxony had also failed to give him an audience. Lüttichau, the intendant of the court theatre, had rejected, at the beginning of 1847, the proposed reforms set out in Wagner's memorandum *Die Königliche Kapelle betreffend.* Wagner had objected to the appointment of Karl Gutzkow, an active member of *Das junge Deutschland*, as theatre playwright; he resisted his interference with the operatic side of the theatre and even threatened to resign on this account. *Tannhäuser* was not a great success; Hanslick had criticized Wagner's 'misuse of diminished sevenths'. 'From now onwards,' wrote Wagner, 'our whole modern artistic public ceased fundamentally to exist for me.' In May 1848 he submitted his forty-page *Entwurf zur Organisation eines deutschen Nationaltheatres für das Konigreich Sachsen* (Plan for the Organization of a German National Theatre) to the Ministry of the Interior, thus bypassing Lüttichau. Its main points were that the intendant should no longer be a court appointment but be elected by the staff and by all members of an association of poets and composers, yet to be founded (another of his recommendations); the setting up of a theatre school and the concentration of authority in the hands of a single *Kapellmeister* (Wagner?). He had feared that one of the first measures of the new democratic government, which popular pressure had forced the king in March 1848 to appoint, would be to cut the subsidy for the royal court theatre, considered by many to be a dispensable, feudal luxury. To obviate this was one of the reasons for his report.

No long afterwards *Lohengrin*, without any word of explanation from Lüttichau, was taken off the court theatre programme although the sets had already been ordered. This, together with the rejection of his report, filled Wagner with bitterness. 'As I saw my last hope of a reconciliation with the theatre, through a good performance of *Lohengrin*, disappear, from now onwards I turned my back, unequivocally and on principle, on the theatre and on any attempts to interest me in it.'

As long as Wagner was immersed in the music for *Lohengrin* he had little time or inclination for other matters – even revolution. Only when the score was completed, at the end of April 1848, could he play his own special part in that year of great liberal movements. He barely commented on the uprisings in Frankfurt and Berlin, or on the revolution in Paris which caused the fall of Louis-Philippe, or on the appearance of the Communist Manifesto, published at the beginning of the year. In January his mother had died unexpectedly, aged seventy, in Leipzig, thus snapping one of the last emotional links which bound him to his family and to Saxony. He dashed off a fiery poem to encourage the insurgents in Vienna and approved King Friedrich August's liberal measures hurriedly enacted in March as an excited populace stormed through the streets of Dresden carrying petitions from different Saxon towns; these measures were abolition of censorship, electoral, legal and fiscal reforms. Wagner's approval was qualified by his fears that these reforms might threaten the subsidy paid to the court theatre from the royal civil list.

What sort of revolutionary was Wagner, if indeed he was a revolutionary at all? He tried as best he could, during the momentous months of 1848 and 1849, to fuse his political and artistic beliefs, to bring together his philosophical and literary reminiscences of Feuerbach, Proudhon and *Das junge Deutschland* with his own musical and theatrical aspirations. As an artist he was both a visionary and a hard-headed realist; he could, like any operator, be ruthless and unscrupulous in seeing to it that his 'visions' took practical shape. No German opera house, least of all the one at Dresden, seemed capable of understanding the essentials of his art. The trouble lay, he thought, 'deep in the structure of our false society'. He wrote, after the disappointing *Rienzi* première, to his friend Ernst Kossak, the Berlin philologist and musical writer, 'What's the point of all this futile preaching to the public? . . . we have to break through the dykes and the means thereto are called Revolution! . . . one single, sensible decision from the King of Prussia regarding his operatic theatre would make everything all right again!' No wonder, therefore, that Bakunin called Wagner a 'Fantast' and took neither his artistic nor his political ideas seriously. Similarly Wagner, as he said in his autobiography, found it difficult to reconcile Bakunin's devastating destruction theories with 'this really lovable, highly sensitive person'.

In June 1848 Wagner, as a member of the revolutionary *Vaterlandsverein*, addressed an open-air mass meeting. His subject was the republican movement and the monarchy. The republican Wagner sang the praises of the Saxon House of Wettin; the King himself must initiate a cultural revolution as 'the first and noblest of all republicans'. He warned his huge audience of 'the absurd and futile teaching' of communism with its lunatic ideas about 'the mathematical division of property and income'. He wanted the abolition of the aristocratic First Chamber and the introduction of universal suffrage. What he wanted, above all things, was an artistic and theatrical reform and the victory of the revolution would mean the victory of the theory and practice of the artist Richard Wagner. A prerequisite to this must be the end of the present age of greed. 'Like an evil hobgoblin (*Alp*) this demonic concept of money, with its loathsome retinue of public and private usury, bond swindles, interest rates and bank speculations, must go. This will lead to the full emancipation of the human species, to the fulfilment of pure Christian teaching.' After this speech Lüttichau removed *Rienzi* from the court theatre programme.

For the rest of 1848 Wagner responded to the prevailing political excitement by writing the sketch for his proposed drama on Friedrich Barbarossa which, in turn, led him on to his first essay about the Nibelungen-Siegfried project in which mythical and historical elements are curiously combined; from there he went on to his prose study *Der Nibelungen-Mythus*, 'Siegfrieds Tod' and the fifty-page sketch of a drama, 'Jesus of Nazareth'. He went for long walks, alone and with Röckel. During them, he says in his autobiography, he tried to visualize the state of human society as it would be as a result of the zealous efforts of the socialists and communists, and how this could then provide the conditions and the platform for the realization of his revolution in art. The *Ring* is nothing less than the musico-dramatic realization of a political Utopia in which man has finally broken out of various forms of bondage to be himself, free and capable of love. It is, maybe, the first and only work of art consciously influenced by political theories. Wagner is unique amongst artists in trying painstakingly to explain to his friends exactly what he was doing in his art. If he left them more confused than they were before he had his awkward style to blame rather than the confusion of his artistic ideas.

The year 1849 opened in an atmosphere of foreboding and uncertainty. The popular parliament in Frankfurt offered the German imperial crown to Friedrich Wilhelm IV of Prussia who refused to accept it from representatives of the people. Nearer home, Wagner wrote an ecstatic essay, 'Die Revolution' for Röckel's newssheet *Volksblätter*. In it he wrote, 'Nearer and nearer rumbles the storm, carrying on its wings the revolution, which will announce a new gospel of happiness.' In April Friedrich August II repudiated the constitution and dissolved both Houses of Parliament. Röckel's *Volksblätter*, which Wagner was ready to take over, was banned and Röckel himself fled to Prague. The king knew that his action would lead to civil war and he relied on his army and on military help promised by Prussia. In Dresden the crowds filled the streets when it was learned that the Saxon government had appealed for Prussian troops. The Saxon infantry fired the first shots on the crowd and up went the cry 'To the barricades! To the barricades!' reports Wagner in his autobiography. He was swept along in the crowd to the town hall where a committee was formed of citizens to defend the constitution. On 4 May at four in the morning the king and his ministers fled to the fortress of Königstein. The citizens' committee appointed a provisional government which announced armed resistance to the royal proclamation. The first clashes with the troops took place. Wagner had leaflets printed – 'Are you with us against foreign troops?' – which he handed out during a truce to the Saxon soldiers. That he was not shot is remarkable. It is also possible that he arranged for the manufacture of hand-grenades.

After abortive negotiations with the few government ministers who had remained in Dresden the fighting started on 5 May. It lasted three days. Gottfried Semper, the architect, supervised the construction of the barricades. From an oriel-window Wilhelmina Schröder-Devrient shouted encouragement to the armed citizens. Wagner was constantly popping up in different parts of the town. He spent the night of 5 May on the tower of the Kreuzkirche; it was his job to observe troop movements and report them to the town hall. On 6 May, early in the morning, he witnessed processions of insurgents coming into Dresden from the Erzgebirge. On the same day the Prussian troops arrived. As Wagner, that evening during a short cease-fire, picked his way through the barricades to his apartment in the distant Marcolini Palace he worked out a drama, *Achilles*. In it, Achilles, like Brünnhilde, rejects immortality in favour of human life. Wagner's attitude, even when in the thick of things, was too detached to be that of a real, hot-blooded revolutionary. He was, after his flight, accused of setting fire to the opera house. This he denied, as he also denied that he had manned the barricades or used firearms.

The insurrection collapsed in the evening of 8 May. Röckel was arrested as ringleader and condemned to death; his sentence was commuted to life imprisonment and he was released in 1862. Throughout all these years Wagner kept in touch with him. That Wagner escaped arrest was due to a fortunate accident; he travelled with Bakunin and the other members of the provisional government as far as Freiberg, a few miles south-west of Dresden, where he lost them. The others were arrested when they arrived at Chemnitz (today Karl-Marx-Stadt). Wagner spent the night alone in an inn at Chemnitz and found his way the next day to Weimar where Liszt, now his great friend and admirer, was ready to help him in every possible way. He wrote to Minna from Weimar, anxious to dispel her fears about him and their future. He told her that he was not a real revolutionary. 'We are revolutionaries in order to *build up* on fresh ground; destruction does not appeal to us, but *creating anew*. We are not therefore the people needed by destiny; they can be found amongst the sediment of the people; we and our heart have nothing in common with them. So, there you are! I now cut myself off from the revolution. . . .' Wagner had nevertheless already revolutionized art by changing the musical language of the nineteenth century and by making his characters Tannhäuser and Lohengrin represent the struggle of the rebel in society.

CHAPTER SIX

In Exile
1849–54

ON 27 MAY 1849, shortly after his thirty-sixth birthday, Wagner reached Lindau on Lake Constance. He had travelled by mail-coach from Jena with the out-of-date passport of Professor Wildmann of Jena University. Liszt, who paid for the journey out of future *Lohengrin* takings, had advised Wagner against taking the more direct route to Paris via Frankfurt; the warrant for his arrest (*Steckbrief*) had been issued a few days earlier, on 16 May, and he would be unlikely to have an easy passage in any of the German states who had treaties amongst themselves to extradite each other's rebels. Liszt had urged him to make for Paris and there find a new field for his work. Being himself more culturally orientated towards France, where his family lived, than towards Germany, he regarded a musical triumph in Paris, or perhaps in London, as the *sine qua non* of a successful career. On top of that, now that Wagner was a wanted man, all theatres in Germany, with the exception of Weimar, would be closed to him. With those heart-chilling experiences in Paris not all that far away, Wagner could hardly be expected to take up this idea with alacrity.

On 28 May, on a wonderful morning, Wagner crossed Lake Constance in a steamer; across the lake he saw, stretching in a semi-circle, the Alpine ridges of the Vorarlberg and of the Swiss cantons of Appenzell and St Gallen. He stepped onto Swiss soil at the little harbour town of Rorschach, sent a message home to report his safe arrival in Switzerland and then proceeded by coach to Zurich, which immediately made a positive impression on him. 'When I entered Zurich from Oberstrasse at the end of May towards six o'clock in the evening and saw for the first time the

Alps of Glarus, that encircle the lake, glistening in the sun, I at once resolved, though without being fully conscious of it, to avoid everything that might prevent me from obtaining permission to settle here.' In his luggage were the poem 'Siegfrieds Tod' and twenty francs in cash. The Swiss mountains were a very different matter from the low hills of Saxon Switzerland where he had gone in his Dresden days whenever he felt the stirrings of a new artistic idea. It is understandable that the Alps made a deep impression on him and inspired loftier masterpieces than the Saxon hills. In fact, much of the *Ring* was written in Switzerland and conceived during his walks in the mountains. 'Let me create the works whose inspiration I received there – in peaceful, magnificent Switzerland – with my gaze directed to the lofty, gold-crowned mountains; they are works of wonder and I could not have conceived them anywhere else. Let me complete them!'

For the Wagnerite Switzerland is sacred ground. As Wagner repeatedly tells us, his life and his work are an indivisible entity; his sensations, big and small, inform his works and his association with that little country covers a period of over twenty-three years. He lived in Zurich from 1849 to 1858 and at Tribschen on Lake Lucerne from 1866 to 1872; the eight years separating these two residential periods were punctuated by long and short visits to Switzerland. This was the period of the *Ring, Tristan und Isolde* and *Die Meistersinger,* of his critical writings, and of his autobiography *Mein Leben.* Eleven years were to go by before he was allowed to return to Germany and thirteen years before he returned to Saxony. For Wagner, the artist, this enforced separation from his homeland did not, as it might have done, dry up the creative springs of his art; rather, the valleys, lakes and mountains of his country of exile seem to combine with his homesickness to give new and dramatic life in his mind to the archetypal Teutonic myths as enshrined in *Der Ring des Nibelungen.*

When Wagner arrived in Zurich wearing a thin brown coat and carrying a very small grey travelling bag he made at once for the home of his friend from Würzburg days, Alexander Müller, a virtuoso pianist and now a music teacher and choir leader in Zurich. It was late at night and Wagner rang the bell furiously. Müller put his head out of the window. 'Who is it at this late hour?' 'It is I, Richard Wagner. Open up, quick!' According to Müller's daughter he rushed upstairs, threw his arms around

Müller's neck and said, 'Alexander, take me in. I am safe here.'

Müller introduced Wagner to the two Swiss cantonal secretaries (*Staatsschreiber*), Jakob Sulzer and Franz Hagenbach, who immediately arranged for him to be issued with a Swiss passport valid for France. The document states that Richard Wagner from Leipzig, 'compositeur de musique', is thirty-six years old, five feet five-and-a-half inches tall (1.63 metres), with brown hair and eyebrows, blue eyes, nose and mouth of medium size and a round chin. 'To my astonishment,' wrote Wagner to his Dresden friend Theodor Uhlig, 'I find that I am famous here, thanks to piano arrangements of all my operas which are repeatedly performed in concerts and musical societies.' Wagner and Sulzer, a highly intelligent and cultivated civil servant, took an immediate liking to each other; they were to remain friends for the rest of their lives. He also met, before going on to Paris, the Swiss musician Wilhelm Baumgartner, a pupil of Müller and an important figure in the musical life of Zurich. He had called on Wagner in Dresden several years earlier and been entrusted with a copy of the score of *Tannhäuser* to give to Müller.

Wagner's delight with Zurich now knew no bounds; firstly the sight of the Alps around the lake as they gleamed in the evening sunshine; then the charm of the town itself, in those days with 33,000 inhabitants, with its old houses and churches along the River Limmat; and finally, those extraordinarily fine, intelligent and sensible men, who sympathized instinctively with his aims! 'They received me with such respectful curiosity and sympathy that I felt at home with them at once. The great assurance and moderation of their simple republican standpoint, from which they commented on my troubles, opened up for me a concept of civil life which lifted me onto an entirely different sphere.' He felt the forces stirring in him to create something exceptional and he had no wish to do this in Paris. Liszt and Minna, however, were determined that Paris should be the scene of his next successes – Liszt had already paved the way with an ecstatic article on *Tannhäuser* in the *Journal des Débats* – and he wearily left Zurich two days after his arrival there. Before leaving he read his new friends his poem 'Siegfrieds Tod'. 'I am prepared to swear that I never had more attentive listeners, amongst men, than on that evening.'

On arriving in Paris his Zurich euphoria quickly gave way to depression. The heat was stifling; there was a cholera epidemic and funeral processions, with muffled drums, passed his house continuously; he noticed, with disgust, the first indications of Louis Napoleon's betrayal of the ideals of the Republic; in Schlesinger's bookshop he bumped into an embarrassed Meyerbeer who asked him whether he proposed to write scores for the barricades. He looked for some of his companions of the barricades and found, to his pleasure, Semper and young Heine who had wanted to design the *Lohengrin* scenery. He then left the plague-infested city for Rueil, a village outside Paris where Belloni, Liszt's former secretary, lived and there he took a single room in a wine merchant's house where he passed the time reading Proudhon's *De la propriété* from which he claimed to derive comfort in his present situation.

At the beginning of July Wagner returned to Zurich; although musically unproductive his stay in Paris had another result – while he was there he had thought about certain of his experiences, personal and artistic, in relation to the political unrest of the time. Back in Zurich he committed these thoughts to paper and gave them the title *Die Kunst und die Revolution* (Art and Revolution). He hoped to get the articles which composed the book published in some distinguished French journal and, with this end in view, he sent them to Paris to be translated into French. They were declared to be too turgid and Teutonic for French tastes and were sent back to him. Wagner then tried his luck with the Leipzig publisher, Otto Wigand, who agreed to publish the manuscript as a pamphlet and sent him five louis d'or for it.

Die Kunst und die Revolution was the first of the many critical works which Wagner wrote during his Zurich period (1849–58). These writings of Wagner have never ceased to cause perplexity to his friends and pleasure to his enemies. Many Germans, friends and enemies alike, describe his style as fustian and prefer to read him in French or English translation. Wagner's 'critical' writings were, of course, absurdly easy to criticize; unashamedly one-sided, often over-simplifying matters despite their prolixity, they are attempts to assess his own spiritual and intellectual situation after the recent revolutionary excitement and also to explain to the intelligent public the principles of his art. That he must have succeeded is shown by the vehemence of the reactions to his writings. It is tempting for Anglo-Saxons to treat these prose writings as exemplifying the ineradicably boring and spuriously earnest side of the German genius. The continental critics fulminated against them. One reason was simple professional jealousy; if a musician is able to philosophize about his art, they said, then his music cannot be spontaneous and natural. As Baudelaire put into their mouths in his essay on *Tannhäuser*, 'Un homme qui raisonne tant de son art ne peut produire naturellement de belles oeuvres.'[1]

Wagner had a mission: to impose on the world his conception of the function of the theatre in a civilized society. In the eighteenth century, when German was coming into its own as a literary language, the theatre was regarded by thoughtful Germans as the perfect vehicle for refining the hearts and minds of men. Schiller, the hero of Friedrich Wagner, both wrote his masterpieces for the stage and also theorized about them, as Wagner was to do half a century later. Since Schiller's day there had been a change in public taste; this taste was less influenced by highminded intellectuals than by the business bourgeoisie with their cheap philistine ideas of entertainment. These people had been, since his arrival in Dresden, the enemies of Wagner's art. Their preference for variety, rather than quality, meant constant changes in the repertoire and the steady degradation of public taste.

Wagner believed that the old German idealism about the theatre still lived. If he could communicate his ideas to a small group of articulate people in sympathy with his aims some progress might be made. He was right. From 1850 onwards, until his death, Wagner was the most discussed musician in Europe. To move from comparative obscurity as a provincial *Kapellmeister* to international notoriety a couple of years later needs further explanation. Wagner's aim was to reform German opera by convincing the public of the equal importance of the dramatic, reflective, poetic and musical elements in the theatre. This seriousness of intent had been understood by a few people in Dresden – the first Wagnerites. That his operas were popular with a wider public was due to melodious parts of the music; his music was still not understood in the way that Wagner wished. The failure of the King of Saxony, Lüttichau and the theatre management to accept any of his suggested reforms, which would, apart

[1] 'Richard Wagner et *Tannhäuser* à Paris', 1861.

from raising the standards of performance in general, also facilitate the production of his operas, turned him into a revolutionary or rebel. The subsequent dramatic flight of the Royal Saxon *Kapellmeister* made him famous throughout Germany. He became a symbol of the new, progressive musical forces; his operas, his writings, the growing number of his vociferous and eloquent adherents, especially Uhlig and Bülow but above all Liszt, his own propagandizing in Berlin and elsewhere – all this was beginning to make a thoughtful public realize that there was a fundamental difference between ordinary repertory operas and those of Wagner. It was also beginning to be realized that music should, like theatre, occupy a central place in the cultural life of an epoch; the political uprisings of 1848 caused many to hope, like Wagner, that a new world of artistic creation and perception would come into being – even if political and social changes were still a long way off. The controversy that raged over Wagner from that time was not simply musical; for Wagnerites he came to represent the deepening and refining of spiritual and intellectual sensibilities; for his enemies he represented, if they were critics, a challenge to their own standards and, if they were not, something uncomfortable that should be suppressed. Liszt's great practical service to Wagner was to show, by putting on *Tannhäuser* and later, in August 1850, *Lohengrin* at Weimar, that his operas were not too difficult to perform in the average German theatre. After that the demand for Wagner scores continued unabated; in 1852 and 1853 his operas were being performed or planned in Leipzig, Frankfurt, Wiesbaden, Würzburg, Breslau, Düsseldorf, Rudolstadt, Hamburg and Riga, the one most in demand being *Tannhäuser*. This was an abrupt and remarkable change after Wagner's unsuccessful efforts to get his operas performed outside Dresden. This success was all the more remarkable since he was an outlawed 'revolutionary'. From almost all these theatres he received a flat, outright fee which enabled them to perform the work as often as they liked; the fee varied between £10 and £30, depending on the size of the theatre. Tichatschek, on the other hand, could command three or four times as much for a single performance. Had composers in those days been given a royalty on each performance of their works Wagner would have been able to live in comparative comfort.

Wagner's theoretical writings are of interest inasmuch as they show the different stages of his grappling with an artistic ideal until he had finally mastered it. This artistic ideal was largely fashioned by his studies of Greek drama which were first stimulated in the Dresden Kreuzschule. Wagner tells us how, one afternoon in the Café Littéraire in Zurich, after a heavy midday meal, in a smoky, jovial, domino-playing atmosphere, he gazed dreamily at the wallpaper depicting certain mythological scenes. This reminded him of a water-colour by Bonaventura Genelli called 'Dionysos amongst the muses of Apollo' which he had admired when a boy in Friedrich Brockhaus's house. 'I conceived at that moment the idea of my *Kunstwerk der Zukunft*' (Art work of the future). Genelli's picture had given him his first clear glimpse of the Greek idea of beauty. What had appealed to him was the union of the Dionysian and Apolline, the demonic and the serene, in art – a concept going beyond the classical ideal of noble simplicity and repose. Wagner wrote this work in November 1849 in a cold, sunless, ground-floor room; he dedicated it to his new hero, the philosopher Ludwig Feuerbach.

Feuerbach is known to Englishmen as one of the formative agnostic influences in George Eliot's spiritual life – she translated his *Essence of Christianity* (Das Wesen des Christentums) in 1854 – and his views on friendship and marriage, had, perhaps, encouraged her to form her 'union' with G. H. Lewes. He had studied under Hegel in Berlin but had grown sick of his teaching. For Feuerbach, Hegelianism was the last refuge of the old theology; Christianity had lost all meaning and a new religion was called for – a de-supernaturalized humanism. Men should discover in their own needs and longings the reality of the ideal worlds of thought and faith. In 1848 Wagner had been introduced to the writings of Feuerbach in Dresden by a Catholic priest and political agitator who wore a Calabrian hat (tall, broad rimmed, white felt hat – in 1848 a sign of republicanism). Feuerbach had influenced *Kunst und die Revolution* before *Kunstwerk der Zukunft*. After Wagner's death his heirs tried to minimize the importance of this influence and even suppressed the dedication to Feuerbach in later editions. Why? Perhaps because of his strong links with atheism and Marxism. Wagner's friend, Sulzer, also disapproved of his interest in Feuerbach whom, as an Hegelian, he did not recognize as a philosopher at all. He said that the best thing Feuerbach had done had been to awaken Wagner's ideas, not having any himself. What Wagner really liked about Feuerbach was his conclusion that the best philosophy was to have no philosophy – 'a theory which greatly simplified what I had formerly considered a very terrifying study'. *Kunstwerk der Zukunft* is a Feuerbachian vision of an artistically aspiring proletariat; in it Wagner hits out at industrialization and utilitarianism and uses for the first time the expression *Gesamtkunstwerk der Zukunft* (collective art work of the future). This phrase led to characteristic misinterpretations: it could either mean a totality of the arts or a totality of artists, with every man an artist. What Wagner appears to have had in mind was the extension of the co-operation of 'the three purely human art forms' of music, poetry and drama to other 'aids to the drama', such as architecture, sculpture and painting. This was to be achieved by a happy band of artists under the leadership of the *Darsteller* (director), who was both the word-and-tone-poet. After the publication of this book, a Professor Bischoff of Cologne coined the derisive word *Zukunftsmusik* (music of the future).

Meanwhile Minna, after many expressions of reluctance, consented to join Wagner in Zurich although she would have preferred Paris. She arrived at Rorschach at the beginning of September 1849 with Peps, Papo and her 'sister' Natalie. He set off on foot to meet this comic band – a distance of at least sixty miles. It is difficult for anyone, who is not a long-distance walker, to understand how Wagner managed these astonishing walking feats. When, in the summer of 1851, his friend Theodor Uhlig, at the age of thirty dying of consumption, travelled from Dresden to Rorschach, Wagner tramped a good sixty miles on foot from Zurich to meet him – through Rapperswyl, the 2900 ft Ricken Pass, Lichtensteig and St Gallen where he picked up Karl Ritter, the son of his benefactress, Julie Ritter.[1] They all three returned to Zurich via the Säntis (8000 ft); on reaching the top Karl Ritter's nerves gave way and it was decided not to descend the mountain on the precipitous side. A few days later Wagner and Uhlig, immersed in conversation about politics and musical conditions in Dresden, went, of course on foot, on a pilgrimage to the William Tell country via Brunnen, Grütli, Beckenried,

[1] Frau Julie Ritter was one of Wagner's Dresden admirers; shortly after his arrival in Zurich she gave him an allowance out of her small income.

Stans, Engelberg, the Surennen Pass, Amsteig into the Maderaner valley, onto the Hüflig glacier and then back to Zurich via Flüelen. A couple of days earlier Wagner had jotted down the theme of the 'Ride of the Walküre' (*Walkürenritt*). On returning to Zurich Wagner and Uhlig parted, never to meet again. For all we know Uhlig's death may have been precipitated by these marathon walks and climbs. There is certainly little doubt that Wagner, whose health was never at all good, taxed himself unduly. He had a need for violent physical exercise; after periods of intense creative and intellectual activity he embarked on some ambitious alpine exploit instead of resting. He enjoyed these climbs for their views and for the exhilaration of being in danger. His biographer Newman wrote that few men had heads as steady as Wagner's. 'The perfect correlation between brain and body, the completeness of nervous control that shows itself in his copper-plate handwriting and in the neatness of the fair copies of his scores, which, for the most part, are as legible as if they were engraved, manifested itself again in an exultant freedom from anything like giddiness at great heights: he would have made an excellent steeple-jack or tight-rope walker.'[1] This passion for vigorous exercise went hand-in-hand with a morbid preoccupation about his health. He took up one 'cure' after another with his usual thoroughness and determination. During his visit Uhlig gave Wagner a book by a Dr Rausse which prescribed water as a cure for every ailment; Wagner had, for some time before that, been experimenting with different forms of water cure. He drank cold water at night and wore a cold wet belt known as a 'Neptune-girdle'. In September 1851 Wagner, weak with dysentery and shingles, started a severe water-curing course at Altisbrunn in the hills near Zurich. He had just finished writing *Eine Mittheilung an meine Freunde* (A Communication to My Friends) and was unable, because of his dejected spirits, to start composing the music to *Der junge Siegfried*. Minna disapproved of this plan, thinking it merely an excuse to leave their new flat in the Zeltweg. He found a fellow-patient to go with him – a Saxon Lieutenant Hermann Müller, a former lover of Schröder-Devrient. The cure was supervised by a Dr Brunner, for some reason much disliked by Minna on her occasional visits. She called him the 'Water Jew'.

This is how Wagner described his hydropathic regime:

[1] Ernest Newman, *The Life of Richard Wagner*, 1933–49.

At five in the morning I was wrapped up and kept in a state of perspiration for several hours; after that I was plunged into an icy cold bath at a temperature of only four degrees; then I was made to take a brisk walk to restore my circulation in the chilly air of late autumn. In addition I was kept on a water diet; no wine, coffee or tea was allowed; and this routine, in the dismal company of nothing but incurables, with dull evenings only enlivened by desperate attempts at games of whist, and the prohibition of all intellectual occupation, resulted in irritability and over-wrought nerves.

Karl Ritter joined him there but failed, as on the Säntis, to emulate Wagner's stamina; he crept away from the cold packs and cold baths and made some surreptitious purchases at the local pastrycook's. At this time his mother Julie found herself able to guarantee Wagner, thanks to the death of her rich uncle, an income of 500 thalers which he continued to receive until 1859. This happy event led him to decide to complete his original sketch of the *Ring* and he wrote to Liszt from Altisbrunn outlining his great plan for a special festival production of the work. He returned to Weimar the advance which the court theatre had given him for *Der kunge Siegfried*.

To return to Minna – no sooner had she set foot in Zurich and furnished their apartment in the Zeltweg, than she pressed Wagner to make a third attempt at an artistic conquest of the French capital. On 1 February 1850 he left unwillingly for Paris. He took with him the prose draft of an opera *Wieland der Schmied* (Wieland the Smith), based on Carl Simrock's version of the Wilkyna saga; his idea was to have it turned into French verse by the librettist Gustave Vaez and then sold to the Opéra, as he had done nearly ten years earlier with *Der fliegende Holländer* (Le Vaisseau Fantôme). 'My stay in Paris is the most loathsome experience that I have ever undergone,' he wrote to his friend Sulzer in Zurich. Before leaving, he had suggested to Minna that they would, with the help of Julie Ritter's allowance of 500 thalers which had started in January, be able to lead a reasonably comfortable life in Zurich. She flew into a rage at this suggestion saying she was not prepared to live with a man who eked out a living as a hack scribbler and conductor in hole-in-the-corner concert halls.

Wagner's bleak Paris mood was not improved by the success of Meyerbeer's *Le Prophète*, an opera which nauseated him. *Wieland der Schmied,* which he turned into a three-act dialogue, was declined by the Opéra, and he suffered from pains in his heart. At this moment he was invited to Bordeaux by Jessie Laussot whom, as Miss Taylor, he had met in Dresden in April 1848 in the company of Karl Ritter. Since seeing *Tannhäuser* in Dresden she had been a devotee of Wagner and his art and she now planned to add 2500 francs to the Ritters' modest allowance. She was rich, attractive and artistic and her husband Eugène Laussot, a wine merchant who had originally been in love with her mother, did not, in her view, share her intellectual tastes. With Wagner things were quite different. In the well-appointed Laussot home he read to her from 'Siegfrieds Tod' and *Wieland der Schmied* and she, in her turn, played to him an accomplished rendering of Beethoven's 'Hammerklavier' sonata. Both felt unhappily married and they decided, in consequence, to leave their respective spouses and start a new life together either in Greece or somewhere in the Middle East.

Wagner returned to Paris; from there he wrote to Minna telling her that he would not be returning to her: 'Where I shall go, I do not know. Do not go in search of me!' Minna and Laussot successfully thwarted the lovers' elopement plans. Jessie had confided in her mother; she, in her turn, passed the news on to her son-in-law and former lover, who now threatened to blow Wagner's brains out. Wagner, brave and serious-minded, wrote Laussot a long letter. 'I told him that I could not understand how a man could bring himself to hold a woman by force when she no longer wished to have anything more to do with him.' He told Laussot that he was coming straight to Bordeaux and would be at his disposal. The cautious or craven Laussot, preferring to avoid this encounter, not only locked up his house and removed Jessie to the country, but also asked the local police to expel his rival for failing to obtain a valid re-entry visa into France. Thus ended the first of Wagner's 'innocent' attempts, as the unhappy artist, to attach to himself the unfulfilled wife of an inadequate husband. After Jessie and Eugène Laussot came Mathilde and Otto Wesendonk and finally Cosima and Hans von Bülow. Minna welcomed him back magnanimously, although writing to a friend in Dresden that 'he can never make up to me for the unspeakable anguish he has caused me'. The Jessie Laussot episode was Wagner's way of protesting at Minna's plans for him to become a Parisian opera composer. She had moved into a new apartment near the lake in the Enge district of Zurich; the future 'conquests' of Paris were to be his responsibility and not hers.

One of Wagner's shorter writings during his critical literary period in Zurich was 'Das Judentum in der Musik' (Judaism in Music). It was published by Franz Brendel in August 1850 in the *Neue Zeitschrift für Musik*. Wagner wrote the article under the pseudonym 'K. Freigedank'. The stimulus had been the expression 'Hebraic art-taste' in an earlier issue of this journal. Brendel was professor of musical history at the Leipzig Conservatory; after the publication of this article a petition to remove him from this post was signed by all the other professors which included the violinist Joachim.

Why did Wagner write his article on Jewishness or Judaism in music and what were the points which he was trying to make? He had noticed expressions like 'Hebrew art-taste', 'Jewish ornamental flourishes' in various journals without any attempt being made to explain them. He had earlier in the year, when in Paris, been disgusted by a performance of Meyerbeer's *Le Prophète*. Furious at the successful perpetration of what he considered a piece of charlatanism he left in the middle of an act and gave vent to his outraged feelings in a letter to Uhlig who later, in a series of articles for the *Neue Zeitschrift*, tore *Le Prophète* to pieces. Wagner's prejudiced conclusion was that a Jew was not capable of creating anything authentic, and he began his essay by mentioning the instinctive distaste for Jews which he proposed to explain in reference to the arts generally and to music in particular.

Why does the involuntary revulsion exist which is awakened by the person and character of the Jew? We deceive ourselves if we classify as bad manners all frank reference to our natural antipathy to the Jewish character ... it is our duty to bring to a state of complete intelligibility our ill-will towards him ... in the present state of things the Jew is more than free – he dominates; and, as long as money continues to be the power before which all our strivings are as naught, he will continue to do so.

Wagner gave his views of Jewish 'characteristics'. No matter, he wrote, what nationality a Jew may belong to, his appearance strikes us as so unpleasantly incongruous that we involuntarily wish to have nothing to do with him; nowadays, in view of his success, this dissimilarity from the rest of us is taken by the Jew to be a distinction. No Jew could be represented in the visual arts unless those traits, which characterize him in ordinary life, are considerably watered down. The Jew speaks any European language in the manner of a foreigner; this makes him incapable of the independent expression of his ideas. Even the greatest genius has found it impossible to write poetry in a foreign tongue.[1] The mere audible twang of the Jew's speech is offensive.

The hissing, shrill-sounding buzzing and grunting mannerism of Jewish speech fall upon our ears as something strange and disagreeable. If ever a Jew becomes excited it is because his material profit or personal vanity is affected; as his excitement has a distorting effect upon his speech it assumes a ridiculous character not calculated to arouse sympathy for the speaker. If therefore a Jew, when allowing himself greater intensity of expression in speech, appears ridiculous, he becomes quite insupportable if he tries to proceed to the height of song.

Wagner's next question is how the Jew, thus incapable by reason of his appearance, speech and song of making any artistic impact, managed to attain in music the position of arbiter of public taste? The answer lies in the ennoblement of money which he has acquired not through honest personal toil but through usury. As the benefits of modern education are now accessible to rich Jews we have a new social phenomenon: the educated Jew who has spared no pains – even submitting to Christian baptism – to obliterate all traces of his origin. This isolates him further; he has lost contact with his former companions in misfortune without obtaining a genuine footing in the society to which he aspires. 'Without friends or sympathy the Jew stands alone in the midst of a society which he does not understand, with whose strivings and inclinations he has no part, and to the history and development of which he is completely indifferent.' Assuming that the Jew should wish to express himself in art, Wagner continues, the substance of what he says could only be trivial or indifferent; all he can do is talk without saying anything and this, argued Wagner, is an art to whose cultivation music offers a great opportunity.

[1] Wagner was writing before the immigrant Jews had had time to establish themselves in the different countries of their choice.

Wagner seemed to assume that a Jewish composer would only find inspiration in a synagogue. He wrote: 'Who has not been shocked and held to the spot, partly by horror and partly by a sense of their absurdity, at hearing those gurgling, yodelling and babbling sounds which no intentional caricature could depict as horribly as the facts themselves and which may be witnessed going on in all naïveté and earnestness.' The Jew, being culturally isolated, cannot have any real passion to impel him to art creation. Without such passion there can be no repose; a genuine and noble stillness is simply passion which has subsided. Jewishness in modern music is therefore restless, dull, trivial and unfruitful.

Meyerbeer has, says Wagner, developed various deceitful artistic means of dispersing the *ennui* of the middle-class opera-going public. He and other Jews only obtained a foothold in the art of music after it had clearly lost its inner life. During the whole period down to the time of Mozart and Beethoven, when music had an organic inner life, we find no trace of a Jewish composer; it is only when the inner death of a body becomes apparent that extraneous elements can seize and destroy it. 'Then the flesh of this body is transformed into a mass of swarming worm-life . . . only in active life shall we able to meet that spirit again; and never by the side of a worm-eaten corpse.'

Following these outpourings which, hardly surprisingly, generated nothing in the way of a serious exchange on musical values, Wagner had to turn his attention to his own affairs.

A week after the publication of 'Das Judentum in der Musik' *Lohengrin* had its première in Weimar on 28 August 1850. Karl Ritter reported from Weimar that it had been musically good but dramatically inadequate. This probably sealed the fate of *Der junge Siegfried*. Wagner wrote shortly afterwards to Kietz in Paris, giving him the first hint of the idea of a festival. If he possessed 10,000 thalers, he wrote, he would erect a wooden theatre in a suitable place, engage the best singers, send out free invitations to all those who were interested in his works, have three performances of *Siegfrieds Tod* within a week, then pull the theatre down and the whole thing would be over. It was at this moment that he learnt of the 'hailstorm' of applications from German theatres to put on *Tannhäuser* and his other operas. These hopeful signs did not shake him in his resolve to plan his *Ring* dramas for a theatre which did not exist as he was sure that the theatre of his dreams would one day come into being.

Although the vast scheme of the *Ring*, which had been in his thoughts since 1848, was beginning to take shape in his mind – he had written the text of *Der junge Siegfried* before Uhlig's arrival – his renewed poetizing did not put an end to his excursion into the realms of criticism. In August 1851 he finished the long auto-biographical foreword to the edition of the poems of 'Der fliegende Holländer', 'Tannhäuser' and 'Lohengrin' which became well known under the title *Eine Mitteilung an meine Freunde* (A Communication to My Friends). In the book he announced to his friends (both personal and those of his art) that he was turning from romantic opera to mythical drama. He declared that he could only be understood by those who loved him; that artistically he was moving away from historical relation-ships to those where the purely human had been released from all conventions (in myth); that his aim was now the gradual dissolu-tion of traditional operatic forms; that he had embarked on the *Ring*. 'On an occasion to be specially arranged I plan in the course of three days and a previous evening to put on those three dramas and a prelude.'

In October he wrote to Uhlig from Altbisbrunn announcing once again three dramas and a three-act prelude. The *Ring* was developing backwards from the final part. He was not satisfied that he had expressed himself clearly enough in *Der junge Siegfried* and this compelled him to go further back to the origins of the myth. At the end of 1851 Wagner was in a state of excitement and elation. He enjoyed entertaining his Zurich friends in his new flat which Minna had made very comfortable. 'She had brought a large and luxurious divan, several carpets for the floor and various dainty little luxuries, and in the back room my writing-table of common deal was covered with a green tablecloth and draped with soft green silk curtains.' These innocuous references to 'green silk curtains' and other 'little luxuries' were seized upon by malicious journalists like the *Daily Telegraph* music critic who called Wagner 'a discordant notoriety-hunting charlatan, in six silk dressing-gowns, who could not write a bar of melody'. His critics delighted to say that he was effeminate and luxury-loving in his tastes. A police spy at about this time reported to the Saxon Ministry of the Interior that Wagner 'lives in ostentatious luxury and purchases the most valuable articles, such as gold watches, at enormous prices. His apartments are adorned with the finest furniture, carpets, silk curtains and chandeliers.' Apart from having a gentleman's liking for the fine things of life Wagner had a physical and emotional need for domestic comforts; in order to compose he needed to feel secluded from the world. To induce the dream condition which he needed when composing he had to have luxurious surroundings – soft carpets and curtains reflecting a mellow light and no object with sharp lines, such as books, which might cut across his dreams. The rooms had to be filled with perfume. He was particularly fond of heavy curtains and portières which gave him a feeling of seclusion. At the same time his marathon walks over the Swiss Alps were a more robust source of inspiration. His Zurich home in the Zeltweg had heavy rich-coloured curtains and hangings. Liszt, Wesendonk, Sulzer and the many others who gave or lent him money to enable him to continue with his work knew that all these luxurious and elegant trappings had been bought on borrowed money. To this Wagner would answer, 'I have excitable nerves; I must have beauty, brilliance, light.' Wagner's enemies, especially Nietzsche in later years, were to give his taste in interior decoration as an example of his own supposed Jewishness; rich Jews were thought to have a predilection for heavy velvet hangings and musty scented atmospheres. The oriental glitter and glow of much of his music was another argument later put forward by Nietzsche to support his case that Wagner was a Jew.

Wagner's high spirits at the end of 1851 were due to his satisfaction with his comfortable new flat in the Zeltweg, to the realization that he was turning into a composer of mythical music dramas, that he was assured of a permanent income from Julie Ritter, and that a new social and political age was about to dawn. His hopes, and those of other liberals, were pinned on the forthcoming elections in France. These were shattered by Louis Napoleon's *coup d'état* on 2 December.[1]

Wagner had written the first prose sketches of *Das Rheingold*

---

[1] To the dismay of democrats who, in 1848, had cast their votes for the Bonapartist candidate as the guarantor of freedom, Louis Napoleon cancelled the impending parliamentary elections with his *coup d'état* on 2 December 1851 (see V. Hugo's *Histoire d'un crime*), thus introducing twenty years of absolutist rule.

and *Die Walküre* in November. It was now absolutely clear to him that this new concept of a tetralogy would mean not only a break with Weimar but with the contemporary theatre as a whole. He wrote to Uhlig saying,

> With my new conception I am withdrawing *totally* from any connection with the present-day theatre and public; I am breaking unequivocally and permanently with the present. . . . I shall only contemplate a production after the revolution; only a revolution will bring me the artists and audiences which I need; the coming revolution will necessarily bring to an end the theatre as at present constructed: it must and shall collapse – that is unavoidable. From the ruins I shall gather what I need; what I need I shall find. On the banks of the Rhine I shall erect a theatre and issue invitations to a great dramatic festival; after a year of preparation I shall give my whole work in *four* days. With it I shall explain to the people of the revolution the *meaning* of the revolution which they will then recognize in its noblest manifestation. *That* public will understand me; the present cannot.

The failure of democracy in France and the after-effects of his exaggerated water cure led to another attack of physical and mental depression. He wrote to Kietz saying that his politics consisted of nothing other than the most intense loathing for our whole civilization, contempt for everything connected with it and a longing for nature . . . he did not, he said, however, quite despair of the *future*, but only the most fearful and destructive revolution could turn our present civilized beasts into 'human beings' again. His thoughts were turning again to America as was often the case in his moments of despairing gloom.

At the end of 1851 Verdi's *Rigoletto* had its première in Vienna and at the beginning of 1852 'a certain family by the name of Wesendonk, who had settled in Zurich a short time before, sought my acquaintance'. They met in the house of Wagner's fellow revolutionary and exile Marschall von Bieberstein. Otto Wesendonk, the thirty-seven-year-old partner in a New York silk business and his twenty-three-year-old wife Mathilde had been at the Beethoven concerts at which Wagner had conducted the music to *Egmont*, the *Coriolanus* overture and the overture to *Tannhäuser*. 'Knowing what a sensation this performance had aroused in Zurich', as Wagner put it, 'they thought it desirable to include me in their circle of friends.'

Wagner's health did not permit him to complete what was now

to be a 'Nibelung' poem in four parts. 'My nerves are desperate and I probably will not last much longer,' he wrote to a daughter of his brother Albert in March 1852. Nevertheless, in the same month he completed the great prose sketch of *Das Rheingold* and, during May and June, when he and Minna were staying at the pension Rinderknecht on the Zurichberg, with a lovely view of the lake and the distant Alps, he wrote both the great prose sketch and the poem of *Die Walküre*. At this time, through Georg Herwegh,[1] Wagner met François and Eliza Wille; Wille was a wealthy Hamburg newspaper proprietor with a face badly scarred in student duels and a tendency to outspokenness. The Willes had a charming old house at Mariafeld on the other side of the lake from the Zurichberg and it was to become one of Wagner's refuges from financial and other storms. The Willes had a large literary acquaintance and their circle included Mommsen, the historian, Semper, Gottfried Keller and Conrad Ferdinand Meyer.

Between the prose sketch and the poem of *Die Walküre* Wagner wrote to Uhlig on 31 May, 'Today I finished the complete draft of *Die Walküre*; tomorrow I shall start versifying. I am spellbound by the comprehensive splendour and beauty of my material in which my whole vision of the world has found its most complete and artistic expression . . . as soon as the verses are written then I shall become a musician again – but only in order to be a producer!' Having written the poem of *Die Walküre*, Wagner realized that he would have to revise many parts of the two *Siegfrieds*, as the mythology had taken on a much profounder and more precise physiognomy. 'I look forward enormously to starting on the music,' he wrote to Uhlig at the beginning of July.

Oper und Drama (Opera and Drama) which, for Wagner, symbolized his liberation from his *Kapellmeister* duties of conducting and writing historical and heroic operas was, for him, like *Eine Mitteilung an meine Freunde*, a kind of covenant or testament. 'The begetter of the art work of the future is no other than the artist of

[1] Georg Herwegh (1815–75), the revolutionary German lyrical poet, took part in the 1848 uprising in Baden and fled to Switzerland at about the same time as Wagner. They saw a lot of each other during the ensuing years. Herwegh accompanied Wagner on some of his marathon walking tours in the Alps; he advised him to read Schopenhauer's *Die Welt als Wille und Vorstellung* and he introduced him to François and Eliza Wille. These services compensated for his refusal to sit through twelve long evenings of hearing Wagner read *Oper und Drama*.

the present-day, who perceives the life of the future and yearns for it to be contained in his being.' *Oper und Drama*, in which he spoke of the new relationship between poetry and music in music-drama and of myth and leitmotiv, was the abstract, theoretical expression of the artistic process which was being worked out in his mind – the shaping of the great *Nibelung* dramas. 'I would never,' he said, 'have been able to define the most important moments in the shaping of the drama of the future had I not as an artist unconsciously hit on them in my *Siegfried*.' This, at least, shows that artistic creation preceded theorizing.

Shortly before the completion of *Oper und Drama* Wagner's beloved parrot Papo died. He was inconsolable. This little bird, who had always greeted him with a cheerful tune and who was a beneficent spirit in the not altogether serene household, was one of the few interests which Wagner and Minna had in common. 'Inwardly I am a stranger to her,' he said to Liszt. 'Oh!' he wrote to Uhlig, 'if only I could tell you what in me, with the death of this little animal, has also died!!! I do not care whether people laugh at me: what I feel, I feel . . . three days have now gone by – and nothing can comfort me. My wife feels just the same.'

It would be as well to summarize the main stages in the development of the *Ring* up to the beginning of 1853 when Wagner had, at his own expense, fifty copies of the completed poem privately printed.[1] A day or two later he read the poem during four evenings in the Hotel Baur-an-Lac to an enthusiastic audience. The musical composition was to start towards the end of the year after the famous 'vision of La Spezia' when, one afternoon, on 5 September 1853 Wagner, lying on a sofa in his hotel bedroom, saw the *Rheingold* prelude rise in all clarity before his eyes; the *Ring* music was born out of the chord of E flat major.

In October 1846 Wagner had written a short prose sketch for a drama about Frederick Barbarossa. Two years later, in the summer of 1848, he took it up again; as he worked on it he was much struck by the similarity of much of the material to that of the saga of the Nibelungen. To him Barbarossa and Siegfried overlapped at many points. He therefore abandoned the Barbarossa project and wrote instead a long essay, 'Die Wibelungen / Weltgeschichte aus der Saga' (The Wibelungen / World History as Seen in Saga). This is a curious, eccentric work, written in an obscure style,

[1] *Der Ring des Nibelungen*, Zurich, 1853.

which shows how many complex uestions, philosophical political and artistic, were occupying his mind. In it he tried to show that the imperial Hohenstaufen dynasty (Wibelings or Ghibellines) are really the Nibelungen of the saga. Pure fantasy, of course, but interesting because it shows how easily history became transformed into myth in Wagner's mind.

Fourth October 1848 is an important date in the history of the *Ring*. On that day Wagner completed the draft of *Die Nibelungen-saga*, the first prose study of the *Ring*, and published later with the title *Der Nibelungen-Mythus als Entwurf zu einem Drama* (The Nibelungen-Myth as Sketch for Drama). On 20 October Wagner finished the prose sketch for *Siegfrieds Tod*; he wrote that the intentions of the gods would be realized when, after this human creation (i.e. Siegfried), they destroy themselves; they must surrender their own power in the interests of the freedom of the human will. The original poem of 'Siegfrieds Tod' was written, in free rhythmic verse and *Stabreimen* between 12–28 November. It does not differ all that much from the later *Götterdämmerung* except that Walhall (Valhalla) does not come crashing down in flames. In December Wagner read his poem to a group of friends in his Dresden flat. Those present were Hans von Bülow, Semper, Karl Ritter, Gustav Kietz, his two friends from the Dresden theatre, Fischer and Heine, and Heine's son Wilhelm. Three years later in Zurich in October 1851 Wagner conceived the *Ring* as a four-part poetic drama. He had earlier thought about composing a cheerful opera based on the Grimm fairy-story about the boy who set out to learn the meaning of fear. This plan threatened to deflect him from his *Siegfried*. 'Think of my amazement,' he had written to Uhlig in May 1851, 'when I suddenly realized that this boy was none other than that very Siegfried who wins the treasure and wakes Brünnhilde.' *Der junge Siegfried* would have, thought Wagner, the great advantage of acquainting the public with the myth, like telling a child a fairy-story, and prepare them for the mighty happenings in *Siegfrieds Tod*.

In the pension Rinderknecht in May 1852 Wagner had written the 'Walküre' poem. Exhausted by this work, which had lasted one whole month, he decided to go on one of his prodigious walking tours over the Alps. Starting at Alpnach on Lake Lucerne, he walked to Interlaken, climbing various glaciers on the way. He climbed the Faulhorn and the Sidelhorn from whose summit he had a sudden and wonderful view of the Italian Alps with Mont Blanc and Monte Rosa. He had been careful, following the example of Prince Pückler-Muskau[1] when he climed Snowdon, to take a small bottle of champagne with him. 'Unfortunately, I could not think of anyone whose health I wanted to drink.'

Back in Zurich, Wagner wrote the 'Rheingold' poem in October and November and in December he rewrote *Der junge Siegfried* and *Siegfrieds Tod* to bring them both into proper relation with the whole. It was only in 1856 that these two works were given their final names of *Siegfried* and *Götterdämmerung*. Important changes were now made in *Siegfrieds Tod*: the tragic themes of redemption through death, the end of the gods and the burning of Valhalla were fully worked out and the poem of *Der Ring des Nibelungen* was completed.

A day or two after the completion of the poem Wagner went with Herwegh to the Willes's house at Mariafeld. He started at once to read the poems of *Das Rheingold* and *Die Walküre* to Eliza Wille, her sister Henriette von Bessing and Herwegh. Next morning it was the turn of *Siegfried* and in the evening he finished reading *Götterdämmerung*. 'I thought I had every reason to be satisfied with the result, and the ladies appeared to be particularly moved. Unfortunately, the effort left me in a state of almost painful excitement; I could not sleep and next morning I was so disinclined for conversation that I left my hurried departure unexplained. Herwegh, who accompanied me back, appeared to understand my mood which he shared by maintaining a similar silence.'

---

[1] Hermann, Prince Pückler-Muskau (1785–1871) was famous for the gardens which he laid out on his North German estates and for his travel notes.

Richard Wagner in 1849, aged thirty-six, by Ernst Benedikt Kietz.
Courtesy, Richard Wagner Museum, Bayreuth.

Ludwig Geyer, Wagner's stepfather.
Courtesy, Richard Wagner Museum,
Bayreuth.

Johanna Wagner, his mother.
Courtesy, Richard Wagner Museum,
Bayreuth.

Minna Wagner and Peps, 1853, by Clementine Stockar-Escher.
Courtesy, Richard Wagner Museum, Bayreuth.

Franz Liszt as a young man.
Courtesy, Richard Wagner Museum, Bayreuth.

Mathilde Wesendonk, by Ernst Benedikt Kietz.
Courtesy, Richard Wagner Museum, Tribschen.

Cosima von Bülow at the time of her marriage to Wagner.
From the author's collection.

Cosima and her father, Franz Liszt.
Courtesy, The Bettmann Archive.

CHAPTER SEVEN

Music and Metaphysics
1855–9

ON HIS FORTIETH BIRTHDAY, on 22 May 1853, the last of three special 'Wagner' concerts was held in Zurich. Wagner had gathered together, from far and wide, seventy musicians paid for by Wesendonk – the Wesendonks had become his closest friends in Zurich – and the Zurich Music Society had provided a choice of 110 singers. The programme consisted of extracts from *Rienzi*, *Der fliegende Holländer*, *Tannhäuser*, and, above all, *Lohengrin* whose music he was hearing for the first time played by a full orchestra. These three concerts, which followed one upon the other, have a place in history as being the first 'Wagner Festival'. The success was enormous; Wagner was presented with a silver goblet and a laurel wreath; the Zurich newspapers declared his music to be 'miraculous'. He refused any form of remuneration, his reward being, he said, the artistic success of the performances. He wrote to Liszt saying, 'I laid the whole festival at the feet of a *certain* beautiful woman.' That woman was Mathilde Wesendonk.

Liszt had many beautiful women in his life and Wagner very few. Vain, weak, snobbish and flamboyant, Liszt does not give the impression of being particularly adult or sensible in his choice of female friends. Marie d'Agoult, the mother of Cosima and of his three other children, went off with him as a gesture of aristocratic defiance to her family and to society. He was susceptible to energetic, well-born women; he lacked, however, the character to drop them when they became unpleasant and unreasonable. The most famous and most monstrous example of this was the Russian Princess Carolyne von Sayn-Wittgenstein,[1] that vindictive,

---

[1] Carolyne (or Karoline) von Sayn-Wittgenstein (1819–87) became Liszt's friend in 1848 and lived with him in Weimar until 1869.

cigar-smoking megalomaniac, whose influence on Liszt was wholly bad. She was jealous of his close friendship with Wagner and also of Wagner's developing musical fame and she did her best, sometimes with success, to poison their relationship.

Wagner's friendships with women were of a very different kind; unlike Liszt he was not a snob – not even when he had triumphed gloriously and kings and emperors came to Bayreuth to pay him homage. Throughout his life he had a compelling need for feminine company and feminine comforts. As a boy he loved his mother and his sisters and took little interest in his brothers. For Wagner the ideal woman was expected to make him comfortable, to create the right conditions for his work, to be attractive and to listen sympathetically and attentively to his theories about his art. Cosima was later to succeed in fulfilling these various functions but Minna could not. As his genius became more apparent and his artistic loneliness more evident Minna failed him more and more as a companion. He recognized her admirable domestic and petit bourgeois qualities but yearned at the same time for a woman who would give him artistic understanding. So it was with Jessie Laussot; Jessie was seventeen or eighteen years younger than Minna, rich, musical, cultivated and attractive. It was early in 1850, when the Laussots and Frau Ritter were planning jointly to give him an annual allowance of 3000 francs, that he wrote to Uhlig saying, 'in not a single trait of my being does my wife comprehend me. . . . I feel crippled, melancholy, wretched; only love can heal me, I feel, and that I shall not find in my home. I have no longer the strength to engage in fruitless daily wrangles with one who should be closest to me. . . .' It was against this background of marital misunderstanding that he had planned to elope with Jessie.

Wagner was not a philanderer at heart; quite the opposite – he was loyal and faithful to Minna for over twenty years and always tolerant of her intellectual and emotional inadequacies. At times she showed, however, provocatively little sympathy with his artistic aims and was responsible for forcing him to seek more congenial feminine company. Such company could be young or old, attractive or plain – preferably young and attractive. Wagner did not mind all that much; he wanted a receptacle into which he could pour the musical, poetic and other thoughts which swirled around in his marvellous brain. There is no doubt that he was, at this period of his life when about forty, a most delightful and fascinating person. He invariably attracted men and women of character and intelligence; women were more able to detect and be affected by what lay behind his magnificent energy, wit, humour and boisterousness. Eliza Wille wrote to Princess Wittgenstein from Zurich in 1857, 'Wagner is indescribably lonely here; but would he not be lonely almost anywhere? For any man whose mind and whose nature raise him above his fellows must stand *alone*, although in exchange he has the company of higher spirits.'

Mathilde Wesendonk has gone down to history as the 'inspirer' of *Tristan und Isolde*. Born a Luckemeyer in 1828 she married her fellow Rhinelander, Otto Wesendonk, in 1848. Wesendonk had made a lot of money and the two of them were leading an affluent life in smart international hotels when they met Wagner in Zurich in 1852. There they were living in the Hotel Baur-an-Lac, the same hotel in which, the following year, Wagner gave his very successful readings of the *Ring*. They were a handsome, serious-minded couple; Mathilde was Madonna-like in appearance, rather languid and given to writing poetry. Long after she had outlived her usefulness as Wagner's 'Muse', she went into the camp of the enemy by taking up Brahms;[1] she asked him to set to music her cantata about cremation, in her view the most important contemporary issue. He refused.

Who was this Mathilde, nominated by popular biographers and the writers of record-sleeve blurbs as the 'onlie begetter' of the most beautiful of Wagner's operas? We do not know what she really thought of Wagner; their friendship was almost certainly platonic and she became for him something ideal and unattainable. It is difficult to see in this cold, middle-class businessman's wife Wagner's spiritual companion. The music and philosophy of *Tristan*, the most intensely philosophical and introverted of all his music-dramas, had been shaping themselves in his unconscious, in accordance with those indefinable organic laws which determined Wagner's creative processes. Wagner himself said, 'We simply do not know how, unconnected with any specific experience or reality, these things happen ... one day I shall know something about the life of the spirit when I hope to show that the

[1] Brahms was not as anti-Wagnerian as his admirers liked to make out.

inner vision of the artist has remarkably little to do with outside happenings.'

The years 1849–54 throw light on the early history of *Tristan*. They were years which, in spite of Wagner's natural ebullience and optimism, brought him much pain and disappointment. Minna was getting older, more carping and with heart-trouble; he was a political exile, with a price on his head; his debts were piling up inexorably and he had to scribble theoretical tracts to bring in some money. Apart from the beauty of its situation and a small number of very nice friends Zurich was a city of philistines and peasants and induced in him a feeling of paralysing artistic inactivity – from April 1848 until the very end of 1853 he did not write a single note of music with one or two trifling exceptions; his theories about the art of music-drama, which were to be triumphantly vindicated before his death, were considered, even by Liszt, to be hopelessly impractical.

In December 1854 Wagner wrote Liszt an interesting letter about Schopenhauer whose great book, *Die Welt als Wille und Vorstellung* (World as Will and Idea), he had been introduced to by Herwegh a couple of months earlier and which he was to read four times by the following summer. He said: 'His main argument, the will's denial of life, is of fearful import but the only one which can release us.' In the same letter he spoke about his conception of *Tristan*: 'As I have never experienced the happiness of love I shall erect a monument to this most beautiful of all dreams in which this love shall, from beginning to end, fulfil itself to satiety; I have worked out in my head a Tristan and Isolde, the simplest but most full-blooded conception; I shall wrap myself in the "black flag", which is unfurled at the end and – die.'

In the peaceful quietness of his house in the Zeltweg, which still stands today and where he lived until he moved into the little Asyl near the Wesendonks's new villa in April 1857, Wagner started reading *Die Welt als Wille und Vorstellung* which was probably destined to be of greater importance to his art than Mathilde Wesendonk. Both Herwegh and Wille were great admirers of the philosopher; Wille so much so that he went to Frankfurt every year to visit the grisly sage. Eliza Wille, who had never forgotten meeting Wagner in Dresden in 1843, when his animated manner, his large head with its immense forehead, his piercing eyes, firm mouth, and granite-like chin made such an impression on her, spoke of the astonishing intellectual ease with which Wagner grasped the essentials of Schopenhauer's philosophy. Schopenhauer's book was first brought to the notice of the German literary world by the translation of an article in the *Westminster Review* of April 1853.

Like many an intelligent man who takes an interest in life, Wagner had long wanted to understand the value of philosophy. In Paris, back in 1841, he had discussed with his friend Lehrs questions such as life after death and the writings of Feuerbach; later he read Schelling and Hegel but, with the best will in the world, soon gave them up because of their obscurity. He liked Schopenhauer at once, less on account of his metaphysical theories than because of the extraordinary lucidity with which he expounded them. On the aesthetic side Wagner was astonished at the nobility of the Schopenhauerian conception of music. On the other hand Wagner, passionately addicted as he was to life despite his worries and his increasing attacks of erysipelas (also known as St Anthony's Fire or 'the Rose' because of its effect on the skin), was alarmed by the philosopher's ethical conclusions – that the annihilation of the will and complete abnegation are our only means of deliverance from the bondage of this world. Certain intellectual critics maintain that Wagner's espousal of Schopenhauer's musical aesthetics, which differed from his 'cheerful' Greek outlook on life as embodied in *Oper und Drama*, forced Wagner into making a series of adjustments, theoretical and practical.[1] Herwegh explained to him that it is upon this very perception of the nullity of the visible world that all tragedy is based; such a perception should dwell intuitively in every great artist.

Wagner now took another look at *Der Ring des Nibelungen*: 'I noticed with surprise that the very things which embarrassed me theoretically had been long familiar to me in my poetical conception. Now at last I could understand my Wotan, and I returned with chastened mind to the renewed study of Schopenhauer's book.' Schopenhauer was helping Wagner resolve the conflict between his intellectual 'Hellenic optimism' and his intuitive artistic pessimism. Whereas his instincts had told him that his operas *Der fliegende Holländer*, *Tannhäuser* and *Lohengrin* were tragedies of renunciation, of denial of the will, his reason told him to look at the world as an imperfect but potentially happy place.

[1] For example, J. M. Stein, *Wagner and the Synthesis of the Arts*, Detroit, 1960.

At the beginning of the year 1854, before he had begun to read Schopenhauer, he wrote to his friend August Röckel, still languishing in a Saxon gaol, 'We must all learn to die and to die in the most complete sense of the word. . . . Wotan raises himself up to tragic heights – but only to bring about his fall. This is all we can learn from the history of humanity: to desire what is needed and to bring it about.' Schopenhauer's teaching therefore fell upon willing ears. Wagner later compared the effects of his reading of Schopenhauer with those of his study of counterpoint under Weinlig back in 1831 in Leipzig; he saw that he had not acquired from either man ready-made theories, but rather new analytical methods and insights. Schopenhauer was no more the lone 'inspirer' of Wagner's art than was Weinlig or Mathilde; what he did was to provide arguments and reasons for what Wagner already apprehended intuitively. In this respect he was the greatest single influence in Wagner's creative life.

Wagner talked, in his usual compulsive and delightful way, to all his friends about his wonderful new discovery. At Christmas 1854 he sent Schopenhauer one of the special fifty copies of the private edition of the *Ring* poem. There was no letter attached – simply the inscription, 'With reverence and gratitude'. Although Schopenhauer did not thank him for this mark of attention – a fact which Wagner never quite forgot – we know what his reactions were, both from his marginal notes in the book and from his comments to Wagner's friend Wille and to others. The crusty old man's musical heroes were Mozart and Rossini; he disliked Wagner's music and disapproved of the liberties he took with the German language in the *Ring* poem. Wagner, he told Wille, was a poet and should hang his music on the peg. This suggests that he rather admired the poem, in spite of his sour marginal notes, some of which are quite funny. At the end of the first act of *Die Walküre*, when the incestuous Siegmund and Sieglinde rush out into the forest, Wagner's stage direction is 'The curtain falls quickly'; Schopenhauer adds, 'And about time, too!'

Tristan und Isolde, Wagner's new monument to his dreams, as he had described it to Liszt, was conceived in that wonderful year of 1854 when Wagner, the musician, was once again conscious of his calling. In that year he had started to write the music to the *Ring* and by the end of it he had completed the score of *Das Rheingold* and the musical sketches of all three acts of *Die Walküre*. 'It was essential for me,' he said, 'to let myself go musically, just as if I had to write a symphony.' Mathilde Wesendonk, Arthur Schopenhauer, his reading of Gottfried of Strassburg's lyrical epic poem *Tristan and Isolt* (*circa* 1210), of Friedrich Schlegel's novel *Lucinde* and of Novalis's *Hymen an die Nacht* – all played their part in the genesis of this sublime opera.

In Wagner's *Tristan und Isolde* the lovers long for night and death; the dying Tristan curses the 'desolate' day as the enemy of the night of forgetfulness and mystic union. In these sentiments Wagner echoes and almost copies certain lines of Novalis. As he was linked in so many ways with his predecessors in German romanticism Wagner was fascinated, as they had been, by the liberating concept of night and death. As for Schlegel's *Lucinde*, that novel also has the theme of eternal longing unfulfilled. 'But at last the fruitless yearning and the empty garishness of the day fade away into a night of love, of endless tranquillity.'

At the beginning of 1855 Wagner accepted, with considerable misgivings, an invitation to conduct eight concerts in London as the guest of the 'Old' Philharmonic Society for a fee of £200. The financial benefits and other gains he could hope to derive from this visit were insignificant and he would be losing valuable time in the composition of *Die Walküre*. Nevertheless he went, pleased at the prospect of handling, once again, a large, well-trained orchestra and persuaded that he was right not to cut all links with the public world of music.

Wagner's second London visit turned out to be very disappointing. The fog was at its worst; he met, for the most part, inferior, uninteresting and unfriendly people; the London music critics were snarling and malevolent; he was not allowed nearly enough rehearsal time before each concert and the concerts themselves consisted of hackneyed pieces arbitrarily assembled and arbitrarily applauded by an uncritical audience. Queen Victoria and the Prince Consort came to the seventh concert; the Queen had expressed a wish to hear the *Tannhäuser* overture which was repeated 'by command'. During the interval Wagner had an animated conversation with the Queen and the Prince which he described as the only stimulating incident of his stay in London. The question came up of putting Wagner's operas on the stage and the Prince suggested that Italian singers would have difficulty in interpreting his music. The Queen, to Wagner's amusement, met this objection by saying that most Italian opera singers in London were German. He wrote to Minna the next day saying that the Queen was 'short and not very pretty' and her nose inclined to be red. Perhaps she had, like him, a touch of erysipelas? He was impressed and rather grateful that he, a proscribed revolutionary in his own country, should be publicly received and treated with such cordiality by Queen Victoria. 'The German police,' he wrote to Minna, 'should now let me pass in peace!' Twenty-two years later, in May 1877, Wagner was once again to meet Queen Victoria when she received him at Windsor. He was back in London to conduct eight concerts of extracts from his works at the Albert Hall, the proceeds going towards meeting the deficit of the first Bayreuth festival held the previous year. On that occasion he left London with earnings of £700, representing one tenth of the Bayreuth deficit.

Wagner realized, to his distress, that the cost of living was much higher in London than in Zurich. He spent most of his money on food, coal and cabs and he took back with him to Zurich at the end of June, four months later, one thousand francs which represented a saving of about £10 a week. He moved into a house in Portland Terrace, near Regent's Park, where he remained until his departure. He managed to borrow a grand piano and a carpenter knocked together a tall desk, like a lectern, which he used for scoring. His frequent companion was Ferdinand Praeger, a German music teacher who had settled in London, whose book *Wagner as I Knew Him*, published after Wagner's death, was described by Newman as 'a masterpiece of mendacity'. Wagner found him 'an unusually good-natured fellow, though of an excitability for which his standard of culture did not sufficiently compensate'. Praeger introduced him to Prosper Sainton, a Frenchman from Toulouse and leader of the orchestra, 'of naïve and fiery temperament who lived with a full-blooded German musician from Hamburg, called Lüders, the son of a bandsman, of a brusque but friendly disposition. . . . I found them living together in a little house like a married couple, each tenderly concerned for the other's welfare.'

Wagner now learned the 'story' behind his invitation to conduct for the 'Old' Philharmonic. The London Philharmonic Society had split some time before into 'Old' and 'New' and the 'Old' were at their wits' end to find a conductor of reputation – Spohr could not come and Berlioz had been engaged by the 'New'. Lüders had read Wagner's '*Oper und Drama*' and apparently exclaimed '*Donnerwetter*! There's something in that.' At Lüder's suggestion, Sainton then recommended Wagner to the committee as somebody who might be a rival attraction to Berlioz. It being agreed in committee that 'a man so much abused must have something to him', they had sent the treasurer, Anderson, to Zurich to make the offer to Wagner in person. Anderson left Zurich, his mission successful, wrapped in a big fur coat which, Wagner learned later, belonged to Sainton.

Wagner was amused and depressed by the neat division in the public musical mind between sacred and secular concerts. The second of his concerts – they were all held in the old Hanover Square Rooms – had several pieces from *Lohengrin*. He had, with his usual thoroughness, written explanatory notes on the *Lohengrin* overture from which the words 'Holy Grail' and 'God' were struck out 'as that sort of thing was not allowed at secular concerts'. On the other hand the oratorio concerts in the Exeter Hall, often continuing for four hours at a stretch, were treated by the public with equal solemnity. 'Everyone holds a Handel piano score in his hand – in the same way that he holds a prayer-book in church.' The choruses of seven hundred voices reached, he thought, quite a respectable standard on several occasions, particularly in Handel's *Messiah*. Their competence and precision was due, above all, to the frequent repetitions of these oratorios. 'It was here that I came to understand the true spirit of English musical culture which is bound up with the spirit of English Protestantism. The oratorio attracts the public more than an opera; an evening spent in listening to an oratorio is almost as good as going to church.'

Miserable as Wagner was in London he thought that Berlioz, who arrived to conduct the 'New' Philharmonic, was in need of even greater sympathy than he. 'When I saw him, a man considerably my senior, coming here in the hope of earning a few guineas I deemed myself perfectly happy, almost floating on air by contrast ... his whole being expressed weariness and despair and I was suddenly seized with deep sympathy for this man whose talent far surpassed that of his rivals.' Berlioz was less distant to Wagner than usual; they cracked jokes about Meyerbeer's sycophancy to the critics and Wagner, surprised at finding himself speaking fluent French, started explaining to Berlioz his new Schopen-hauerian artistic theories. 'I endeavoured to describe the powerful effect of vital impressions on our temperament; how they hold us captive until we rid ourselves of them by the development of our inmost spiritual visions which are not called forth by these impressions but only roused by them from their deep slumber. The resulting artistic image is not a result of these vital impressions but rather a liberation from them.' Berlioz smiled patronizingly throughout all this and, when Wagner had finished, commented, 'Nous appelons cela: digérer.'

Apart from one or two little diversions, like getting jostled in Regent Street during the state visit of Napoleon III and Empress Eugénie and familiarizing himself with 'the imaginative way in which the English find their amusement' by seeing a non-stop series of pantomimes, subtly merging into one another, starting with *The Goose that Laid the Golden Egg* and ending with *Cinderella*, Wagner's months in London in 1855 were profoundly gloomy. Only once did an Englishman invite him to a meal and that was when John Lodge Ellerton, a brother-in-law of Lord Brougham, entertained him and his friends at the University Club. His host, an early Wagnerite who hoped that Wagner might succeed in curbing the dreadful Mendelssohn adulation, had to be carried home by two men after lunch – 'quite as a matter of course,' said Wagner. Throughout his stay his health was bad and he could not keep himself warm. He managed, somehow or other, to finish scoring the first act of *Die Walküre* and to start on the second, although he had hoped to proceed much further. In his wretched mood he could not even decipher his original compositional sketches. He plunged into Dante's *Inferno*; he read a canto every day and it became for him, in the London atmosphere, a never-to-be-forgotten reality. To Liszt he wrote that he was living like the damned in hell; to Minna he congratulated himself on his forty-second birthday in some comic, bitter doggerel:

> Im wunderschönen Monat Mai
> Kroch Richard Wagner aus dem Ei:
> ihm wünschen, die zumeist ihn lieben,
> es wäre besser drin geblieben.[1]

[1] 'In the wonderful month of May Richard Wagner crept out of the egg. Even those who like him most wish that he had stayed inside.'

He also told her that he had conducted Mendelssohn's 'Italian' Symphony wearing white gloves which he took off for Weber's *Euryanthe* overture. His enemies in the Press managed to associate this behaviour with his essay 'Das Judentum in der Musik'.

Wagner made two more quite important acquaintanceships when he was in London. The first was with Karl Klindworth, a young pupil of Liszt, who was later to write piano scores for many of Wagner's operas. He was so handsome that Wagner regretted he was not endowed with a tenor voice as he would have made an admirable Siegfried. (Klindworth later adopted the English orphan Winifred Williams and often took her to Bayreuth where she met Wagner's son Siegfried whom she married in 1915.) Secondly, he met Malvida von Meysenbug, like him a political exile from Germany. She was one of Wagner's earliest admirers and later belonged to the select Wahnfried circle as well as being a friend of Nietzsche.

At the end of June he shook off the servitude of being a guest conductor – a reminder of his Dresden *Kapellmeister* duties. He was given a heart-warming send-off by the members of the Philharmonic orchestra. Both players and members of the audience crowded round him and mobbed him with loud cheers. This was not enough to stop him from waiting impatiently for the hour of his deliverance. He hurried home to Zurich with his hard-earned thousand francs in his pocket. On the way he stopped in Paris. 'It was clothed in its summer glory and I saw people really promenading again, instead of pushing their way through the streets on business.' As for the thousand francs, 'This is the hardest money I have ever earned,' he wrote to Sulzer; 'In comparison my drudgery in Paris in days gone by, humiliating as it was, was child's play. I assure you that I have had to pay for every one of these thousand francs with a feeling of bitterness which I hope I shall never again experience.'

Wagner returned to Zurich to find his little dog Peps dying. He went with Minna to Selisberg on Lake Lucerne where she took a sour-milk cure. He hoped to derive some benefit from being in this beautiful place, the nearest thing to paradise which he had met with on this earth, so he said. But, alas, his nervous disorder, erysipelas, plagued him more and more; each attack, resulting from a slight change in diet or in the weather, caused him violent pain; he attributed his woes to the awful London climate.

Although all this meant a regrettable slowing down in his work on *Die Walküre*, he managed, before the year 1856 was out, to score the first two acts and to complete the third act early the following year. He wrote to Liszt saying that the true nature of his poetry only came to him when composing. In December 1855, after returning from a walk, Wagner sketched the contents of the three acts of *Tristan*; he wove into the last act an episode which was later dropped: Parzival, in search of the Grail, visited Tristan on his sick-bed. Wagner could not help but identify Tristan, wounded and yet unable to die, with Amfortas of the Grail legend. For the time being he forced himself to stop thinking further about *Tristan* in order not to be diverted from the monumental *Ring*, that gigantic musical myth which, in the words of Professor Closs,[1] arose 'from an unfathomable flood of reality and dream, of superhuman heroism and modern psychoanalysis'.

The growth of a huge Wagner literature in the last hundred years, both polemical and critical, written for the massed ranks of Wagnerites and anti-Wagnerites is due, above all, to Wagner's intellectual versatility. The nineteenth century was *his* century more than that of any other individual; he reacted instinctively to new fashions and forces in literature, art, music, philosophy and politics, and he felt compelled to comment on them in his writings, letters and music. He was, before everything else, an artist. Musical and poetic concepts were more real for him than the world of the senses – although to his mysticism was adjoined the sharpness of observation of the man of the world with his feet on the ground.

The year 1856 opened with Heine dying in Paris, with Freud's birth in Moravia and with Wagner making a determined attempt to return to Germany. The idea of Wagner as a political revolutionary is exotic and fascinating. He cannot be classed with those people who take to revolutionary politics deliberately or by impulse. His brief appearance on the political stage, characterized by wayward, eccentric and amateurish speeches and actions, underlined his total unfitness for a revolutionary rôle. It is odd that Friedrich August II and his ministers and officials, all of whom knew Wagner's volatility well, should have taken his behaviour so seriously. Had he not fled it is possible that he might have been let off with a light punishment and Switzerland and

[1] A. Closs, *The Genius of the German Lyric.*

Frau Wesendonk would never have claimed to be the inspiration of Wagnerian music-drama. They must surely have known that, in his behaviour during the uprising, he was acting true to form – contradictory, changeable and unexpected.

The King of Saxony, who had most reason to feel hurt by Wagner's 'ingratitude', appears to have treated his inflammatory utterances which were violently republican and monarchical at the same time with good-natured understanding. His brother Johann,[1] who succeeded him as king in 1854, was much more unyielding and legalistic than his sympathetic predecessor whose excellent qualities were respected by his political enemies. The German historian Treitschke called him 'the most amiable of the house of Wettin'. In spite of his magnificent brain Wagner was an out-and-out sentimentalist; his exuberant emotionalism drove him into situations from which he often had difficulty in extricating himself. It also enabled him, in darkest hours, to write his masterpieces, first as poetry and then later united to music.

Wagner's inconsistency and opportunism in matters outside his art made him unpopular in certain circles. In musical matters he was attacked, with much less justification, for being both an innovator and a traditionalist. In London the music critics were consistently hostile to him. When his appointment as the 'Old' Philharmonic guest conductor was announced Henry Chorley, music critic of the *Athenaeum*, complained that, 'even if no competent conductors existed in England, why pick a man whose avowed and published creed is contempt for all such music as the English love ... the appointment of Herr Wagner can be regarded as nothing short of a wholesale offence to the native and foreign conductors resident in England'. Those were symptomatic of views expressed from that Mendelssohnian backwater. Wagner's intelligent conservatism, like (as Baudelaire said) his ability to theorize about his works, provoked the critics. They could not brand him as an ignorant iconoclast; he appreciated and understood the music of his great predecessors – Bach, Mozart, Gluck and Beethoven – possibly better than any contemporary musician; he was a master of traditional harmonic and melodic forms. He knew, unlike the critics, that after Beethoven and Schubert a certain musical rigidity set in and that it was his

[1] Johann, King of Saxony (1801–73) was a Dante scholar and translated *La Divina Commedia* into German.

mission, despite his profound conservatism, to lead the world into a realm of new musical experiences. It was Wagner who turned the music of the nineteenth century – with its harmonies, sonata form, operatic structure, orchestral treatment – into that of the twentieth. He invented the 'new music' – a triumph of genius and character – by joining the revolutionary virtue of impatience with the conservative one of stubbornness. As late as 1880 *The Nineteenth Century* declared, with relief, in its October issue that 'the Wagner bubble has burst and music still remains!' The article went on to say that Wagner was a controversialist and man of action rather than a studious and retiring composer; it was through a caprice of destiny that he was a musician. Wagner knew, however, in his heart (continued the article) that he was no musician and he therefore took to writing for the opera house rather than for the concert room,

... in whose pure air music stands alone of its own merits ... on the opera theatre he planted his banner ... he proclaimed that all music, except operatic music, was now at an end. Such astounding audacity from the lips of any other man would have brought eternal ridicule on its propounder. But in the case of Wagner with such passion did he defend his obstinate opinions that he actually persuaded a number of well-meaning people to believe him ... finding that Meyerbeer, Auber, Spontini and others, despite his clear demonstration of their errors, continued to engross public favour and exclude him from his dearly sought popularity, he discovered a new means to invalidate their pretensions by roundly declaring that no man could be a musician unless he were at the same time a poet; consequently these pampered pets of the public, who did not have the good fortune to know the art of rhyme, were not merely egregiously wrong-headed and trans-gressing musicians, but, in the strict sense of the word, were no musicians at all.

The article went on to ridicule Wagner's verse: 'Such sorry stuff has scarcely ever entered human head as the metrical jargon which forms the librettos to his operas.' *Tristan und Isolde*, written to give vent to this imprisoned passion of his soul, opens with Isolde, the eternal woman, introducing herself to the public:

    Isolde (jeeringly):
    In shrinking trepidation
    His shame he seeks to hide,

While to the king, his relation,
He brings his corpse-like bride.

'By sheer indomitable perseverance and force of will Wagner con-
trived to palm this stuff off upon hosts of believers as celestial poetry.'

The above is an example of the spite and venom meted out to
Wagner by the greater part of the English press until he died.
The press campaign against him continued unabated although
the public had been flocking for a quarter of a century to hear his
operas in every European capital and in most important cities in
the United States. When Wagner conducted his works in London
in 1877 *The Times* found the overture to *Der fliegende Holländer* 'a
mere inflated display of extravagance and noise'. At that time a
small group of Wagner enthusiasts were fighting hard to establish
his reputation in England. The most famous of these was Bernard
Shaw whose *The Perfect Wagnerite* was published in 1898 and who
had, during the preceding years, been writing intelligently about
Wagner in his excellent pungent prose. Nor should Queen
Victoria be forgotten when speaking about Wagner sympathizers;
she summoned him to Windsor in 1877 and 'helped to alleviate
his feelings of disappointment and isolation by her gracious
words and encouragement'.

In the spring of 1856 Wagner decided to send a personal
appeal for clemency to the King of Saxony, a step from which he
had hitherto recoiled. His letter to the king, starting 'Most
illustrious King and Lord', states, seven years after the event, his
reasons for sympathizing with the uprising. It was not, he said,
out of cowardice that he fled from Saxony rather than stand his
trial. It was because he saw no possibility of his artistic views
being accepted in Dresden; a new more receptive climate could
only, he then thought, be brought about by a transformation of
political and social conditions after which his ideal of the proper
relation of art to life might be realized. Politics and the events of
the day only concerned him in so far as they affected his artistic
purpose; he never gave serious support to any political undertaking. Whatever conclusions were drawn from his behaviour
during the Dresden riots he was so little conscious of any criminal
intention, least of all against the King, his benefactor, that when
he fled the country he had no idea of the nature of the charges
preferred against him. Later he learned that he had been accused

of the blackest ingratitude against his royal benefactor and of crimes of which he was innocent, although he could not disprove them. 'The only thing that sustained me in this painful situation was a truly morbid feeling of exultation to which I gave myself over with a sort of desperate eagerness during the first years of my exile.' The books which he had subsequently written in Switzerland, proclaiming his theories on art and life, gave his detractors the opportunity of saying that his criminal conduct, far from being spontaneous and unconsidered, was actually the result of a philosophical system. He then referred to the inward change which he had experienced. 'I began to have a deeper insight into the nature of things which made me realize that my former views were mistaken.' He would cheerfully submit to a continued exile were it not that his art bound him with indissoluble ties to his Fatherland: 'only there can I hope to see my music-dramas produced and that is an experience indispensable to the future progress of my art'. Wagner ended by acknowledging his guilt in 'deserting the proper sphere of art for the field of politics', and pledging his word never again to indulge in any form of political activity.

After seven years of internal struggle Wagner had finally swallowed his pride and brought himself to write to the King of Saxony acknowledging his guilt and begging forgiveness. The King handed his petition to the Ministry of Justice. Wagner heard that his petition had been unsuccessful in August 1856, just after finishing his cure with Dr Vaillant at Mornex near Geneva. He had been talking quite cheerfully about the expected amnesty to the point of planning to move to a Swiss summer resort and keeping a small *pied-à-terre* in Zurich (as he would frequently be visiting Germany). His disappointment must have been great; the good offices of Liszt and the intervention of the Grand Duke Carl Alexander of Weimar, Wagner's admirer, had been unavailing.

There were, however, one or two gleams of light in the darkness of Wagner's affairs. Dr Vaillant had succeeded in curing his erysipelas. 'Monsieur, vous n'êtes que nerveux', he told him, putting him on a mild water diet and promising that he would be cured within two months – which he was, at least for the next twenty-four years. Wagner spent his time in Vaillant's establishment reading Sir Walter Scott in French (he was one of Schopenhauer's favourite authors) and designing, with an architect's thoroughness, a house for himself which he hoped to build out of the proceeds of the sale to the publishers, Breitkopf & Härtel, of his *Nibelungen* scores. His original plan, a fantasy, had been to produce the *Ring* dramas for himself, Liszt and a few friends of his art in an 'instant' theatre on the banks of the Rhine – a four-day operatic event after which the dream would have vanished and all be over. He himself now believed that there was a chance of a wider public appreciating these works. 'It is not possible', he told Härtel, 'that I shall ever again conceive or execute anything resembling my *Nibelungen* dramas; they constitute the most complete and magnificent achievements of my life and in the poetry alone I may claim to have presented the nation with a work whose quality the future will endorse with pride.' In view of this he asked Breitkopf & Härtel for two thousand louis d'or or ten thousand thalers in gold. He would immediately hand over to them, against payment of half the fee, the first two complete parts of the tetralogy (*Das Rheingold* and *Die Walküre*) and he would receive the balance upon the completion of *Siegfried* and *Siegfrieds Tod*. The publisher, after some reflection, refused this offer thereby losing a fortune. The scores of the *Ring* were finally published not by Breitkopf & Härtel, but by Schott.

Although Wagner had now written the music for *Das Rheingold* and *Die Walküre* the belief still persisted that his *Ring* poem was unrealizable in music and that, as a result of his long period of seclusion in Zurich, he was losing touch with reality. Even his friend and admirer, Liszt, had failed to see the dramatic and musical possibilities inherent in the *Ring* poem. He and the Princess were due to arrive in Zurich in October 1856 and Wagner hoped, if the Princess did not turn out to be too distracting, to show Liszt what musical progress had been made. This would be Liszt's second visit to Zurich during Wagner's exile. The first had been in July 1853 just after Wagner's three highly successful concerts. The week which they had spent together was, for Wagner, of 'almost stunning delight'. Wagner had cried, laughed and stormed with joy on seeing Liszt again; words had poured out of him in torrents. Liszt had admired the *petite élégance* of Wagner's home and the piano scores of *Rienzi*, *Tannhäuser* and *Lohengrin* 'superbly bound in red'. He had written to the Princess of Wagner's behaviour:

He loves me heart and soul and never stops saying, 'Look what you've made of me?' when the conversation touches on his fame and popularity. Twenty times during the day he fell upon my neck; then rolled on the floor with his dog Peps, caressing and talking gibberish to it in turns; then started cursing the Jews, with him a generic term of wide meaning. In a word, his is a grand and grandissimo nature, like a Vesuvius letting off fireworks, emitting sheaves of flame and bouquets of roses and lilacs.

During that visit Wagner got to know Liszt better as a man and as a composer; they went to the William Tell country and, with Herwegh as the third in the party, drank *'Brüderschaft'* (brother-hood) to each other from the springs on the Rütliberg. They settled that Zurich should be the place for a festival of Wagner's music-dramas.

Now, three years later, Wagner was disenchanted with Zurich; he refused to conduct any more concerts for the Music Society and he knew that the town would never provide him with a temporary theatre for the *Ring*. From now onwards the Swiss were, for Wagner, 'smug bourgeois' and 'suburban Philistines'. He withdrew from public musical life and spent his time orches-trating the *Ring*, studying Buddhism, brooding about *Tristan* and seeing a few friends – Semper, Herwegh and Gottfried Keller. Shortly before Liszt's second Zurich visit Wagner started on the orchestration of *Siegfried*; the noisiness of the Zeltweg was getting more and more on his nerves. He had several rows with a tinsmith who lived opposite and who, with his hammerings, unwittingly inspired the motif of Siegfried's outburst against the bungling Mime (G minor theme in Act I).[1]

The great day arrived and Liszt, the Princess and her daughter Marie took up their quarters in the Hotel Baur-au-Lac – this time to stay for six weeks. Liszt played Wagner his *Faust* and *Dante* Symphonies from the score; Wagner urged him to replace the crude and pompous ending of the *Dante* Symphony by something softer and more shimmering. Liszt agreed but later let the Princess overrule him. 'And this,' said Wagner, 'was exactly typical of my relations to Liszt and to his friend Carolyne Wittgen-stein!' This frightful woman at once turned Zurich into a social

[1] The writer knows the daughter of this tinsmith – a very old lady who lives a few streets away from the Zeltweg.

whirlpool. Carriages came and went; footmen ushered in and out the most 'interesting' people in Zurich; the university professors were ferreted out of their holes to dance attendance on this aristocratic blue-stocking who had plaster medallions of Liszt distributed amongst her guests. Wagner was appalled by what he described to Bülow as 'this eternal racket'. The highlight of the 'racket' was Liszt's birthday party in the Baur-au-Lac; before a large gathering Wagner improvised a 'performance' of the first act and of Brünnhilde's 'death message' (*Todesverkündigung*) in *Die Walküre*. The performers were Liszt, on the piano, Wagner as Siegmund and Hunding and Emilie Heim, a Zurich singer, as Sieglinde and Brünnhilde. At the end Liszt, overwhelmed with admiration, stretched out his hands towards Wagner; next day a letter in the *Neue Zürcher Zeitung* claimed that this poetic music, amongst the most magnificent ever written, represented the realization of Wagner's reforming endeavours. 'It marks a new epoch in the world's history.'

More agreeable than the frenzied soirées in the Baur-au-Lac were the unceremonious evenings at Wagner's home where the Princess behaved less pretentiously. 'With Polish patriarchal friendliness she would help the mistress of the house in serving.' On one of these occasions Wagner spoke to his guests, spread out half-sitting, half-lying in front of him, about his two newly conceived poems 'Tristan und Isolde' and 'Die Sieger' (The Victors). The latter was a Buddhist drama based on the themes of renunciation and redemption, certain features of which later found their way into *Parsifal*.

The Princess was gracious enough to express an interest in certain curious aspects of the gods' behaviour in the *Nibelungen* dramas; as he answered her precise arithmetical questions Wagner felt as if he was explaining some French society play. Liszt's harmonies began to exert, during this visit, their influence on Wagner; the Princess was later to do her best to persuade people that Wagner's reputation as an harmonic innovator was based upon what Liszt had taught him. Shortly after seeing them off at Rorschach on Lake Constance at the end of November 1856, Wagner finished the score of the first act of *Siegfried*; it had succeeded beyond all his expectations and he believed that he had at last achieved what had hitherto escaped him – a continuous, unbroken flow of melody, as opposed to the alternating 'arioso' and recitative of *Das Rheingold* and *Die Walküre*. Whether he thought he had reason to be grateful to Liszt for the development of this new technique of composition we do not know. He was later to recognize the influence of Liszt's music in *Tristan und Isolde* and in *Parsifal*.

At one time during his stay in Zurich Liszt dropped his saintly mask thus indirectly stopping Wagner's pension from Frau Ritter. Wagner had already learnt that the gentle Liszt could be at times bad-tempered and quarrelsome. It was dangerous to cross him on the subjects of Louis Napoleon, Goethe and the Russian character. He flew at Wagner during a discussion about the nature of Goethe's *Egmont*. 'We never actually came to blows,' said Wagner, 'but from that moment onwards, for the rest of my life, I had a vague feeling that this might one day happen and that the encounter would be terrific.' Liszt was holding forth about his hero, Louis Napoleon, one evening in Wagner's house and Karl Ritter fixed on him an inane, but contemptuous, smile provoking Liszt into shouting at him, 'Baboon face!' Karl Ritter left in a fury and was angry with Wagner for not avenging this insult to his person in his own house. Wagner felt that he could no longer, in these circumstances, accept financial help from Karl's mother and he wrote her a dignified letter renouncing the pension which he had been receiving for the last five or six years.

Wagner's main consolation, now that Liszt had gone, lay in the company of the Wesendonks. He was attached not only to Mathilde but also to Otto who offered him, early in 1857, a little house, the Asyl, for life at a nominal rent. It was in the Enge district of Zurich on the Grünen Hügel (Green Hill) and adjoining Otto's new estate on which he was building a large and splendid villa on classical lines. (The Villa Wesendonk[1] still stands in its elegant park – the Asyl has been pulled down – but no traces whatsoever remain of the cultured occupancy of the Wesendonks.) This German couple managed, thanks to Wagner's attraction, to turn their house into a meeting place for artists and men of letters and to lure to it those withdrawn and stuffy intellectuals – a feat of which only the Princess had hitherto been able to boast.

In the spring of 1857 the Wagners moved into the Asyl. His mood was now one of soaring optimism and happiness; he had

[1] Now the Rietberg Museum specializing in oriental antiquities.

at last found the perfect home; here he would be able to write his music-dramas and lay them at the feet of his muse, Mathilde, who conveniently lived a stone's throw away, the other side of a carriage drive; her husband Otto had found him a house and paid his debts. 'A pretty little garden,' he wrote Liszt, 'affords my wife the pleasantest of occupations and keeps her from getting notions in her head about me; a good sized kitchen garden demands her most solicitous care.'

On Good Friday Wagner woke up to find the sun streaming into the little house. He thought once again of Wolfram's *Parsifal.* 'Since my stay in Marienbad, when I conceived *Die Meistersinger* and *Lohengrin*, I had never given another thought to that poem; now its possibilities struck me with overwhelming force and, out of the thoughts about Good Friday, I rapidly conceived a whole drama of which I then and there dashed off a sketch dividing the whole into three acts.' This first prose sketch of *Parsifal* has disappeared.

'The last move in this world,' as Wagner called it, was now over. He longed to invite his friends to share his pleasure in his new home, furnished 'with pedantry and elegant cosiness', and see from his study window the marvellous view of the Lake of Zurich and the Alps. Frau Ritter had written him a conciliatory letter and renewed his allowance. 'This letter warmed us through and through and made the first day in our Asyl a glorious sun-flooded festival.'

Breitkopf & Härtel's rejection of Wagner's offer to sell them the *Nibelungen* scores made him feel like giving up this 'obstinate undertaking'. On 28 June 1857 he wrote Liszt those lines which most Wagnerites know by heart: 'I have led my young Siegfried into the forest solitude; there I have left him under a lime tree and, with tears from the depths of my heart, taken my leave of him.' (*Siegfried*, Act II.) The second act of *Siegfried* is the 'nature' section of the *Ring par excellence*; the forest murmurs and the birds sing: those birds he had heard a few weeks earlier on his birthday (22 May) on his woodland walks in the nearby Sihltal. On the same evening, as he sat on the verandah of the Asyl, he heard the music of the Rhine-maidens drifting towards him; he inserted it lightly with a pencil into that part of his compositional sketch where Siegfried emerged from Fafner's cave, with ring and Tarnhelm, the magic helmet, not having any idea what to do with either. And so Wagner said farewell to his Siegfried whom he loved so much; it was in 1869, twelve years later, that he resumed the orchestration of Act II.

Wagner's decision to stop work on the *Ring* and take up *Tristan*, 'a manageable and thoroughly practicable opera', was not due solely to his chagrin with his publishers. He may have felt that he was not yet musically ready for the complex orchestration of *Götterdämmerung*; before that he needed to absorb the harmonies of *Tristan* and the contrapuntal technique of *Die Meistersinger*. The *Ring* had been occupying his thoughts, on and off, for the last nine years; he had to give organic musical unity to this mass of mythological dramatic material; the themes and motifs had to be susceptible to contrapuntal treatment and to an infinite number of variations and combinations as the psychological complexities of the work developed. He realized also that he was in danger of becoming a forgotten composer if he did not soon produce something 'easily performable' on an ordinary stage. It is one of the most endearing things in Wagner's career that *Tristan*, whose 'new harmony' marks the beginnings of modern music and which is considered by many to be his most 'difficult' opera, should have been regarded by him as a money-making project. He had by now sketched out some of the first musical themes in *Tristan* – the love scene in Act II and the chromatically rising yearning motif (*Sehnsuchtsmotif*).

A curious episode followed when Wagner was visited by a certain Dr Ernesto Ferreira-França, a Brazilian living in Dresden, with an invitation from his master, the Emperor Dom Pedro II, to go to Brazil and produce his operas there. Wagner at once thought of producing *Tristan und Isolde* in Rio de Janeiro in an Italian translation. He followed up this *démarche* with his usual eagerness. He persuaded himself that 'Tristan', being a passionate musical poem, would sound much better in Italian than in German and, to show his enthusiasm for the proposal, he sent the Emperor, via Ferreira, expensively bound copies of the piano scores of his early operas. He never heard another word from the Emperor, nor from Ferreira, about this matter. Dom Pedro remained, however, a Wagner enthusiast; nearly twenty years later he attended the first performance of *Das Rheingold* at Bayreuth. He came quietly, writing in his hotel visitors' book under 'occupation' the single word 'Emperor'.

Eduard Devrient,[1] his friend from Dresden days and now *régisseur* at Karlsruhe, visited Wagner at this time. He told him of the Grand Duke of Baden's enthusiasm for his operas and suggested Karlsruhe, rather than Rio, for the production of *Tristan und Isolde* as it was going to be a 'practical' opera. Wagner was delighted; he forgot all about Rio and Dom Pedro, and, in his pocket-book, sketched out the 'Tristan' poem and the tonal sequences. Devrient did not realize, any more than perhaps Wagner did, that his preoccupation with the Tristan subject was a result of his growing mysticism. Although always ebullient, his instincts were now to withdraw from the world of garish day into one of mystic night. He finished the 'Tristan' poem as Bülow and Cosima arrived in Zurich on their honeymoon, a few weeks after their unfortunate marriage had taken place in Berlin. Cosima used to say to her grandchildren, seventy years later, 'Herr von Bülow should never have married'.

The three important women in Wagner's life – Minna, Mathilde and Cosima, were now all together in the Asyl. He played them bits from *Siegfried* and read the poem of 'Tristan'. By this time Mathilde had become his official muse, to whom he was dedicating all his creative work. 'What he composed in the morning,' said Mathilde, 'he would play over on my piano in the afternoon, to see how it sounded. This was between five and six o'clock. He called himself "the twilight man".' How did the three ladies react to the 'Tristan' poem? Minna found the hero and heroine 'an odious, tear-jerking couple'; Mathilde took the passionate love declarations in the poem personally; Cosima kept her thoughts to herself.

Some Wagner biographers give love and others financial anxiety as the main-spring of his creative activity. Assuming that love in this context was more important than money, which of these three women played the decisive rôle in his life as an artist? The accepted answer is Mathilde Wesendonk; 'She is and remains my first and only love! I feel that more and more definitely. It was the zenith of my life,' said Wagner later. When he knew her in Zurich he was in his early forties and at the height of his powers; Minna, his wife, was ageing, carping, unhealthy and incapable of

---

[1] Eduard Devrient (1801–77), producer, stage manager and writer, held theatrical positions in Dresden and Karlsruhe and was a close friend of Mendelssohn.

understanding his artistic aims. He was strongly sensual by nature and he derived pleasure, when a little boy, from the touch of a woman's hand and from feeling his sisters' clothes. Later, love meant for him, as for his Tannhäuser, sensual gratification; he gave himself over to a life of moderate dissipation and had a number of straightforward affairs, such as those at Würzburg with Thérèse Ringelmann and Friederike Galvani. As Minna became less attractive, and his marriage more and more nightmarish, his sensual feelings turned into a *yearning* for that indulgence. His effeminate, self-pitying nature cried aloud for love which became merged with a yearning for redemption. Love and Death are intermingled in Wagnerian dramas; love is not, as in the days of *Das Liebesverbot* a happy, earthly union, but a means of redemption through death. Lovers can only be united by death. Sensuality is not a happy sensuality à la *Liebesverbot* but a hateful orgy, as with Tannhäuser and Kundry, which could only be redeemed by chaste virginity and renunciation, as with Elizabeth and Parsifal. Wagner needed, he thought, emotional torments and deprivations to unlock the treasures of his genius. *Tristan und Isolde* was a monument to the love he had never enjoyed. 'If we could really live, art would be unnecessary,' he once wrote. 'Art begins precisely where life leaves off.'

In addition to this unfulfilled voluptuous yearning, Wagner also needed – all the more so as the years went by – more and more exotic and extravagant aids to creation. These 'needs' of his were to land him in a lot of trouble and ridicule in the future; they aroused the Puritan wrath of his creditors, of the music critics and even, in 1865, the King of Bavaria's ministers. The modest luxuries of his home in Zurich were nothing when compared with the sophisticated elegance of some of his future establishments. When he worked he needed heady perfumes, soft lights and colours, the brilliant shimmer of the heaviest silks, soft furs and rich satins – to touch these caused him violent excitement. Twenty years later, in 1877, when he was writing *Parsifal*, that Christian drama of renunciation and farewell to this world, Wagner badly needed new stimulants for his senses, dulled by ten years of Cosima's domestic attentions. He found them in a brief love affair with Judith Gautier and in various external aphrodisiacs. In earlier days, in Munich and Vienna, his dressmaker had made him silk dressing-gowns and down pillows and he had intoxicated himself with colours, rich materials and the touch of glimmering satin. Now he needed to supplement this tactile satisfaction with other stimulants such as voluptuous scents. Judith conveniently lived in Paris, the home of all these delights. Here are some characteristic passages from some of his love letters:

Sweet glowing soul! What a great creative urge I feel when I am in your arms . . . but let's talk business. First of all, the boxes haven't yet arrived. I will keep the silk brocade. I want to order ten yards but perhaps there are other colours more to my taste – I mean silver grey instead of chamois and pink (*my* pink, very pale and delicate) instead of blue. You frighten me with your perfumes. They'll make me do all kinds of silly things . . . never mind about the money; above all with the bath perfumes – the amber, for instance. My bathroom is underneath my study and I like it when the fragrance mounts up to me from there . . . everything has arrived safely, the slippers and the milk of iris. First rate! But I need a lot, a half bottle for a bath; and I bathe every day. Please bear this in mind. Rimmel's 'Rose de Bengale' is better than the 'White Rose'. I'll continue with that; please send me a large quantity as I use a lot. . . . I want some satin. That's the only sort of silk I like because the light plays so softly on its folds. For my sofa I need a very lovely cover in a striking pattern which I shall call Judith! Try and see if you can find some of that material they call 'Lampas', or something like that. A background of yellow satin, as pale as possible, covered with a network of flowers – roses. I need all that for the lovely morning hours when I am occupying myself with *Parsifal*!

'And thus the sweet memories of Judith's embraces and the exotic, sensual atmosphere generated by Rimmel's sweet perfumes, the iridescent satins, silk dressing-gowns, and soft, gay-coloured slippers were the midwives of the fascinating harmonies that Wagner drew forth from his genius in his *Parsifal*.'[1]

From this glance at the increasing voluptuousness of his tastes in the future we return to the Asyl where the three women in Wagner's life find themselves together. Cosima was silent when asked to comment on his reading of 'Tristan'. She was clearly not enjoying her honeymoon with Bülow who was more devoted to Wagner than he was to her. She had had a miserable upbringing in Paris, not being allowed by Liszt to see her mother; behind each act of inhumanity lay the vindictive hand of the

---

[1] J. Kapp, *The Loves of Richard Wagner*, 1951.

Princess. It seems that Cosima was depressed and frightened by Wagner's strong personality and by the tragic nature of 'Tristan'. When he asked her more questions about 'Tristan', she began to cry. 'I am silly enough still to be shy towards him,' she told Minna.

The Bülows returned to Berlin at the end of September 1857 and Wagner started at once to compose *Tristan und Isolde* in earnest. He did a compositional sketch of Act I in which he unconsciously developed a new harmony. At this time he also set to music five of Mathilde's songs, now known as the 'Wesendonk Lieder'. These poems were one of the very few exceptions to Wagner's rule not to set other people's texts to music; steeped in the harmonic mood of *Tristan und Isolde*, they belong to that brief period when Wagner and Mathilde had a relationship of, for him, pure unclouded happiness. Soon afterwards, in January 1858, came the 'moment of truth' and Wagner felt he was standing on the brink of a fearful decision – to renounce either Mathilde or Minna. The nature of this crisis is not clear; it is probable that Wagner had a row with Otto who was getting irritated by the billing and cooing going on between his wife and Wagner. In any event Wagner went to Paris for a few weeks hoping thus 'to allay somewhat the sufferings of the good-natured Otto Wesendonk'. He wrote to Liszt saying, 'I am at the end of a conflict in which everything that a man holds sacred is involved and every choice before me is so cruel that, before making my decision, I must have by my side the one friend that heaven has sent me.'

When Wagner returned to Zurich it was Minna's turn to make trouble. She had been watching the developing intimacy of Wagner and Mathilde whose visits to each other grew steadily longer; the servants' tongues wagged and her friends, especially Herwegh's wife, whispered innuendoes in her ear. 'I couldn't help noticing that Richard always went over when the good man was out ... this woman sent messengers to enquire whether "Herr Wagner had slept well" or asking him to come over: "the conservatory is heated". .... She visited him secretly and forbade any servant, when he let her in, to say that she was upstairs.' Straightforward Minna cannot altogether be blamed for failing to understand that Wagner could have one woman as his muse and another as his wife. For her Wagner was simply having a love affair with their neighbour's wife; for Wagner it was something quite different – he and Mathilde were 'mystical' lovers, finding spiritual happiness in mutual abnegation. To Minna all this was a lot of rubbish, particularly after she had intercepted on 7 April 1858 a parcel which a servant was taking from the Asyl to the big house. It was a scroll containing the original pencil sketch of the *Tristan* prelude and tucked into it was an eight page letter which Wagner later described as 'a little note in which I communicated to her, seriously and calmly, the mood that filled me at the time'.

Most of this famous letter referred to a conversation about Goethe the previous night. At the end he wrote, 'Today I'll come into the garden; as soon as I see you I shall hope to find you alone for a moment. Take my whole soul as a morning greeting!' For Minna this was conclusive of his guilt; without telling him she took the letter to Mathilde, warned her against any further intimacy with her husband and told her that she was fortunate that she, Minna, was not a common woman, otherwise she would have gone straight to Otto with the letter. Wagner said that Minna's behaviour 'represented a brutal and vulgar intrusion into the tenderness and purity of our relations and many things had to change'.

It was not long before these changes took place. Otto took his wife to the Italian lakes for a change of air and Minna went to Brestenberg, near Zurich, to find a cure for her heart ailment. Wagner was now alone in the Asyl; he composed the second act of *Tristan und Isolde* marking, at the end, 'Still in Asyl'. Minna returned from her cure in July and recriminations again started. Her irritability had been increased by insomnia and drug-taking; life for Wagner in the Asyl was now 'a veritable hell'; he could not make any further progress with *Tristan* and he was determined to leave as soon as he could. Before this could happen they had certain obligations to fulfil. The Bülows were again expected; they arrived in July, this time with Cosima's mother, the Comtesse d'Agoult. The atmosphere on the Grünen Hügel was oppressive; Mathilde had taken exception to the erection of a floral triumphal arch by the servants to celebrate Minna's return from her cure. The three women had, for a second time, come together just as the Asyl household was about to be broken up. Once again Wagner's presence had an inhibiting effect upon Cosima who was sombre and silent. 'I seem a little repellent to her,' he wrote to

Liszt. Cosima left Wagner and Bülow together and went to meet
her step-sister in Geneva. Karl Ritter accompanied her. Quite
apart from the effect of Wagner on her, Cosima was in a very
strange state at this time. In Geneva she asked Karl to kill her;
he agreed to do so provided he could die with her. This she would
not allow. She rowed out in the lake in order to drown herself,
only refraining from doing so because of Karl's determination to
drown himself as well. Back at the Asyl she behaved more
demonstratively towards Wagner; on the day of her departure,
Wagner tells us, 'She fell at my feet and covered my hands with
tears and kisses so that I gazed at this, puzzled, amazed and
startled, without being able to find the key of it.'

Bülow, in his 'thank you' letter to Wagner, told him that 'a
man like you belongs to another world than this vulgar and
trivial one. . . . I am willing to become your bootblack. . . . I
haven't the impudence to claim to be your friend'. He signed the
letter, 'your true vassal and servant'. Bülow, then, gave Cosima
the lead in her growing admiration for Wagner.

Wagner and Minna left the Asyl forever on 17 August 1858;
before going their different ways, she back to Dresden and he to
Venice with Karl Ritter, she accompanied him to the station in
Zurich. 'It was a brilliant summer day,' wrote Wagner, 'with a
bright cloudless sky. I remember neither looking back, nor
shedding a tear on leaving her, which almost terrified me. As I
travelled along in the train I couldn't help noticing that my spirits
were steadily lifting; it was obvious that the totally futile
anxieties of the last few weeks could not have gone on any longer
and that I needed, to fulfil my life's purposes, a complete severance
from them.' He now needed a prolonged period of calm to
orchestrate *Tristan und Isolde*, Act III. The rows with Minna and
the other disturbances on the Grünen Hügel had, in a way
peculiar to Wagner, by raising his emotional temperature, released
a flow of music and poetry.

Venice was to be the scene of this brief period of tranquillity.
After a couple of days in Danieli's Wagner moved into the
dilapidated Palazzo Giustiniani, a fifteenth-century Gothic
palace next to the Palazzo Foscari, on the Grand Canal. Venice –
sad, beautiful, dreamlike – was suited to his present mood.
'You will one day hear a fairy story dream,' he wrote to Mathilde,
'which I there turned into sound.' Wagner's first sight of a

gondola filled him with apprehension; as he stepped under the black awning he remembered that there had been a recent cholera scare. 'I felt as if I was taking part in a funeral procession during a pestilence.' Like every visitor to Venice he was soon caught in the melancholy spell cast over the lagoon by these slim, black-draped vessels, skilfully guided by *gondolieri*. During one sleepless night Wagner leant over the balcony of the palazzo and heard an old folk-song like a rough lament, drifting towards him across the Rialto and being answered by a distant voice in another direction. This mournful dialogue affected him greatly. Late one night, as he was being rowed home along the gloomy canal, the moon broke out, illuminating the palaces, and his gondolier suddenly uttered a deep wail, like the cry of an animal; it gained in strength and forced itself, after a long drawn-out 'Oh!', into the simple musical exclamation 'Venezia'. These musical impressions remained with him as he completed *Tristan*, Act II and suggested the mournful call of the shepherd's horn at the beginning of Act III.

Wagner was the only occupant of the Palazzo Giustiniani. He took a few furnished rooms on the first floor. His working surroundings were becoming more important to him and he had the walls of the large room covered with dark red hangings. The Hungarian landlord provided some gilded chairs; his grand piano arrived from Zurich and now all was ready for work on *Tristan und Isolde* to be resumed. His work was impeded, however, by an attack of dysentery and by a carbuncle on his leg which he called a specifically Venetian complaint. Another irritant was the police supervision; although Venice did not belong to the German Federation, it was part of the Austrian Empire and the Saxon government made it clear that his presence on Austrian territory was unwelcome. Wagner's movements in Venice were the subject of detailed police reports for the benefit of the Austrian Chief of Police, Lieutenant-General Baron Kempen von Fichtenmann, an implacable republican-hunter. On learning of Wagner's arrival in Venice he sent a telegram in cipher to the Venetian police: 'The Saxon refugee, Richard Wagner, author and composer, is said to be in Venice. If this is so, how did he get permission to travel and what is his motive?' The reports about Wagner for Kempen were written by a Police Commissioner Crespi; he was clearly a music lover and their sympathetic tone has earned him a place in the Wagnerian hall of fame. Here are some extracts from his first report:

... as composer, musical essayist and critic he has shown genius of a high and original order; as the begetter of the so-called 'music of the future' he stands at the head of the musical and aesthetic movements of the day ... his physicians have strongly recommended that he move to some southern climate but he was too occupied with composition to follow their advice. When it became clear his health would be endangered by further delay he decided to make a long stay in Venice where he now lives quietly and in retirement. As proof of his overwrought nerves we may mention that, on the day of his arrival at the Palazzo Giustiniani, he asked his landlord's permission to repaper the apartment. ...

The harsh Baron Kempen von Fichtenmann was unimpressed by Crespi's pleading and reminded him sharply in his reply that 'far too little importance is attached to the political nature of the case'.

Crespi deliberately forbore to mention in his report that Wagner had become friendly with Austrian soldiers. He had been startled to hear the overtures to *Rienzi* and *Tannhäuser* played by the military bands in St Mark's Square. He was invited to attend their practices in the barracks where the Austrian officers treated him with great respect. He was struck by the total absence of applause after these stirring concerts. The reason was that 'the least sign of approbation of Austrian military music would have been looked upon as treason to the Italian fatherland'. As the political situation became more acute, with Cavour and Garibaldi doing their best to make trouble, and war between Austria, France and Savoy looked, and indeed was, imminent, Fichtenmann redoubled his efforts to get Wagner, that dangerous Saxon refugee, off Austrian territory. In February 1859 he was ordered to leave Venice, a move which he attributed to the 'monstrous spite of the Saxon government'. The co-operative Crespi advised him to appeal for an extension of his stay, on the grounds of ill-health, to the Governor-General of Lombardy, the Archduke Maximilian, who later became the unfortunate Emperor of Mexico. Maximilian agreed immediately to his request.

Wagner could at last work in peace on *Tristan*. He drew up a careful daily routine for himself. The morning he spent working on *Tristan*; in the afternoon a gondola brought him over to the Piazzetta where he lunched with Karl Ritter who was staying elsewhere in Venice; afterwards he walked, alone or with Karl, in the Giardino Publico or along the Lido; at nightfall the gondola brought him back to the Palazzo Giustiniani where a lighted lamp greeted him in the darkness. He then worked again and read until Karl appeared at eight. With his usual voracity he read history, poetry, philosophy and biographies. After reading Daru's *Histoire de la république de Venise* he dropped his prejudices about the cruel, secretive governments of the Doges, being persuaded that their methods, although harsh and inhuman, were in the interests of the Republic. Once again he turned to Schopenhauer and found himself able to resolve, through more careful reading of the great man's book, two problems which had perplexed him. One was on the metaphysical aspect of sexual love – why should two people who are in love wish to commit suicide and thus renounce the highest felicity? – and the second was concerned with the metaphysics of music in relation to the other arts, in particular poetry. He alone, he thought, was qualified to pronounce on this as there had never before been anyone who was both poet and musician and therefore able to understand the inner processes of both arts.

The only people apart from Karl that Wagner was prepared to see in Venice were Winterberger, a pupil of Liszt, Tessarin, a Venetian piano teacher with a passion for German music, and the Russian Prince Dolgosuki. He wrote to the distant Mathilde, who returned his letters unopened.[1] He also kept a diary for her; in it he wrote, after he had been unwell for several days, 'Since yesterday I have been busy again with *Tristan*. I am still in the second act. But – what astonishing music it is going to be! I could spend my whole life just working on this music. . . . I've never done anything like it . . . it is the highest point that my art has ever reached.'

A day or two before leaving Venice, towards the end of March 1859, Wagner finished scoring *Tristan*, Act II. By giving the deepest philosophical and psychological thoughts musical and pictorial form he turned *Tristan* into a manageable opera for the man in the street, unaware of its poetic depths.

Wagner left Venice and travelled to Lucerne, spending a few days sightseeing in Milan on the way; he scrambled over the Duomo and admired Leonardo's *The Last Supper*. He stayed in

[1] It is not clear why she did this; probably because of the trouble which her friendship with Wagner had led to.

Lucerne, at the Hotel Schweizerhof, until he composed *Tristan*, Act III. On 6 August 1859 at half past four in the afternoon he completed the opera in the presence of Felix Draeseke.[1]

[1] Felix Draeseke (1835–1913) was a German musician, a pupil of Liszt and a composer of several symphonies and choral works. He takes his place with Weissheimer, Damrosch and other semi-forgotten composers whose acquaintance with Wagner brought them a modest fame. Draeseke insisted upon being present when Wagner wrote the last bars of *Tristan*. They spent four weeks together going on walking tours and talking at length about art, philosophy, religion and politics. He declared Wagner to be the wittiest and most intellectually stimulating person he had ever met.

CHAPTER EIGHT

The Wandering Years
1859–64

WHERE WAS WAGNER TO GO after delivering himself of *Tristan und Isolde*? Germany and the Austrian Empire were out of bounds for him; Zurich was now unbearable and he had no wish to return to London after the hideous experiences of 1855. He no longer needed the solitude which he had found in Venice and Lucerne. The paramount need in his life was to 'hear a good orchestra and first-class quartets', to find a theatre where *Tristan* could be performed and to bring his music to the notice of a wider public. There were still only two people in the world who properly understood his music – Bülow and Liszt; his estrangement with the latter was now perceptible. Liszt was going through a difficult time and chinks appeared, once again, in his mask of selflessness and urbanity; his small son had just died; the Princess had gone to Rome to try and get a dispensation from the Pope to marry him; a manifesto, declaring his music to be a pernicious influence in Germany, had been published, signed amongst others by Brahms and Joachim; and he was resorting to narcotics and stimulants to keep himself going.

Wagner decided to make a second serious assault on Paris. He had, in fact, no choice. With his banishment from Germany still in force there was really no other town, with lively orchestral traditions, where he could go. He thought again of emigrating to the United States but decided against undertaking such a step. As for Paris he remembered only too well the misery of his time there twenty years earlier and his contempt for its false and corrupt musical standards. It was unlikely that the intervening years had brought much improvement; the materialism of the Second

Empire had replaced the materialism of the 'Bourgeois' Monarchy; the rich Jew, Meyerbeer, still had, by the careful use of bribes, the theatre and press in his pocket. Paris, however, still ranked as the 'musical capital' of Europe. A Paris 'success' had very great influence in Germany; the last traces of the cultural domination of Louis xiv, who was a model for most German princelings, lingered on.

Since Wagner left Paris in April 1842, intending never to return, he had been back for several brief visits. In June 1849 he had gone there, at the urgent request of Liszt and Minna, after his flight from Dresden. In February 1850 he was back there again from Zurich before his intended elopement with Jessie Laussot. On that visit he wrote an essay 'Kunst und Klima' (Art and Climate) and was nauseated by a performance of Meyerbeer's *Le Prophète*. In October 1853 he dined in Paris with Liszt and his three children, including the sixteen-year-old Cosima. In 1855 he passed through Paris to and from London and in January 1858 he fled there from the first of the Wesendonk crises; on this last occasion he had taken legal advice about protecting the French copyrights of his operas, been given an Erhard grand piano by the widow of the manufacturer (the very piano which he had with him in the Asyl, Venice and Lucerne) and was perilously near the scene of Orsini's attempted assassination of Napoleon iii.

On his way to Paris in September 1859 Wagner spent a few days at the Wesendonks; Mathilde must have relented soon after returning his letters to Venice unopened. On this occasion he sold Otto the publishing rights in his *Ring* operas for 6000 francs. Mathilde still had her uses as his muse but only when she was a long way off. He found himself surprisingly unaffected by her presence. Louis Napoleon's Italian campaign had by this time resulted in the humiliation of Austria. At the Wesendonks Wagner had to mediate in a violent argument on this subject between Gottfried Keller and Semper who deplored the defeat of Austria as the defeat of the idea of German nationality. He had a far-fetched notion that Louis Napoleon represented a Romance element in which he saw a hateful type of Assyrian despotism.

Wagner reached Paris in the middle of September 1859 and he started looking for somewhere to live near the Champs Elysées. With Otto's 6000 francs in his pocket he was, for once, not short of money. He took a small house, 16 rue Newton near the Etoile, and put down three years' rent; he engaged a maid as well as a manservant. The maid was intended for Minna who had been living in Dresden since they parted in Zurich. He was prepared to live with her again, he said, provided she made no sexual claims on him as they were bad for her health and his nerves.

In Paris Wagner could not persuade the important people to take an interest in *Tristan und Isolde* and he soon abandoned the idea of a French performance. Meanwhile, Carvalho, the director of the Théâtre Lyrique, was seriously interested in producing *Tannhäuser*. During their meeting, when the project was discussed, Wagner played the finale of *Tannhäuser* Act II with such frenzy that Carvalho hurried away, quite unnerved. He gave an account of this extraordinary performance: Wagner wore, for the occasion, a blue jacket with red braid and a yellow cap adorned with a green fringe. He was waiting in the drawing-room where there were two grand pianos. He began by playing parts of *Tannhäuser* on one of the pianos; he shouted, threw himself about, banging the keyboard with his wrists and elbows. Then, dripping with perspiration, he disappeared to reappear in a different costume. Now he wore a yellow coat with blue braid and a red cap with yellow braid. He continued throwing himself about, beating the piano, hitting hundreds of wrong notes, howling and, said Carvalho, 'to crown it all, he sang in German! And his eyes! The eyes of a madman! I did not dare to cross him; he frightened me.'

Wagner's next idea was to start a German theatre in Paris where all his operas, *Tristan und Isolde* included, might be performed. He was unfortunate in that, being both a musician and a dramatist, he encountered every possible kind of incompetence, stupidity and shortsightedness. It was rare for him to meet a theatre director, conductor, designer, critic, or indeed, musician who had any understanding of his art. To realize his idea of a theatre he needed, above all, influential friends. After the arrival of Minna in Paris with her dog and her parrot – a reminder of the circumstances of her arrival in Rorschach ten years earlier – Wagner threw open their house in the rue Newton every Wednesday evening. These soirées were very successful; given the host's radical political and artistic views it is hardly surprising that his guests were, on the whole, of a liberal persuasion and therefore hostile to the régime of Napoleon III. They reflected, in their attainments, the versatility of Wagner's interests; poets, artists, musicians, writers, scholars and politicians all came to his Wednesday evening gatherings. Malvida von Meysenbug tells how he dominated them; his guests, in spite of their individual eminence, had eyes and ears for him alone. Klindworth was summoned over from London to accompany Wagner as he sang, with his usual zest, passages out of *Lohengrin*, *Das Rheingold*, *Die Walküre* and *Tristan*. The few scraps of French at Minna's disposal during these soirées were of little use in this sophisticated milieu. She complained that the guests treated her as the housekeeper who had access to the drawing-room where she could show off her new silk dresses.

It would oversimplify matters to bestow upon Baudelaire the distinction of being the only Frenchman to perceive the greatness of the German composer in their midst. His essay 'Richard Wagner et *Tannhäuser* à Paris', written after the *Tannhäuser* fiasco in March 1861, was a clarion call to his countrymen to recognize Wagner's genius and an attempt to counteract the influence of his denigrators in the press and in society.

By 1860 the ground had, however, been prepared, for the growth of Wagnerism in France, by a small group of disciples. The foremost of these was Auguste de Gaspérini, a naval surgeon, music lover and versifier. He had a remarkable understanding of Wagner and his music and he has left us with an agreeable description of him at this time. Wagner was forty-six but he looked ten years younger. De Gaspérini was at first struck by his coldness, his reserved manner and the severity of his features. As he warmed to the conversation, however, his features lit up and he became the person that de Gaspérini had visualized from his music. All his features bore the signs of that indomitable will which was the basis of his nature and which revealed itself in the massive forehead, strong chin, compressed lips and hollow cheeks which betrayed the excitements of a tormented life. 'In the extraordinary mobility of his features, which his dominating will tried in vain to control, I recognized the born dramatist and the tireless explorer of the human soul into its innermost recesses.' At times de Gaspérini saw, in Wagner's changing expressions, the frantically tormented Tristan or the follower of Buddha and Schopenhauer. When the conversation took a turn which engaged his interest and enabled him, as he battled bravely with the French language, to propound his plans for the future – then he looked young and animated and, in defiance of his theories, was a far cry from

Buddha and his unrewarding meditations. Wagner had no more
social airs and graces than he had had twenty years earlier; this
blunt son of a petty Saxon official never became, like Liszt, a
smiling charmer with well-born ladies swooning at the sight of
him. He continued to speak with a thick Saxon accent, even in
the most elegant and intellectual of *milieux*, until the end of his
life.[1]

Another important early French Wagnerite was Jules Champfleury, a painter and sculptor, who was profoundly affected by the
thought of Wagner's struggles and who wrote a little essay about
him which was greatly to Wagner's liking. 'He displayed such a
comprehension of my music, and even of my personality, that I
have never since come across anything to equal it, except perhaps
Liszt's elaborations on *Tannhäuser* and *Lohengrin*.' Champfleury
had written, 'I cannot recall a martyrdom comparable to that of
Richard Wagner; and yet there are no traces of this in his works.'
Wagner himself noticed this fact with a certain pride; after completing *Tristan und Isolde* he told the Princess that his bitterness
expressed itself in his behaviour, his letters and his writings, but
never in his art which was undefiled by practical worldly cares.

Wagnerism became a lively movement in France, at first after
the three concerts which Wagner gave in the Théâtre Italien – the
same building as the former Théâtre de la Renaissance which
dashed his hopes for a production of *Das Liebesverbot* – and then
after the notorious command performance of *Tannhäuser* at the
Opéra in March 1861. He was most anxious to present *Tristan*, his
'workmanlike' opera so recently completed, to the world, even
if not in France. The Grand Duke of Baden and Eduard Devrient,
the intendant of the Karlsruhe theatre, both of whom had
promised to put on *Tristan* in Karlsruhe and had given him vague
assurances that it would be possible for him to supervise the
rehearsals personally despite his banishment from Germany, now
went back on their word. It turned out later that Devrient, out
of jealousy and shortsightedness, had played a double game from
the start. The Grand Duke took his place with that other German
princeling, Carl Alexander of Weimar; both talked big about
their intentions to stage Wagner's operas but did nothing when
the time came. Wagner then decided to acquaint the Parisians with
his new work by hiring the Théâtre Italien. He communicated

[1] His Saxon accent was less noticeable when he read aloud.

to Mathilde Wesendonk his thoughts about *Tristan*: 'I would say that the finest and most profound aspect of my art is what I call the art of transition, since the whole tissue of my art consists in these very transitions . . . my masterpiece in the art of the subtle, gradual transition is undoubtedly the great scene in the second act of *Tristan und Isolde*.' Wagner meant by this the linking passages between the musical expressions of totally dissimilar emotional states. 'This, then, is the secret of my musical form which, I venture boldly to suggest, in its resolution and clear, yet detailed development, has never before been foreshadowed, let alone achieved.'

Schott, the music publishers in Mainz, unexpectedly and without haggling, agreed to pay Wagner ten thousand francs for *Das Rheingold*. As he had just sold it to Wesendonk, the latter's agreement to this transaction was necessary. This the compliant Wesendonk duly gave. Wagner's concert in the Théâtre Italien was a great success. He impressed the audience of 1500 by conducting without a score and the *Tannhäuser* march was interrupted by bursts of applause. The *Tristan* prelude left them perplexed. Amongst the audience on that first night on 29 January 1860 were Auber, Gounod, Berlioz and Meyerbeer. The critics were more hostile than ever in their notices; knowing that they would be angry Wagner had deliberately not invited them which made them all the angrier. The second and third concerts were less well attended than the first; they brought him some distinguished new admirers, however, who came in future to his Wednesday evening gatherings. Of these the most illustrious was Baudelaire who wrote to Wagner, after the concerts, an immensely enthusiastic letter praising the grandeur and naturalness of his music. He felt that he always knew it. 'You have led me back to my own being.' Baudelaire tactfully did not write his address on the letter in case Wagner should think he had some motive in writing. 'Needless to say I knew how to find him.'

Although the critics' comments were of no interest to Wagner he took seriously an article by Berlioz, in the *Débats*, published when the concerts were over. In it Berlioz said that he neither understood *Tristan* nor believed in the 'music of the future'. 'If this is the new religion,' he wrote, 'I raise my hand and swear *Non credo*.' Wagner replied in the next issue of the same journal deploring the use of the ludicrous phrase, 'music of the future', coined by a

Professor Bischoff of Cologne, and regretting Berlioz's mis-understanding of his 'theories'. A weary Berlioz, his jealousy worked upon by an odious wife, wrote later to Wagner saying: 'Vous êtes . . . plein d'ardeur, prêt à la lutte. Je ne suis moi prêt qu'à dormir et à mourir.'

The immediate result of Wagner's three concerts was a deficit of 11,000 francs; this put an end to his plan of a culminating performance of *Tristan und Isolde*. Once again he was deeply in debt; it was doubtful whether he would be able to save from the wreckage the comfortable home which he had created for Minna and himself in the rue Newton. His solution to this crisis was to go to Brussels and there give another set of three concerts whose profits would compensate for the Paris losses. Although the first two concerts, held in the Théâtre de la Monnaie, were very successful and Wagner was entitled to half the receipts, he had overlooked a clause in the contract under which he had to pay the costs of the musical part of the proceedings. Realizing that this would leave him with no money he cancelled the third concert and returned to Paris. His visit to Antwerp had been another Belgian disappointment for him; he had gone there to pay his respects to 'Madame Lohengrin, née Elsa' and he had visualized the citadel on some commanding height. Instead, all he could see from the other side of the Scheldt was a dreary plain with some sunken fortifications. 'After that, whenever I saw *Lohengrin*, I could not restrain a smile at the scene painter's castle, perched aloft in the background on its stately mountain.'

On returning to Paris Wagner was rescued from his latest financial embarrassments by a 'noble-hearted' lady, Marie Kalergis, née Countess Nesselrode. This cultured, cosmopolitan woman – her father was German and her mother Polish, her education Russian and her husband Greek – had been at the première of *Tannhäuser* in Dresden in 1845. She was a pupil of Liszt and Chopin and Wagner had last seen her with Liszt in Paris in October 1853 on the same occasion as he had met Cosima. Marie Kalergis now invited Wagner to call on her; she had not been able to attend his concerts but she had heard that they had been, for Wagner, a financial disaster. She begged him to let her pay the losses of 10,000 francs. 'I felt,' said Wagner, 'as though something were now being fulfilled which I had always been entitled to expect.' Remarks of this kind have been seized upon by Wagner's detractors when looking for examples of his egoism and ingratitude. He was, in fact, profoundly appreciative of any kind of attention, material or otherwise, if made in the right spirit. He saw benefactresses like Marie Kalergis and Julie Ritter as collaborators in a joint cause – that of the reform of the theatre and the transformation of public taste. He was exceptionally conscientious, even by the standards of a well-bred man of the world, in thanking people, however unimportant their social standing, for small kindnesses. If he took his time in paying his tradesmen's bills there is nothing particularly reprehensible about that. He knew that the friends of his art – Pusinelli, Wesendonk and many others – did not really expect their loans to be repaid. Their reward was to be the ultimate victory of Wagner's artistic ideas. It is, indeed, astonishing how little money Wagner was obliged to 'borrow' when the size of his income is considered. Ernest Newman pointed out that Wagner would have been a rich man before he was fifty if he had been born Italian and not German. In the ten years Verdi had amassed an enormous fortune which normally could only be made on the stock exchange. Compared with Verdi Meyerbeer was a poor man; *Robert le Diable*, at that time the most successful opera ever staged, brought him 45,000 francs over a period of twenty-five years whereas Verdi made 80,000 francs out of *Il Trovatore* in a single year. And yet Wagner would have been happy to have received a portion of Meyerbeer's earnings.

As an expression of his thanks to Marie Kalergis for paying the losses incurred by his concerts Wagner improvised a special showing for her of *Tristan* Act II with the famous Pauline Viardot-Garcia as Isolde and himself as Tristan; he summoned Karl Klindworth over from London, at his own expense, to play the accompaniment. Apart from Madame Kalergis the only other person present at this most select performance was Berlioz. The audience was not exactly carried away by enthusiasm; Marie Kalergis, according to Wagner, 'remained dumb' and Berlioz merely complimented him on the 'chaleur' of his delivery. She later told her daughter that *Tristan* was 'plainly impossible; it is an abstraction, intriguing to study . . . as a dramatic work it will be rejected by the public everywhere'. This shows that even his most loyal adherents had difficulty in following the turn which his musical language was taking.

In March 1860 Wagner called on Rossini; in 1868, a month after Rossini's death, he published an account of this visit, 'Erinnerungen an Rossini' (Recollections of Rossini) in an Augsburg newspaper. Rossini, the composer of *William Tell* and *The Barber of Seville*, had first visited Paris nearly forty years earlier; he returned to live there, an elderly invalid suffering from neurasthenia, in 1856. A cure at Bad Kissingen had restored him to health and he now delighted in the rôle of a revered and jovial sage. Wagner had, in *Oper und Drama*, written some harsh things about Rossini's technique. 'With Rossini the opera died,' he had said. 'Italy's voluptuous son lolled in the rankest lap of luxury, cast his wanton, roving eye over the European scene looking for folk-melodies. . . .' On his way to Paris, Wagner continued, Rossini had rested awhile amidst the snowy Alps of Switzerland, there to hearken how the sturdy peasants divide their musical pastimes between their mountains and their cows. Upon arriving in Paris, with a happy father's pride, he showed the world his youngest child which he had, in a lucky moment, christened *William Tell*. This turned Rossini, in the eyes of the critics, into a 'national' composer. He had found a new recipe for galvanizing the half-paralysed body of opera – some fossilized piece of national peculiarity. This would only be permissible if the composer himself belonged to that particular folk-culture. Rossini swept away drama in opera; from now onwards all that mattered was Melody, naked, ear-delighting, delicious Melody. Form was also of no interest to him; the singers and instrumentalists could do what they liked to win public applause. These were some of the sarcastic, laboured criticisms levelled by Wagner against Rossini's music ten years earlier.

During their half-hour conversation Rossini assured Wagner that he had not, as the press asserted, made caustic remarks about Wagner's 'unmelodic' music; that, in any event, he would never criticize another composer who was trying 'to extend the frontiers of our art'; that he had during his cure at Bad Kissingen listened with enjoyment to the march from *Tannhäuser* – the only bit of Wagner's music that he knew. Wagner left, delighted with his reception. 'Of all the musicians I met in Paris Rossini is the only truly great one.' As he had also met Berlioz and Liszt in Paris this remark should not be taken too seriously although he had no reason to feel well-disposed towards these two fellow composers

Both displayed towards him at this time a certain petulant ill-will, nutured respectively by wife and mistress.

In the middle of March 1860 the Emperor commanded that *Tannhäuser* be performed at the Opéra. Four months later Wagner learned from the Saxon ambassador in Paris, Baron von Seebach, of his partial amnesty; he could enter any part of Germany with the exception of Saxony. These two events, each of which was the fulfilment of a fervently held wish, were, in various ways, connected. The immediate cause of the fateful command to produce *Tannhäuser* was Princess Pauline Metternich, both wife and niece of the Austrian ambassador and grand-daughter of the great Metternich. She was a coarse, monkey-faced little woman, given to smoking, drinking, swearing and lavatory jokes. She had many enemies in Parisian society who disliked her close friendship with the Emperor and Empress and her efforts to bring about a *rapprochement* between France and Austria after the Italian campaign. She decided to take up Wagner and told the Emperor about him and his music. According to Wagner, Bülow deserved as much credit as Princess Metternich for bringing him and his works to the notice of Napoleon III. He arrived in Paris from Berlin, carrying with him a letter of introduction from Princess Augusta of Prussia, an old admirer of Wagner's music, to Count Pourtales, the Prussian ambassador. His attaché, Count Hatzfeld, was another admirer of Wagner and it was he who, at a masked ball at the Tuileries, recognized the Empress Eugénie under her mask, led her into an adjoining room and there asked her to use her influence to bring about a performance of *Tannhäuser* at the Opéra. She asked him to put the details of this request on paper. Hatzfeld was later Prussian ambassador in London and he told this story to his legation secretary Prince Ernst zu Hohenlohe-Langenburg who was to engage in a long correspondence with Wagner's widow Cosima.

Now that Wagner had important friends in political and diplomatic circles, both in Paris and in Berlin, now that there was an imperial order to produce *Tannhäuser* and the Saxon ambassador himself had been pressing Wagner's claims for an amnesty in Dresden, there was a good chance that the obdurate King Johann of Saxony would soon bow to the inevitable and give the errant composer a pardon. It further needed the persuasive intervention of Princess Augusta of Prussia at a meeting of kings and princes in Baden-Baden before King Johann finally issued an ungracious, qualified pardon. On 22 July 1860 Seebach informed Wagner that he was free to enter Germany.

The much wanted amnesty had been granted and Wagner once more crossed the Rhine into Germany. He did not, as he had done in April 1842, weep on seeing his fatherland again. 'I did not feel the slightest emotion, alas, on setting foot, once again, on German soil. God knows I must have become a cold fish!' He wrote to Liszt, 'Believe me, we have no country; if I am really "German" I carry my Germany inside me.' He could not feel much professional enthusiasm about returning to Germany; although he was demoralized by the financial failure of his Paris concerts and by the impossibility of having *Tristan und Isolde* performed there, he knew that a long, hard struggle would be awaiting him in German theatres and that the one town, Dresden, where he could expect success and understanding, was still out of bounds. Besides that, he now had to prepare for the French performance of *Tannhäuser*, although with a heavy heart. He had a small but growing côterie of French friends to whom he was 'at home' on Wednesday evenings; these soirées were about to come to an end, as rue Newton was scheduled to be demolished as part of Baron Haussmann's grandiose scheme for the 'improvement' of Paris. Poor Wagner had been tricked by his landlord into paying the sum of 4000 francs as three years' rent in advance. He only knew about this scheme when his street was pulled up and he could not even approach his house on foot. He never recovered the two years' rent which he had paid in advance but he had to pay the legal fees for attempting to do so. He then looked for somewhere nearer the Opéra and found 'a poor cheerless spot' in 3 rue d'Aumale. It was a second-floor apartment in a crowded house in a dark noisy street. Malvida von Meysenbug tells in her memoirs how her heart ached when she first saw it: 'I felt how dreadful it must have been for him to live in such an unpleasant apartment.'

Wagner only spent a few days in Germany. He went with Minna to see his brother Albert at Frankfurt and thought of visiting Schopenhauer but was restrained from so doing by a 'singular timidity'. The old man died the following month. They went to Baden-Baden; leaving Minna at the roulette table he went to pay his respects to Princess Augusta, later the German Empress, and to thank her for the part she had played in securing his amnesty. She reacted coldly to his approaches; he learned later that his Saxon accent might have put her off.

Back in Paris, Wagner threw himself into the preparations for *Tannhäuser*. The articles of the Opéra provided that operas by foreign composers must be performed in French and that no composer, whether a Frenchman or not, could conduct his own work. He had, then, first of all to have the text of *Tannhäuser* translated. He chose for this task a young customs official, Edmond Roche, who knew no German! He had helped Wagner clear his furniture from Zurich through the customs. 'Pale and seedy-looking', but full of life, he had made a careful study of Wagner's piano scores and he supplemented his exiguous salary by playing the fiddle in small vaudeville theatres. To help Roche Wagner found a German, Rudolf Lindau, who in his turn knew very little French. In the end Wagner and Roche hammered out the translation together, working from early in the morning to late at night, Wagner, wild-eyed and gesticulating, pacing up and down, singing, hitting the piano and shouting at Roche,[1] 'Allez! Allez!'

At last Wagner presented the French text to the director of the Opéra, Alphons Royer, who rejected it on the grounds that it was the policy of the Opéra only to accept libretti that rhymed. He recommended that this rhymeless verse be turned into rhyme by Charles Truinet, the young keeper of the archives at the opera. Roche's efforts provided the basis of this new versification which was regarded by all as 'acceptable'.

Wagner wished, in his thoroughgoing pedagogic manner, to prepare the Parisian public intellectually for *Tannhäuser*. The critics had said that his art was hidebound by theories and that everything he wrote had been fitted to a 'system'. The dangers of being labelled a theorist or systematizer had been pointed out to him by Frederic Villot, the conservator of pictures at the Louvre, whom he had met in Flaxland's music-shop when he overheard him order the score of *Tristan und Isolde*. Villot possessed the scores of his other operas which he had played to him by Saint-Saens who could play all Wagner's scores by heart. Wagner was impressed by Villot, who knew no German, telling him that the music of his operas was the best guide to an understanding of the poems. To Villot, then, he dedicated 'Quatre poèmes d'opéras, traduits en prose française, précédés d'une lettre sur la musique

[1] Roche died a few months later.

par Richard Wagner'. The four operas which he had translated in prose without the music were *Der fliegende Holländer, Tannhäuser, Lohengrin* and *Tristan und Isolde*. The translator was Herwegh's Paris friend, Paul Challemel-Lacour, who did not at all relish the job. Wagner decided that the public could best be disabused of the notion that he was first and foremost a theorizer by producing prose rather than verse translations of his poems. They could then be read and understood for their dramatic and psychological content. The long foreword, addressed to Villot, summarized the main arguments of *Oper und Drama* and emphasized the melodic character (*unendliche Melodie*) of his work. Beethoven had, he wrote, created, with his symphonic music, new possibilities for the opera and these he was trying to exploit in his dramatic poems. His *Tannhäuser* poem vividly described a situation whose dramatic, poetic and psychological truths were brought out by the harmonic and melodic subtleties of the new symphonic music. Shortly afterwards this essay was published in Leipzig with the title 'Zukunftsmusik' (Music of the Future). At this time the violinist Joseph Joachim and others signed a protest against the 'music of the future' of the New Germans Wagner and Liszt.

The Emperor had given instructions that all Wagner's wishes should be met. No expense was to be spared in achieving an artistically and musically satisfying production of *Tannhäuser*. For the first time in his life Wagner had at his disposal a magnificent orchestra and first class chorus master, stage manager, choreographer, scene painters, costume designers – everything one would expect from the world's leading opera house. He should have been happy but he was not. Contact with the theatre had, it is true, the usual vitalizing effect upon him and his demonic will lashed into action the many people who were part of this great enterprise. Beneath this surface energy he was morose and brooding; in his dingy little apartment in the rue d'Aumale, where he trained the singers individually, he wrote long philosophical and pessimistic letters to Mathilde Wesendonk, profoundly dejected in tone – 'God knows for what I still exist!' – and in content full of thoughts about *Tristan und Isolde*, Schopenhauer and Buddha, of reincarnation, of Day's illusion and of Night's redemption. He had no money and his health suffered from the noise and stench of Paris after the calm of Venice and the pure air of Lucerne. He had come to Paris in the hopes of staging *Tristan*, and *Tannhäuser*, composed fifteen years earlier, was very much a second best. It embodied, nevertheless, certain cardinal principles of his art with which he was determined not to compromise.

It was an unwritten rule of the Opéra that every opera should have a ballet in the second act. The blue-blooded members of the Jockey Club considered this to be their inalienable right and no director or composer had hitherto dared to defy these formidable and unsuitable patrons. Royer, the director, insisted therefore that there be a ballet in the second act; it was the practice of the aristocratic *abonnés*, after dining well, to arrive at the opera at ten, missing the first act, in time to see their mistresses and girl friends glide langourously about the stage. Wagner, indignant and dangerously confident of the unswerving support of the Emperor and Princess Metternich, refused. His drama could not be tampered with in such a way; he did not write operas for the effete and philistine members of the Jockey Club but for a more reflective public. He consented, in the end, to rewrite the Venus-Tannhäuser scene in Act I and call it a ballet; if this was not accepted he would withdraw the work. He did not reckon with the combined mischief-making capacities of the press and Jockey Club whose members were motivated more by political than by artistic considerations. Their political attitudes seem to have been confused and contradictory. They were out for Wagner's blood because he was reputed to be a revolutionary and a friend of the enemies of the Second Empire; at the same time they disapproved of his influence at the Court. An upstart German composer was being foisted onto them by the repulsive *intrigante*, Princess Metternich, who was scheming to bring about a *rapprochement* between France and the enemy Austria. Ballet or no ballet, in the first act or the second, the Jockey Club members were out to destroy the Paris *Tannhäuser*.

Wagner's willingness to compromise with the Opéra management by expanding the Venus-Tannhäuser scene in Act I reflected his secret wish. He had always thought the Venusberg scene to be the weakest part of the opera, insufficiently expressing the conflict between the sensual and the spiritual in Tannhäuser's soul. Now, since the musical achievements of *Tristan und Isolde*, he felt a new surge of creative power; he believed that he possessed the melodic equipment to write passionate, voluptuous, bacchanalian music; he had, for the first time, choreographic opportunities to illustrate such music. So, in spite of his pennilessness, his Buddhistic gloom and his squalid lodgings, he wrote in a few weeks the shimmering, sensual Venusberg music. The remodelled *Tannhäuser* is known to history as the 'Paris version' and is now more generally performed than the older 'Dresden version'. In his mind for the new Venusberg scene he may have had Goethe's 'Klassische Walpurgisnacht' in *Faust*, Part Two, with its mingling of classical and Nordic mythology. Wagner had, until now, never thought much about ballet as an art; he barely touched on its functions in *Oper und Drama*. Now, with the zeal of a convert, he gave unbridled rein to his phantasmagorical fantasies in his sketch of the new Venusberg scene. He wanted to bring into his Bacchanal the entire mythological rabble, animal as well as human, all dancing frenziedly to the furious fiddling of a *Strömkarl* or Northern water-sprite, a character out of Grimm's *Deutsche Mythologie*, who emerges from a waterfall carrying an outsize fiddle; his tones conjure out of the darkness an army of cupids, nymphs, griffins, sphinxes, panthers, centaurs. Dionysian revelry all of a sudden gives way to Apolline dream pictures of Europa and the bull and Leda and the swan. Unfortunately, Wagner dropped the *Strömkarl* and other ingredients in the final Bacchanal. They were too much for the dancers and their dainty 'petits pas'. Wagner asked Petipas, the ballet master, for the dancing to be more in the untamed yet noble spirit of the music. Petipas said that if he were to ask this of his dancers they would simply dance the can-can – 'and then we would be ruined'.

Wagner finished scoring the Venusberg Bacchanal at 3 a.m. in the morning on New Year's Eve, 1860, just as Minna was returning from a ball. During this time his health had been poor and his doctor prescribed for him a diet of beefsteak in the morning and a glass of Bavarian beer at night. A month or two earlier, at the end of October, he had fallen seriously ill with typhoid and brain-fever. He was unconscious, partially blind and had strange hallucinations, one being that he could only be cured in Naples by Garibaldi. On 20 November he was able, still very weak, to drag himself back to the theatre. Rumour had gone around that he was dead and the rehearsals had drifted irretrievably. Albert Niemann, whom Wagner had fetched from Hanover to sing *Tannhäuser* for a nine-month engagement at a fee of 6000 francs a month, had let him down grievously both as man and singer.

He scoffed at Wagner's directions and refused to depart from the crude and vulgar gestures and phrases which had won him applause as Tannhäuser in many small German theatres. During Wagner's illness he had lent a willing ear to the press campaign of denigration of him and his works. Albert Niemann cut an altogether horrible figure of stupidity, vanity, and egoism during the *Tannhäuser* rehearsals. There were 164 such rehearsals before the première of the 'Paris version' on 13 March 1861. The conductor Dietsch, the composer of the 'original' *Vaisseau fantôme*, was incapable of conducting Wagner's complex score; during the rehearsals Wagner had sat behind him beating the time with his hands and feet. In desperation he asked to be allowed to take over from Dietsch; his request was turned down by Count Walewski, minister of the household. 'All is over,' said Bülow, 'Wagner is not to conduct. One of the most contemptible blockheads ... a stupid old man [aged fifty-three], without any memory, utterly unteachable, with no ear and no sense of time ... is to hold the baton.' The three performances of *Tannhäuser* on 13 March, 18 March and 25 March, the first two in the presence of Napoleon III and the Empress Eugénie, are enshrined as one of the great scandals in theatre history. The members of the Jockey Club had also rehearsed their parts; at a given sign they raised to their lips special *Tannhäuser* silver whistles which they had been holding in readiness in their white kid gloves. Their intervention was noisier and more vicious at each performance as there were sure signs that this Paris *Tannhäuser* was going down well with most of the audience. It is extraordinary that a small group of louts should have got away with wrecking this production of *Tannhäuser* specially commanded by the Emperor and on which so much public money had been spent. Even the presence of the imperial pair did not restrain their whistles and cat-calls. Wagner tells us that the Emperor tried in vain to negotiate with them. 'The Emperor and his consort stoically kept their seats through the uproar of their own courtiers.' This suggests that poor Louis Napoleon felt socially insecure on his parvenu throne even when at the height of his popularity and power.

After the third performance, from which Wagner stayed away, his friends found him alone with Minna at 2 in the morning quietly smoking his pipe and drinking tea. Malvida von Meysenbug saw that his hand was trembling. The next day he decided to withdraw the score and forbid any further performances. The Jockey Club now felt avenged on evil foreign influences at court and on the revolutionary composer who despised their Meyerbeer. The costs had been, in all, 250,000 francs; the takings on the third evening were nearly 11,000 francs, a record sum. The opera would certainly have become a box-office success. As it was, the only winner was Niemann with 54,000 francs. Wagner's fee was 750 francs which he handed over to Roche.

When Gounod heard the news of Wagner's defeat he exclaimed, 'Que Dieu me donne une pareille chute!' Princess Metternich, when taunted about the *Tannhäuser* catastrophe, foretold that Paris would be applauding him twenty years hence. She was right. In the 1880s, after his death, Paris was completely under Wagnerian domination. Mallarmé, in 'Richard Wagner, rêvérie d'un poète francais' called him a god; Eduard Dujardin, author of the early 'stream of consciousness' novel, *Les lauriers sont coupés*, founded in 1885 the brilliant *Revue Wagnérienne* which was a powerful force in French artistic life. Wagner was already writing to Bülow of sects which were being formed where he was straightforwardly venerated – even by the ordinary people (*Volk*). Baudelaire had written after the *Tannhäuser* performances, 'What will Europe think of us and what will they say in Germany about Paris? A handful of louts have brought us national disgrace.' The German musical public began at this time to take him to its heart as a national composer.

The three years from April 1861 to May 1864 were years of erratic, labyrinthine wanderings for Wagner. They were unhappy years for him and perhaps even unhappier for Wagnerites. They saw him exposed to intolerable sufferings and anxieties. Ernest Newman writes, 'For more than three years after the Paris catastrophe he was a wanderer on the face of the earth, his main occupation ... being a desperate hunt for money – money from anyone, contracted by any means, at whatever cost of decency or dignity.' The *Tannhäuser* disaster meant financial ruin for Wagner. Impecuniosity was the background of his life for the next three years. Out of the innumerable journeys he made and people he saw, two episodes stand out – his final separation from Minna which led to one or two temporary liaisons, and the composition of *Die Meistersinger*, that serene and peaceful opera and perfect example of that delicate controlling mechanism in his mind whereby his consciousness, unable any longer to bear a crushing load of cares, moves automatically into a joyous inner world of music-making.

In April 1861 Wagner went to Karlsruhe; the Grand Duke was once again interested in staging *Tristan und Isolde* and 9 September 1861 was the date fixed for its performance. He went on to Vienna to look for soloists for the Karlsruhe *Tristan*. There he heard *Lohengrin* for the first time at a rehearsal under *Kapellmeister* Eiser. Wagner was most affected. 'I sat motionless through it all; as one tear chased another down my cheek ... finally orchestra and chorus broke into loud applause.' He thought he had found in the tenor, Aloys Anders, and in the soprano, Luise Meyer-Dustmann, a suitable Tristan and Isolde. The intendant of the opera refused permission for them to go to Karlsruhe, suggesting instead that *Tristan* be produced in Vienna. Wagner brooded over this tempting idea; as he descended the steps of the Hofburg, he was approached by a 'stately gentleman', Dr Josef Standhartner, physician to the Empress Elizabeth and an admirer of him. From this moment Standhartner was one of his most dependable friends. Before leaving Vienna, Wagner went to a public performance of *Lohengrin* where he received a tremendous ovation, 'such as I have only experienced from the Viennese public'. He spent his remaining days in Vienna in the company of Tausig and Peter Cornelius, composer of the *Barber of Baghdad* and an enthusiastic but not uncritical admirer of Wagner. Both were raving about Bülow's piano arrangement of *Tristan* and wanted Wagner to start rehearsals then and there. Wagner returned to Paris via Winterthur, Zurich and Karlsruhe. He made this detour in order to put off for a day or two the embarrassing disclosure to the Grand Duke of his new plans for *Tristan*. He wished, so he said, to spend his forty-eighth birthday in the company of his old Zurich friends, the Wesendonks, Sulzer, Semper, Herwegh and Gottfried Keller. The Grand Duke of Baden acquiesced quite calmly to the abandonment of a Karlsruhe *Tristan* and Wagner, accompanied by Tausig, who unexpectedly turned up, proceeded to Paris. Tausig wished to see Liszt and Wagner wished to superintend the break-up of his Paris household. Liszt had reverted to his snobbish habits of dancing attendance on the great; even his daughter Blandine could only snatch an occasional word with him in his carriage. He spared Wagner one evening and paid a few of his debts. Liszt was invited to dine with the Emperor at the Tuileries, 'to which,' said Wagner, 'it was not thought necessary to invite me to accompany him'. After they had disposed of their apartment in the rue d'Aumale Minna went off on a cure to Bad Soden and Wagner was invited to stay with Count Pourtales, the Prussian ambassador. Just before this their little dog Fips died of poisoning, but not before biting Minna on the mouth. Wagner was, as usual, inconsolable and he buried his pet tenderly in a friend's garden so that he would escape the fate of being handed over to the scavengers. In his view, 'the sudden death of this lively and lovable animal acted as the final rift of a union which had long become impossible . . . in our childless life the influence of domestic pets had been very important'.

Wagner's room in the Pourtales's residence looked onto a garden with the Tuileries in the distance. In the pool were two black swans which gave him a dreamy satisfaction. Inspired by them he composed for his hostess, Countess Pourtales, an *Albumblatt* in A flat major, 'Ankunft bei den schwarzen Schwänen', based on Elizabeth's 'Sei mir gegrüsst' in *Tannhäuser*, Act II, although steeped in the mood of the introduction to *Tristan*, Act III. At the same time he wrote another *Albumblatt*, in C major for Princess Metternich which foreshadowed the melodies of *Die Meistersinger*. His monkey-faced benefactress, with other well-wishers, had raised some money for him to pay urgent debts. The two *Albumblätter* were his first compositions since the Paris Venusberg music. During his stay with the Pourtales's Wagner experienced 'a profound sense of well-being in the midst of a condition of total impecuniosity'. When the day came for him to leave Paris he spent an evening with his trusty French friends – de Gaspérini, Truinet and Champfleury – in a café in rue Lafitte. On his way back he enjoyed the effect of the bright moonlight on the deserted Paris streets.

At the beginning of August 1861 Wagner was in Weimar on the occasion of a meeting of the Tonkünstlerversammlung (Society of Musicians). He went there solely to please Liszt, some of whose works were being played. When Wagner appeared at the gathering he was tumultuously applauded; at the gathering there were most of the lesser 'New German' musicians – Cornelius, Brendel, Weissheimer, Draeseke and Damrosch – whose music Wagner undoubtedly listened to with boredom and distaste. The only thing which he found 'really excellent' was Liszt's 'Faust' Symphony. From Weimar Wagner travelled with Emile Ollivier and his wife Blandine, Liszt's daughter, to Vienna via Nuremberg, Munich and Bad Reichenall where Cosima was taking a sour-milk cure. He found her in better health and spirits and, on his leaving for Vienna, she gave him a look 'of almost timid questioning'. Wagner then drove to Salzburg in a one-horse carriage (*Einspänner*) and next day went on to Vienna.

'My situation was, as I now plainly saw, quite hopeless as everyone seemed to have deserted me.' This was Wagner's mood when finding himself back in Vienna in August 1861. Standhartner lent him his house for six weeks, whilst he was on holiday with his family, and he left his niece Seraphine Mauro to attend to his wants. Wagner found this 'sweet doll' a consolation during these frustrating weeks in Vienna; she had a pretty figure, a face pale as marble, framed in the blackest locks imaginable which tumbled about her rounded bosom. A year later Wagner was still pining for his poor *Puppe*.

The Vienna *Tristan und Isolde* was now set on the same arduous course as the Paris *Tannhäuser*; Wagner lacked, this time, powerful patrons and the Emperor Franz Josef did *not* order a command performance. The seventy-two rehearsals culminated, not in an artistic catastrophe, but in Wagner's second flight to Zurich – this time to avoid being arrested for debt. Anders, the tenor, had lost his voice and the *Tristan* rehearsals had to be postponed; he had, in fact, developed a terror of the part which lent credence to the stories put about by Hanslick and other critics that not only was *Tristan* unsingable but Wagner was also destroying the voices of all the best singers. The next twenty years were to prove something quite different: under Wagner's inspired guidance and by dint of his demonic will he taught singers to sing as they had never sung before; he invented a new type of singer. The weeks of Anders's indisposition turned into months; the management, alarmed by the insulting remarks in the press about Wagner and *Tristan*, used this as an excuse to drag its feet. They had never quite believed that Wagner would keep the appointment and be back on 14 August to start rehearsals. Esser, the director, also lent a willing ear to suggestions that the opera was 'unperformable' (*unaufführbar*). Wagner's only ally was the Isolde, Frau Meyer-Dustmann. 'She will sing the part to perfection,' he wrote to

Minna. 'She is the most talented of the lot.' She was also later to let him down, angered by his friendship with her sister Friederike Meyer whom she considered disreputable.

Finding himself with very little to do Wagner was in need of distraction. Suddenly there arrived an invitation from the Wesendonks to join them in Venice at the beginning of November. 'God knows what I had in mind as I, on a grey November day, started off in a casual sort of way . . . for Venice.' He went by train to Trieste and from there by boat to Venice where he stayed, once again, at Danieli's. To his disappointment he found the Wesendonks relaxed and happy in each other's company – the good Otto had guided Mathilde with a firm hand through the reefs of the *Tristan* episode and she had gratefully born him a son a few months earlier – and surprisingly unconcerned about his difficulties in Vienna. Mathilde now became for him *only* a friend. Some say that the world should thank her for *Die Meistersinger*. She possessed the original draft which Wagner had sketched in Marienbad in 1845; in Venice she suggested that he return to this subject as a way out of his depression. Otto then took him to the Accademia where the sight of Titian's *Assumption of the Virgin* exercised, so he tells us, such a sublime effect upon him that he determined on the spot to take up *Die Meistersinger* once more. In fact Wagner had written to the publishers Schott a fortnight earlier announcing his scheme for a popular comic opera. He urgently needed a new advance. He wanted, he told Schott, to undertake something artistic which would at once occupy and divert him. 'The opera is to be called *Die Meistersinger von Nürnberg* and the jovial, poetical principal hero is Hans Sachs.'

After 'four dreary days' Wagner surprised the Wesendonks by suddenly leaving Venice. During the long train journey back to Vienna, which took a day and two nights, Wagner composed 'with the utmost distinctness the principal part of the overture in C major'. Back in Vienna Wagner summoned Cornelius who, 'frantic with delight', procured from the Imperial Library a copy of Cornelius Wagenseil's *Nuremberg Chronicle* (1697), from which Wagner derived the terminology about the Meistersinger rules of rhyme. Within the space of five days, 14–18 November, Wagner wrote two separate prose drafts, known to Wagner scholars as drafts B and C, of the opera. Both differed in many important respects from the 1845 Marienbad draft A, which now belonged to Mathilde. On 20 November Wagner sent draft C to Schott. 'You will now see what it is about and you will undoubtedly agree with me when I anticipate its becoming, if not the most original, certainly the most popular of all my works.' He said how he had intended to reserve the composition of this opera for a later period in his life as his present bustling existence was not conducive to the right mood. He had now decided, however, that the many difficult problems which beset him could best be resolved by carrying out this cheerful project. The completed opera would be ready for posting to all German theatres under the one important condition that Schott have confidence in him and remove, for the coming twelve months, all material cares from his shoulders.

Wagner needed somewhere comfortable and peaceful where he could write the poem and compose the music. The Metternichs, who were now in Vienna, offered him, in the Paris embassy, just the retreat he wanted – a suite of rooms overlooking a quiet garden. He left Vienna for Paris, stopping at Mainz to negotiate the fee for *Die Meistersinger* with Franz Schott. After contracting an advance of 10,000 francs, a respectable sum, he read the prose draft of *Die Meistersinger* to Schott, his artistically-minded wife Betty, and some invited guests.

The Metternichs withdrew, to Wagner's great disappointment, their offer of accommodation because of the death of her mother, Countess Sandor. The text of *Die Meistersinger* was born, not in the Austrian embassy, but in a small room on the third floor of the dingy little Hotel Voltaire on the Seine. (At about this time Liszt settled in Rome where he practised certain devotions which, in 1865, entitled him to take up minor orders and call himself Abbé Liszt.) The poem 'Die Meistersinger' took exactly thirty days and was finished on 25 January 1862. He later called these weeks the happiest of his life. Every day the libretto increased its swelling volume of rhyme. 'How could I not find myself in a humorous mood when I, after reflecting on the quaint sayings and verses of the Meistersinger, raised my eyes from the paper and saw out of the window the tremendous crowds moving along the quays and over the bridges and a view which embraced the Tuileries, the Louvre and even the Hotel de Ville.' Sometimes laughter, sometimes tears caused him to lay his pen down and stop working. 'Protect your heart against Hans Sachs,' he wrote to Mathilde. 'You are going to fall in love with him.'

Wagner led a withdrawn life; almost the only person he saw was Truinet – who had turned the French translation of *Tannhäuser* into verse – with whom he lunched most days in the Taverne Anglaise. On his way there one day, as he was strolling along the galleries of the Palais Royal, the music of the 'Wach auf' chorus, with which the people greet Sachs in Act III, came to him. He asked Truinet, who was waiting for him, for some pencil and paper to jot down the melody which he hummed to Truinet as he went along. All Truinet could exclaim was, 'Mais, quelle gaité d'esprit, cher maître!'

Now Wagner needed somewhere more comfortable and permanent where he could write the music for *Die Meistersinger*. His former Parisian friends and acquaintances were a little distrustful of him; they could not understand why he had returned so soon to the scene of the *Tannhäuser* débâcle. His requests for accommodation met with frightened refusals. He therefore left Paris for Mainz where he hoped to find a quiet spot and be under Schott's financial protection. 'The music is all in my head,' he wrote to him. 'God must give me four sturdy posts within which I can house my dear old Erhard piano . . . and awaken it again into sound.' On 4 February he read his poem before a large gathering in Schott's publishing house; Peter Cornelius came all the way from Vienna, braving snow and floods, to hear it. It was admired by all as a brilliant virtuoso performance.

Wagner chose Biebrich on the Rhine, between Mainz and Wiesbaden, as his domicile for composing the *Meistersinger* music. He rented some rooms in a villa, with a view of the Rhine, belonging to an architect called Frickhofer. He was about to get down to his work when Minna unexpectedly arrived, from Dresden, ostensibly to help him settle in. After ten frightful days of quarrels and recriminations she returned to Dresden. 'They were,' said Wagner, 'ten days of Hell.'

Minna had, by now, become intolerable. She showed hilariously little understanding of her husband's complex nature. Tristan and Isolde were, for her, a couple of neurotic chatterboxes and every woman that Wagner met became an object of her prurient suspicion. The very mention of the name 'Mathilde Wesendonk' turned her into a screeching, venomous, lower-middle class housewife. As luck would have it, a belated Christmas parcel from Mathilde arrived just after Minna; it had been sent to Vienna and then returned to Zurich. The 'bitch' (*Mistweib*) had sent him, according to Minna, an embroidered pillow, a packet of tea and toilet water, all wrapped in violets. The episode of the parcel led to violent scenes. 'The woman was just as she was four years before. The same rantings and coarse accusations . . . suspicion, mistrust, false interpretations put on every word . . . these ghastly ten days were a good thing in that they brought on my final decision.' Wagner determined not to live with his wife any longer. Some biographers, put out by the coldness and snobbery of Cosima, have been unnecessarily charitable to Minna. There is no need to be, although her domestic virtues were self-evident. Wagner praised them incessantly and he persuaded himself for years that they compensated for her other shortcomings. Now he was through with her; at this moment he heard from their doctor Pusinelli that her efforts to get his amnesty extended to Saxony had been successful. The last thing he now wanted was to live with her in Dresden. Pusinelli sounded her out on the question of a divorce. 'If he wants a divorce, then I say No! He should have the patience to wait until God divorces us.'

Wagner, alone at Biebrich, his nerves much disturbed, was badly in need of the gentle solace of feminine company. He found it with two young women of quite different characters and attainments; one was called 'Maier' and the other 'Meyer'! The first, the twenty-nine-year-old Mathilde Maier, he met at an evening party given by the Schotts for their Mainz friends. She had blue eyes and wavy blonde hair; she was innocent, educated and charming. Wagner and Mathilde Maier were immediately drawn to each other; she felt his obvious sufferings in her heart and she did what she could, to the extent that local proprieties permitted, to add a feminine touch to what he called his *Biebernest* (beaver's nest). They had no love affair; he was Sachs and she was Eva and his letters to her breathe the cheerfully serene *Meistersinger* mood. He was entranced by the idyllic simplicity of her household in Mainz where she looked after her mother, two aunts and a sister and her family acquaintances included Schopenhauer's only friend, *Gerichtsrat* (notary) Becken. Under her beneficent influence he started to write the *Meistersinger* music.

From my balcony, as I beheld, in the sunset, the incomparable spectacle of 'golden Mainz', with the majestic Rhine flowing by in a glory of light, the prelude of my *Meistersinger* made itself distinctly felt in my soul. I had seen it, once before, in a sorrowful mood as a distant mirage. I proceeded to write down the prelude exactly as it appears today in the score containing the outlines of all the main themes in the opera.

On his birthday, on 22 May 1862, he wrote the prelude to Act III. 'It is clear to me,' he told Mathilde Wesendonk, 'that this work is going to be my most perfect masterpiece and that I shall finish it.' On the same day Mathilde Maier presented him, as she was to do on all his future birthdays, with six standard rose trees in full bloom.

The other young lady was Frau Dustmann's sister, the actress Friederike Meyer, whose 'delicate and tender acting' Wagner had admired at Frankfurt. She turned out to be the mistress of Guaita, the director of the Frankfurt theatre, who collected her from Biebrich after she had fallen ill staying with Wagner. Her commitment to Guaita disturbed neither Wagner nor Friederike and she joined in many jolly gatherings and expeditions; in the summer of 1862 these mingled with unforgettable hours of music with Hans and Cosima von Bülow, Ludwig and Malvina Schnorr von Carolsfeld and Wagner's old friend August Röckel, released from gaol after thirteen years. The Bülows spent two months as Wagner's guests at Biebrich during which time his relations to Cosima underwent a definite change. She had lost her old shyness of him although her thoughts and feelings were still 'shrouded in silence and mystery'. When he sang, in his fashion, Wotan's *Abschied* (Farewell) from *Walküre*, Act II, she had the same expression on her face as at Zurich on a similar occasion – only this time 'the ecstatic element had been transfigured into something higher and more serene'. These expressions of Cosima convinced him, perhaps understandably, that she belonged to him and this certainty, added to his present over-excitement, led him into pranks of 'boisterous gaiety', such as asking Cosima whether he might wheel her back into her hotel in an empty wheelbarrow. So the cheerful weeks in Biebrich passed; the conduct of this 'theatre crowd' caused many a local Philistine to raise his eyebrows in indignation. The most unhappy member of the group was Bülow; in the presence of Wagner he felt miserably inadequate.

Those sublime hours of music-making which evoked the enchanted world of *Tristan* and *Die Meistersinger* made him realize that he could never be a composer. Cosima, ambitious for her husband, had even written an opera libretto for him. At Biebrich he felt that everything he had written was wretched, shoddy and worthless. He lost faith in himself and Cosima lost faith in him. She was now setting her sights on the 'better man'. Wagner found himself pleasantly poised in the year 1862–3 between three women: Mathilde, Friederike and Cosima, while the other 'sublime' Mathilde was given the rôle of a resigned Hans Sach. To satisfy a whim of his wife, Otto Wesendonk sent a painter, Cesar Willich, to do a portrait of Wagner. To keep him still Cosima read to him during the long sittings. Bülow began, at this time, to wonder whether there might be anything between Wagner and his wife.

Work on *Die Meistersinger*, which had been proceeding slowly, came to an abrupt halt when Schott's bulldog Leo bit Wagner on the thumb of his right hand. Schott refused to pay any further advances and Wagner therefore gave up work on the opera, his life thereby taking a turn which was to bring him to disaster. The following eighteen months, with no money forthcoming from Schott, was a bleak uncreative period in his career. He travelled about frenziedly giving concerts. The Vienna *Tristan* fiasco slowly came to an end. The *coup de grâce* was given by Frau Dustmann, who refused to have anything more to do with Wagner, accusing him of exploiting her sister, Friederike, both sexually and financially. For him, the positive and pleasurable aspects of the concerts which he conducted during these gloomy months – in Frankfurt, Vienna, Prague, Petersburg, Moscow, Budapest, Karlsruhe and Breslau – was the opportunity of hearing his own music played. It was also an opportunity for the public to hear extracts from some of his latest works which had never been seen before in opera houses. He gave the first of these concerts in the Theater an der Wien, Vienna's second largest theatre after the opera house, in the presence of the Empress Elizabeth. The house was full; with the exception of *Die Meistersinger* prelude, which he had conducted a few weeks earlier in the Leipzig Gewandhaus before an almost empty house, every piece was having its first performance: the gathering of the Meistersinger, Pogner's address from *Die Meistersinger*; the ride of the Walküre, Siegmund's spring song (*Lenzlied*) and Wotan's farewell; from *Das Rheingold* the rape of the gold (the second part of the first scene), Donner's conjuring up of the storm and the entry of the gods into Valhalla (*Walhall*). The applause was overwhelming; after the ride of the Walküre the Viennese audience could no longer contain itself. In Vienna, as in every city where Wagner's works were performed, with the exceptions of Leipzig and Berlin, the results were always the same – public enthusiasm and deplorable reviews. Why his birth-place should have been a centre of anti-Wagnerian prejudice is not quite clear – a legacy, perhaps, of Mendelssohn and his con-temptuous attitude to Wagner's music and of Leipzig's cultural hostility to Dresden where Wagner had been *Kapellmeister*. After the first performance of *Die Meistersinger* prelude one of the leading Leipzig critics wrote, '*Die Meistersinger* is intended, so we understand, to be a comic opera; its flatulent prelude hardly suggests that Wagner is capable of writing a comic opera'.

From Leipzig Wagner went to Dresden for the first time since the events of May 1849. He found that most of his theatre col-leagues were dead or retired. He trod once more the familiar streets of that beautiful city. 'My first impression was one of extraordinary boredom and emptiness; I had last seen them filled with barricades when they looked unusually interesting.' He stayed with Minna and saw his old friends Pusinelli, Heine the scenery painter and the two Schnorrs. In Minna's drawing-room he read 'Die Meistersinger' 'for the benefit of those people who did not know it'. Wagner read his dramatic poems so brilliantly that he was able to envelop them with an atmosphere of theatrical and symphonic magic which quite carried away some of the listeners. Others could hardly sit through them. Minna lived in an apartment in the Walpurgistrasse; she had furnished it, as she always did, tastefully and comfortably. At the entrance she had embroidered the word 'Salve' on the doormat. 'I recognized our Paris drawing-room in the red silk curtains and furniture.' After three days Wagner left Dresden; he and Minna never met again. As they said farewell to each other at the railway station she had forebodings that this might be the case. Her life dragged on until, early in the morning of 25 January 1866, she was found lying dead on her bed, her lips covered in foam. She continued writing hysterical letters in which Wagner was a 'wild beast' and she a 'poor helpless woman'.

In Vienna, Standhartner gave a party in his house on

23 November 1862; the occasion was Wagner's reading of 'Die Meistersinger'. Amongst the guests was Eduard Hanslick who apparently decided that he was being caricatured in the figure of Beckmesser. 'As the reading proceeded,' said Wagner, 'the dangerous critic looked more and more pale and depressed.' He left abruptly afterwards. Hanslick had grounds for this suspicion as Wagner had, in an earlier draft, given Beckmesser the name Veit Hanslich. On the other hand Wagner had invented Beckmesser, as the pedantic enemy of the new musical art, in his Marienbad sketch of 1845. In any event, Hanslich became, from this moment onwards, Wagner's enemy and, because of his surprising ability to intimidate everybody in the Viennese musical world, he may share, with Frau Dustmann, the honour of sabotaging the Vienna *Tristan und Isolde*.

At the end of 1862 Wagner wrote a preface to the first public edition of the *Ring* poem. In it he stated that it would be impossible to entrust his works to any of the inferior German repertory theatres of the day, 'because of the grotesque inadequacies of their performances'. His solution was the construction in some medium-sized town of a provisional theatre, shaped like an amphitheatre, where the artists would have an unified style and purpose. In such a theatre his opera-dramas would be performed; in order that the public should enjoy the illusion of reality it was most important that the orchestra be invisible. Who should finance this undertaking? A German prince would be the most likely person to make possible model performances of his *Nibelungen* dramas. 'Will this prince ever be found?' he asked.

At the beginning of 1863 Wagner cried out for female company. 'I need a woman,' he wrote to Mathilde Maier, 'who is willing, in spite of everything, to be to me what only a woman, in these wretched circumstances, can be – if I am to survive.'

The third, and last, of his Vienna concerts which included, this time, the *Faust* overture, went off successfully. Brahms, who had, with Cornelius and Weissheimer, helped Wagner to give concert endings to the ride of the Walküre and other passages from his operas, sat in a box, looking impassive and withdrawn. He did not join in the general applause; neither did the dramatist Friedrich Hebbel who had written his own *Nibelung* dramas which Wagner found 'unnatural, vulgar and affected'. Hebbel disliked all Wagner's operas, particularly *Lohengrin*, which reminded him how his dog had been killed by a swan. He did not go up in Wagner's estimation when he called on him, in his absence, leaving a card on which was printed, 'Hebbel, chevalier de plusieurs ordres'. 'Later I learned that he had died of softening of the bones and I then understood why he had affected me so unpleasantly.'

With *Die Meistersinger* advances from Schott cut off and the futile *Tristan* rehearsals dragging to a standstill Wagner had no choice but to continue giving concerts. The three Vienna concerts, although very popular, ended in a deficit which Wagner had increased by erecting a sound-wall (*Schallwand*). The Empress Elizabeth, at the instance of Madame Kalergis, gave a thousand gulden to help cover the losses. In February 1863 he gave a concert in Prague where he conducted a Beethoven symphony and some of his own works. In Prague he alarmed young Lilli Lehmann, later to sing Woglinde in the first Bayreuth performance of *Das Rheingold* in 1876, by hugging and kissing her inordinately. He was dressed in a manner unusual for Prague; he turned up at rehearsals wearing a yellow damask dressing-gown, a red or pink tie and a wide black velvet cape lined with rose-coloured satin. 'I stared at him in open-mouthed astonishment,' said Lilli Lehmann.

The Prague concert, which had earned him 1100 gulden, was followed by concerts in St Petersburg and Moscow arranged by Madame Kalergis. The programme at the St Petersburg concerts, held under the auspices of the Philharmonic Society, consisted of what was coming to be an almost standard repertoire: Senta's ballad, the overture and sailors' chorus from *Der fliegeonde Hlländer*; the overture, Wolfram von Eschenbach's hymn (Act III) and the march (Act II) from *Tannhäuser*; the *Lohengrin* prelude; the customary extracts from the *Ring* and some Beethoven! His Russian concerts were a great triumph for him. After the first St Petersburg concert he wrote to Mathilde Maier: 'It was quite frightful; I've never known it so hot as here in Russia!!! The public of 3–4000 almost gobbled me up ... my triumph is unbelievable.' He was given a splendid orchestra of over 120 players picked from the best imperial orchestras; they included sixty violins.

In St Petersburg Wagner met Editha von Rhaden, a lady-in-waiting to the Grand Duchess Helena Pavlovna who was a princess of Württemberg and widow of the Grand Duke Michael.

She occupied a leading position in the court of Tsar Alexander II and her apartments were an important intellectual and political centre. Editha von Rhaden introduced Wagner to this august lady who expressed the wish to be better acquainted with the poem of the *Ring*. Wagner did not need asking twice; he saw her at once as the benefactress of his dreams and hastened to obtain from the publisher J. H. Weber in Leipzig the proof-sheets of the still unpublished *Ring* poem.[1] He read the poem to the Grand Duchess and her friends at four successive tea parties. Before the arrival of the proof-sheets from Leipzig he read her the 'Meistersinger' poem which Schott had published in 1862; the Grand Duchess Marie, a daughter of the late Tsar Nicholas, was also present at this reading throughout which she feared that Hans Sachs would end up by marrying Eva. The Grand Duchess Helena did not wish to patronize Wagner on the scale that he had hoped; she contented herself by giving him 1000 roubles to compensate for the disappointing results of one of his concerts which suffered from being announced simultaneously with another of his concerts – a charity one for the inmates of debtors' prisons – a cause which should have been close to Wagner's heart. Afterwards General Surverov, the governor of the city, handed him a silver drinking-horn as a thanks-offering from the imprisoned debtors.

Wagner moved to Penzing outside Vienna on 12 May 1863. Within two months he had spent all his hard-earned Russian roubles and he was once again in the hands of money-lenders. It is difficult to justify the senseless, wanton expenditure on which Wagner now embarked. He yielded with voluptuous delight to his most fanciful sybaritic cravings. In his own words, 'I had to spend some money in order to make my long-desired asylum fit and cosy both for rest and work.' He kept on the caretakers Franz Mrazek and his wife Anna, both of whom later worked for him in Munich, and he engaged a maid Prucha; for the rest, his money disappeared in a flurry of expenditure on dressing-gowns, silks and velvets, carpets, cushions, plush sofas, braid and lace. The milliner, Bertha Goldwag, now known to history because of Wagner's 'Briefe an eine Putzmacherin' (Letters to a Milliner), and two upholsterers, worked day and night to carry out his minute and constantly changing instructions. Bertha decorated his study

[1] The limited private edition was published in 1853.

of which she has left us a description: 'The walls were festooned with silk; from the ceiling hung a wonderful chandelier giving out a soft light; the floor was covered with a very heavy, unusually soft carpet, into which your feet literally sank; the furniture consisted of a small sofa, armchairs and a table, all covered with the most costly rugs and cushions. . . . I made them all!"

Wagner needed a new set of clothes to avoid any possible disharmony between the trappings of his body and those of his home. She made him, in addition to twenty-four dressing-gowns of different colours, many pairs of satin trousers with matching jackets and fur-lined slippers. The other rooms were given the same detailed attention; his bedroom was largely of red plush with blue silk blinds and a violet *passementerie* for the white quilted bed-cover; the green room had chairs of violet silk and velvet.

What Wagner now needed was a woman, a consort for his fairy kingdom. He asked Mathilde Maier to come to him from Mainz and 'remedy this deficiency in a becoming manner'. Mathilde was not prepared to join Wagner in Vienna unless he was free to marry her. A certain Marie, the daughter of a pork butcher, did not have Mathilde's qualms. He described her to Mathilde Wesendonk as 'experienced, sedate, gentle and pleasing'. She knew what Wagner wanted of her as we can see from a letter to his 'dearest, little Marie', announcing his return from a concert tour: 'My sweetheart . . . see that my pretty study is in apple-pie order . . . perfume it nicely. Buy the best perfumes so that it will really be fragrant . . . look pretty and charming. . . . I deserve to have a really good time.' This little flutter is known to historians as the Penzing Idyll.

On 22 May 1863 Wagner had what he called his 'half hundredth birthday'. He felt lonely; Marie had gone and no other love-bird had yet arrived to luxuriate with him in this colourful, scented arbour of silks, satins and velvets. His only visitor on this day was Standhartner. A few days later a torchlight procession was held in his honour by students and by members of various choral societies. Reassured by these expressions of his popularity with the Viennese public and comforted by the frequent visits of Tausig and Cornelius he settled down to finish scoring the first scene of *Die Meistersinger* Act I. At last he felt in the right mood to make up for lost time and to immerse himself in the serene and joyful glow of the music. The pressure of his debts compelled him, however, to embark upon another round of concert giving. Until the end of the year he gave three concerts in Budapest, two in Prague, two in Karlsruhe (Turgenev was present at the first), one at Löwenberg in Silesia with the private orchestra of the Prince of Hohenzollern-Hechingen, one in Breslau and one in Vienna. These were five exhausting weeks for him and the financial results were disappointing. Wagner was now living from hand to mouth; after his two Karlsruhe concerts he was paid 200 marks which he spent at once on a fur coat. The Grand Duke also gave him a gold snuff-box with fifteen louis d'or; this he sold for 270 marks to his friend Weitzmann, who gave Cosima lessons in the theory of music, in Berlin on his way to Löwenberg. He joked with the Bülows over dinner at the Hotel Brandenburg about this addition to his reserves. The next day, when Bülow was preparing to give a recital, Wagner and Cosima went for a drive. 'This time', he says, 'our jocularity died away in silence; we gazed speechless into each other's eyes. With tears and sobs we sealed our confession to belong to each other alone.' This was the turning point in Wagner's relations with Cosima. There is no record of their development up to this point.

In Löwenberg the old invalid prince paid him a handsome fee of 4200 marks, almost all of which he had to remit at once to Vienna to meet urgent bills, or to Minna. He was surprised to find at Löwenberg the rich sister of Eliza Wille, Henriette von Bessing; she promised to let him have large sums of money and followed him to his next concert engagement in Breslau. It turned out that her motives were neurotic and dishonourable; she wanted to possess the man rather than assist the artist. Two months later, when Wagner was swamped with short-dated bills that had become due and was on the point of ruin, she scornfully rejected his desperate plea for help. 'Even if I do save him', she admitted to her sister, 'he will still love the Wesendonk!' Apropos the Wesendonks he went to Zurich and stayed with them for the last time. 'The idea of assisting me did not ever seem to occur to these friends of mine although I informed them quite frankly of my position.'

The year 1863 ended with a Christmas party at Penzing with his friends Cornelius, Porges, Tausig and Schönaich, 'to each of whom I gave an appropriate trifle'. Cornelius described to his sister the 'trifle' which 'the mad Wagner' had given him. 'Just imagine – a wonderful, heavy greatcoat (*Paletot*) – an elegant grey dressing-gown – a red scarf – a blue cigarette case and lighter – lovely silk handkerchiefs – splendid gold shirt studs – the *Struwwelpeter* – elegant pen-wipes with gold mottoes – fine cravats – a cigar-holder with his initials – in short, what only an oriental imagination could think up. It made my heart heavy. . . .' We do not know what 'trifles' his other friends received.

Wagner was now advised by Eduard Liszt, a local judge and an uncle of Franz Liszt, to flee to Switzerland before payment became due on any more bills. This was his only way of escaping arrest and being thrown into prison, the treatment given to defaulting debtors in Austria. On 10 March 1864 the eighteen-year-old Ludwig II succeeded his father Maximilian II on the Bavarian throne. A fortnight later Wagner fled from Vienna. He made for Zurich, confident that he would find shelter with Eliza Wille, if not with the Wesendonks. On the way he stopped at Munich; the town was in mourning for the late king. 'I saw a portrait of the young king, Ludwig II, in a shop window and I experienced the peculiar emotion which is aroused by the sight of youth and beauty placed in a particularly difficult situation.'

Eliza Wille, whose husband was in Constantinople on holiday, had hardly had time to prepare his rooms. Fifteen years had gone by since Wagner last crossed Lake Constance and arrived, breathless and penniless in Zurich, looking for shelter. The Wesendonks flatly refused to accommodate him, Mathilde going so far as to return to Eliza Wille, unopened, a letter which he had written her.[1] Cold and feverish, Wagner wrapped himself in his Karlsruhe fur coat and read Jean Paul, George Sand, Walter Scott, his hostess's 'Felicitas', Frederick the Great's diaries and the German mystics like Tauler. He was visited by both serene and nightmarish visions; at one moment he was Lear in the storm; at another he was summoned to join Voltaire in Potsdam at the court of Frederick; in another he was in a renunciatory mood on the Ganges. To Cornelius he wrote, 'My situation is dismal, a good, truly helpful miracle must happen; otherwise I'm finished . . . a light must show itself; a person must appear who will

[1] The contents of this letter have been the subject of several learned Wagnerian monographs.

support me energetically – I still have the energy to requite such help: otherwise not!'

On 28 April Wagner left Zurich and travelled to Stuttgart via Basel. In Stuttgart he called on his friend *Kapellmeister* Karl Eckert who could do nothing for him. From his hotel he wrote to Weissheimer, 'I am now at the end.' His home at Penzing had been broken up and his property held in pawn. His career appeared to be in ruins and he contemplated suicide. Then, like his Elsa, his prayer for succour from some unknown heroic friend was answered and Ludwig of Bavaria, the 'Dream-King', entered his life.

CHAPTER NINE
A Royal Patron
1864–5

AT TEN O'CLOCK on the morning of 3 May 1864 Franz Seraph von Pfistermeister, the cabinet secretary of the young King of Bavaria, called on Wagner at the Hotel Marquardt in Stuttgart. He had been round the previous day but Wagner, suspecting him to be one of his more determined and enterprising Viennese creditors, refused to see him. He had had a sleepness night, preparing for the worst. In the morning he steeled himself to meet the stranger who presented him with a photograph of Ludwig and a ring, together with a message from the King that he had always been one of his fervent admirers. The King had heard about his difficulties and wished to be able to relieve him in the future of all material cares but he wished, above all, to meet the man to whom he owed the noblest thoughts and emotions of his life. Pfistermeister, whose search for Wagner had taken him to Penzing and to the Wille's house at Mariafeld before he finally tracked him down in Stuttgart, proposed that they both leave the same evening for Munich. Wagner, then and there, penned the first of his many letters to the king, thus starting a correspondence comprising about six hundred letters and covering a period of nearly twenty years. 'Beloved, gracious King! I send you these tears of most heavenly emotion, to tell you that the wonders of poetry, like a divine reality, have now entered into my poor lovelorn life; and this life, its poetry and its music, now belongs to you, my gracious young King; dispose of it as if it were your own property. In highest ecstasy, loyal and true, your subject, Richard Wagner.'

Ludwig wanted to meet the composer of *Lohengrin*. Pfistermeister's exact words to Wagner, as he handed him the ring, had been: 'As this jewel glows, so he (the king) burns with desire to see the poet and composer of *Lohengrin*.' Ludwig was born in Nymphemburg on 25 August 1845, a few days after Wagner had, in Marienbad, in a feverish flow of creativity, written complete prose sketches for *Lohengrin* and *Die Meistersinger*, a couple of months before the première of *Tannhäuser* in Dresden. This, said Wagner later, was more than a coincidence; it showed that God had made Ludwig especially for him. Ludwig's happiest days had been spent in Hohenschwangau, an ancient, squat, simple castle on the edge of the Bavarian Alps, now overshadowed by Neuschwanstein, the most spectacular of his later building follies. His father, Maximilian II (1811–64), had, in 1848, succeeded his grandfather Ludwig I (1786–1868), whose infatuation with the Irish adventuress Marie Gilbert, better known as the 'Spanish' Lola Montez, had so shocked the powerful conservative and clerical circles in Bavaria that he had been forced to abdicate. Ludwig I had worshipped beautiful women and classical antiquity; his taste in the former can be judged from the Schönheitsgalerie at Nymphenburg, that delightful collection of portraits of nobly born and peasant beauties (it includes a portrait of Lola Montez by Josef Stieler) and in the latter by Munich's public buildings and thoroughfares. Ludwig I, a nineteenth-century Lorenzo the Magnificent, had, over a period of thirty years, transformed the face of Munich, turning it into Europe's most remarkable neo-Florentine city. The fall of Ludwig I occurred at the same time as that of Louis-Philippe – the difference being that the French had dropped and the Bavarians acquired a King with middle-class virtues.

Maximilian II and his wife Marie, who had been a Hohenzollern princess, led lives of impeccable domesticity. He had inherited neither his father's building mania nor his penchant for actresses – the elderly king had, long before Lola Montez had danced her way into his heart, been in the habit of calling on actresses in the evenings whilst his wife, the handsome *Hausfrau* Theresa of Saxe-Hildburghausen and mother of his seven children, sat knitting at a window of the Residenz, waiting patiently for his return. Maximilian was serious-minded and educated but lacked the Wittelsbach charm and eccentricity. His building activities were confined to restoring Hohenschwangau, the Bavarian Balmoral, where he relaxed in leather shorts rather than in a kilt. Apart from Hohenschwangau the royal family lived, when in Munich, in the Residenz and in Berg, a quaint little castle on the Starnberg See near Munich.

Ludwig was brought up in a harsh, inhuman way which is often the lot of princes. His father was a terrifying martinet and his mother a frail, commonplace neurotic (although qualifying for inclusion in her father-in-law's 'Schönheitsgalerie') who understood neither of her sons but preferred Otto, the youngest. A French governess filled Ludwig's mind with stories of Louis XIV and Marie Antoinette, of the deference due to kings and of the splendour of Versailles. This was not enough to satisfy the imaginatively starved prince. Hohenschwangau, overlooking the Alp See, in its setting of firs and larches, was the capital of the Swan-Country; here Lohengrin lived with Elsa and pictures of the legend of the Swan-Knight adorned the castle walls. Swans glided in the lake and the royal apartments had the swan as their dominating decorative motif: chairs, cushions, inkstands, ornaments, clocks – whether in precious stones, gold or silver, in embroidery or in oils – the swan was ubiquitous. As a boy Ludwig sealed his letters with a cross and a swan; one of his early drawings was of a fantastic, crenellated castle in front of which floated a swan which dwarfed everything else in the picture.

In 1861, at Ludwig's urgent request, his father had commanded a performance of *Lohengrin* in the Hoftheater in which Ludwig Schnorr von Carolsfeld sang the title part. Ludwig was so affected that it was thought he might have hysterics; the courtiers feared that this neurotic, melancholy youth, over-disciplined by tutors, might become irretrievably committed to a world of reverie and solitude and unwilling, or unable, to perform his princely, social duties. In the Residenz he could pace the *Nibelungen* rooms and enjoy the company of Siegfried and the Teutonic gods. He had read the public edition of the *Ring* poem, published at the beginning of 1863, and Wagner's long preface ending with the ringing words 'Will this prince ever be found?' This prince was to build a theatre suited to a new, genuinely German, style of musico-dramatic production in which model performances of Wagner's music-dramas would be given. When Ludwig read this preface he had pocket-money of a few pence a week. A year later he was king of the richest, most important state in southern

Germany with enormous personal power, with freedom to indulge in any fantasy and with no experience whatsoever of the responsibilities of government.

Maximilian had died unexpectedly, at the relatively early age of fifty-three, worn out, it was said, by anxiety about the intractable Schleswig-Holstein question, a subject which was not to cause his successor many sleepless nights. Ludwig was eighteen when he came to the throne and already certain features of his character had, as the courtiers feared, taken shape. He loved the solitude of the lakes and forests of the Bavarian Alps; he hated Munich and the very sight of the mob; he disliked the chatter of women; he had no use for priests, politicians, soldiers, government servants or for any of the ceremonial aspects of monarchy; when he went to the theatre he preferred to be the only member of the audience rather than be stared at by the repulsive rabble. 'In short,' says Wagner's biographer Newman, 'he exhibited so many signs of exceptional sanity that it was a foregone conclusion that the world would some day declare him to be mad.'

Old King Ludwig I was in Sicily when his son Maximilian died; he hurried back to Munich hoping that he would be asked to return to the throne. This was not to be; he witnessed, with mixed feelings, the coronation of his grandson, the beautiful Swan-Prince who, for some reason or other, hated his grandfather. The apparent similarities in the eccentric careers of grandfather and grandson are very obvious. The 'wholesome' eccentricities of the elder Ludwig – fresh young women with white bosoms and ringlets, velvet hats and ribbons, and glacial, neo-classical, architectural extravaganza which gave a new character to Munich, seem to be of less interest to a prurient, 'romantic' posterity than those architectural 'sick children' of his grandson – Neuschwanstein, Herrenchiemsee and Linderhof – whose goings-on with stable boys, guardsmen and actors, chronicled in his bizarre diaries, have led people to question the exact nature of his relationship with Wagner. Ludwig, in his diaries, mentions several times his guilty association with 'Richard'; Wagnerian research has happily proved that this 'Richard' was a casual acquaintance and not to be confused with our hero.

The friendship between the morbidly romantic boy king and the great composer in his early fifties, and at the very height of his powers, must be one of the strangest and most touching in history.

Its quality is best shown in the letters and other communications, such as poems and telegrams, which the two exchanged between 1864 and 1883. There is no doubt whatsoever that Wagner represented all that was best in what became the increasingly disturbed and wretched mental world of the 'Dream-King'. His admiration for Wagner and his determination that his works be fittingly performed and produced had an ennobling effect on his mind and character. He saw his own dramatic ideals exemplified in Wagner's works and he shared Wagner's belief in the vital role of the theatre as a centre of culture rather than as a futile place of entertainment.

It is my intention [he wrote to Wagner later in the year] to induce in the Munich public a more elevated and reflective mood by producing serious and significant works like those by Shakespeare, Calderon, Goethe, Schiller, Beethoven, Mozart, Gluck and Weber, to help it wean itself gradually from common, frivolous, fashionable works and thus prepare it for the marvels of your genius. Its understanding of these will be made easier by first presenting it with works of other distinguished men; for everyone must be aware of the seriousness of art.

Before leaving Stuttgart with Pfistermeister Wagner went to say goodbye to *Kapellmeister* Eckert; a telegram arrived with the news of Meyerbeer's death the previous day. Weissheimer broke out, said Wagner, into 'boorish laughter' at this 'wonderful coincidence'.

The fateful meeting between Ludwig and Wagner took place in the Munich Residenz early in the afternoon on 4 May 1864. Ludwig, pale and nervous, awaited the man whose music-dramas and whose writings (he had read all Wagner's important prose works) had comforted his years of loneliness. 'You should have seen how his gratitude shamed me,' Ludwig wrote to his cousin, later his fiancée, Sophie, younger sister of his friend the Empress Elizabeth,

when I offered him my hand with the assurance that he would not only be able to complete his great *Nibelungen* work, but also have it produced in complete fidelity to his wishes. He bent low over my hand and appeared to be moved by what was so natural; he remained a long time in that position without uttering a single word. I had the impression that our roles were reversed. I stooped down to him [Ludwig was six foot three inches tall and Wagner five foot and six inches] and pressed him to my heart with a feeling that I was swearing an oath to be true to him for the rest of time.

Wagner's joy and excitement were just as great; he was bowled over by the boy king's pathos and beauty. He wrote to Eliza Wille,

Today I was taken to the king. He is, alas, so fair and spiritual, so soulful and wonderful, that I tremble lest his life should dissolve like a fleeting celestial dream in this mean world. He loves me with all the fervour and passion of a first love; he knows everything about me and he understands me like my own soul. He wishes always to have me by his side.

To Mathilde Maier he wrote the next day,

Yesterday's meeting was a love scene which neither of us wanted ever to end. He has the profoundest understanding of my nature and of my needs. He offers me everything I want – for my life, for my work, for the production of my dramas. I am just to be his friend: no appointment, no functions. He is the ideal fulfilment of all my wishes ... that this should happen now – now – in this night of death, this very blackest moment of my existence!! I am overwhelmed!

Ludwig's subjects shared Wagner's infatuation with their new ruler.

His wavy black hair curled slightly and was as thick as a woman's, and his blazing blue eyes revealed a capacity for suffering surprising in one so young: the mouth was proud and pouting, the features too finely chiselled, the expression obstinate but disarming. He had a youthful arrogance, a grave beauty, an almost feminine grace, and Bavaria, fascinated, fell in love with her young king. And when, a few weeks later, he again appeared in public, in the solemn Corpus Christi procession, walking bareheaded and carrying a taper, people said that his beauty was supernatural.[1]

In his first letter to Wagner, written the day after their meeting, Ludwig wrote,

Believe me that I shall do all in my power to indemnify you for what you have suffered in the past. The tedious cares of everyday life I shall rid you of for ever; I shall procure for you the peace you long for in order that you may be free to unfold the mighty wings of your genius in the pure climes of your blissful art. Although you did not know it you were the sole source of my joy from my tenderest youth, my friend who spoke to my heart as no other, my best teacher and educator. I shall repay you everything as far as I can. Oh, how I have longed for the day when I could do this! I hardly dared to nourish the hope to be able so soon to prove my love to you.

[1] Henry Channon, *The Ludwigs of Bavaria*.

Before the honeymoon of king and composer could start in earnest, and their joint plans for the musico-dramatic regeneration of Bavaria and Germany be worked out, Wagner had some urgent debts to settle. He went to Vienna with 4000 florins given to him by Ludwig, the king's first move to free him from the 'tedious cares of everyday life'. A month later the king gave him a further 16,000 florins to pay the remainder of his Viennese debts and to buy back some of his favourite pieces of Penzing furniture which his friends had bought to avoid the publicity of a distraint. Wagner returned to Munich bringing back with him his servants, the Mrazeks, and his old dog Pohl who had replaced the one that died in Paris. Ludwig rented for him the Villa Pellet in Kempfenhausen on the Starnberg See, only fifteen minutes' drive from Ludwig's little castle at Berg.

The Starnberg idyll now started. Ludwig sent a carriage every day to bring Wagner to Berg. Hours of rapturous conversation followed. Wagner was astonished to find that Ludwig knew all his writings intimately and his poems by heart. Ludwig was the first German prince who instinctively knew how to treat Wagner. For an annual salary of 4000 florins he was simply to be himself – Richard Wagner! He had no title, no functions, no duties. He no longer had to let his operas be mutilated in mediocre little German repertory theatres; the only object of the king's patronage was to preserve him from compromising his own integrity. Their joint mission was to be the regeneration of Germany through the theatre. The theatre which Wagner visualized had yet to be built; the singers that he needed had yet to be trained; his works which were to serve as models both for operatic production and operatic composition had yet to be written or, at any rate, completed. This was Wagner's programme which he hoped to carry out in Munich, with the king as his intimate collaborator, during the years ahead. He did not know that, before eighteen months were out, he would have incurred the odium and envy of being the king's favourite and be hounded out of Munich by the combined clamour of press and politicians.

At the end of May Wagner presented Ludwig with a 'Programme for the King', which ended with 'my happy death' in 1873: 1865 would see performances of *Tristan* (with Schnorr) and *Die Meistersinger*; 1866 *Tannhäuser* in a partly revised version; 1867–8 the complete *Ring*; 1869–70 the *Sieger* (Ludwig was anxious for Wagner to proceed with this Buddhist piece); 1871–2 *Parsifal* (with his friends Wagner always referred to Ludwig as 'Parsifal').

When Wagner returned to his loveless bachelor's villa after those intoxicating hours with Ludwig he felt the loneliness all the more. He was still sending off letters in all directions acquainting his friends (but not his creditors) with his new piece of good fortune. 'He has been sent me by Heaven – it is through him that I exist and create. I love him . . . never, never has history chronicled anything so marvellously beautiful, profound and exquisite as the relation of my king to me!' he wrote to Marie Kalergis. He badly needed, however, feminine company. He would presumably, in view of their recently sealed union in a Berlin carriage, rather have had Cosima at his side than anybody else. As she was the wife of his best friend he preferred to avoid, or defer, that fateful course of action until after he had tried his luck elsewhere. The Penzing Marie refused to come. Mathilde Maier also refused although he wrote a long letter to her mother to reinforce his pleas and to emphasize the purity of his intentions. He explained that he had two floors, one for himself and one for the woman who will run the place for him. 'Sensuality will play no part whatsoever in this arrangement.'

In the end Wagner was compelled to send a desperate message to Bülow in Berlin, 'as the last testament of a dying man'. He urged him, his wife and children to come and spend the summer with him. On 29 June 1864 Cosima turned up at the Villa Pellet with her two children, Daniela and Blandine. Bülow joined them a week later. During this week the fate of the three persons in the triangle was determined. Wagner and Cosima had made their decision and nine months later, in April 1865, Wagner's first child, Isolde Josepha Ludovica was born on the day that Bülow was conducting the first orchestral rehearsal of *Tristan und Isolde*. (Isolde was to marry the conductor Franz Beidler; she died in 1919 worn out with fury and bitterness at her failure to obtain a legal ruling that she was Wagner's daughter and not Bülow's. Her motives were less pride in her paternity than determination to have her share of the Wagner children's inheritance.) At Wahnfried, the Wagners' house at Bayreuth, it was forbidden to mention Isolde's name in Cosima's presence and mother and daughter only corresponded through lawyers. This was the first and most serious of the family feuds which have, since the establishment of the Wagner dynasty at Bayreuth, cast their shadows over the temple of Wagnerian art. Wagner himself, civilized and carefree about money, would not have approved of his daughter's rapacity. Nor could he have foreseen that his lonely mission to transform the world of German theatre would end up as a vast concern with many people anxious to get their hands on some of the profits.

Hans von Bülow arrived at the Villa Pellet in a pitiable condition; his nerves were shattered through overwork and other anxieties in Berlin and he was on the verge of a breakdown. He moved a few weeks later to a Munich hotel where he lay paralysed in both legs and in one arm. Wagner's succinct comment in his diary on this unhappy state of affairs was, 'Hans to Munich: ill and furious in hotel.' Cosima, oddly enough, left the same day to see Liszt in Karlsruhe. It is probable that she wished to tell her father about the new situation that had arisen between Wagner, Bülow and herself. Ludwig, by going to Bad Kissingen to meet some Russian and Austrian royal personages in the middle of June, was unwittingly responsible for what had happened. His carriage could no longer bring Wagner once or twice a day to Berg for their intoxicating chats. Wagner felt suddenly alone and Cosima, knowing just what she wanted, stepped into this gap. This tortured, strong-willed woman was happy at last. Three days after arriving at the Villa Pellet she wrote to her friend Marie von Buch, later Countess von Schleinitz, an indefatigable champion of Bayreuth, how

… in the little village of Starnberg on the lake everything seems remote to me as if the world forgets me and I have forgotten the world. When I have explained everything to you, you will not misunderstand my words. I have been here three days and it seems as if it was already a century and that it will last – how long, I do not know. My spirit is sunk in peace and I have an infinite longing never to see or hear a town again.

From this moment Cosima's grip on Wagner tightened inexorably. She had succumbed to the force of his genius and she knew that she was, like Ludwig, destined by fate to play a vital part in his artistic mission. Cosima was now twenty-six; her life until now had been neither easy nor happy. She was not as attractive as her mother, Marie d'Agoult, who eloped with Liszt in 1835 and who had, during their five-year liaison, a son and two daughters by him; Cosima was born in Cosmo on Christmas Eve 1837. Marie d'Agoult came from an old family, de Flavigny, although her grandfather was a Jewish barber from Frankfurt, a fact which Cosima never mentioned. Her affair with Liszt over, she re-established herself with her children in Paris. Under French law she had no legal rights to them and Liszt used his authority to keep them away from her. When Wagner dined with Liszt and his children in Paris in October 1853 he was surprised to find him tense and unnatural with them. He used them to vent his spite upon their mother who had, under the pseudonym Daniel Stern, lightly mocked him in one of her novels. The Princess, who became his mistress in 1847, fanned his hatred of Marie d'Agoult. The children were handed over to the Princess's former governess, specially brought over from Russia, and her sister, both over seventy. Cosima was given a strict education in music, deportment and other subjects which her governess had formerly taught her aristocratic Russian charges.

When Wagner first met Cosima in Paris she was tall and angular with a sallow complexion and a long nose; she had beautiful golden hair and to these qualities was later added a deep resonant voice. She gave to many the impression of desperately yearning for some great passion; she also gave the impression of consider-able conceit and vanity. 'Now and then her lips would curl con-temptuously with the inborn mockery of the Parisienne,' said the Princess's daughter Marie, who later married Prince Constantine of Hohenlohe-Schillingsfürst, Chamberlain at the court of the Emperor Franz Josef. Cosima and her sister were moved to Berlin and placed in the care of the unpleasant mother of their piano teacher, Hans von Bülow. Two years later she married him; both were pleased – she to make a good marriage and lose the stigma of illegitimacy and he to be the son-in-law of his master Liszt. Pop-eyed, chinless and unstable he cut a sorry figure. He was a clever fool. He had exceptional musical gifts and never wavered in his championship of the music of Liszt and Wagner whose causes he brilliantly served as a conductor and pianist. With his rudeness, peevishness and temper he made enemies wherever he went; his language could be wounding and pungent. He never thought before he spoke; he was unimaginably tactless. Poor Bülow lacked the stamina to deal with the consequences of his excesses; when things went wrong he went to pieces, either screaming or fainting. Cosima hoped, as a proud, able and ambitious wife, to make a man of him. But with his rudeness and vanity went an ineradicable sense of inferiority. He was convinced, from the beginning, of his unworthiness of Cosima, telling Liszt, on the eve of his marriage, that he would 'set her free if she should discover that she has been deceived in me'. As for Wagner, the mere glance at one of his scores sufficed to remind Bülow of his nothingness. 'My God!' he said, after dipping into the *Die Meistersinger* score, 'all that is still ideal and worth preserving in the German spirit lives in this one head.'

Bülow was not, in a conventional way, jealous of Wagner taking Cosima as his mistress. He understood only too well why she should consider it her destiny to give herself to the man he worshipped. Although Wagner and Cosima have been accused by biographers of concealing the truth of their relationship, for at least two years, from the trusting Bülow it is probable that he was told that week in Starnberg when his nerves were in a more shattered state than usual. The subsequent conspiracy of silence was a triangular conspiracy not to protect the reputation of any member of the trio but to prevent news of the scandal from jeopardizing Wagner's friendship with Ludwig and from threatening the accomplishment of their artistic aims in Munich. Bülow's presence in Munich was essential to Wagner both for the 'model' performances of his operas and for ensuring the proximity of Cosima. Wagner obtained for him, at a salary of 2000 florins, the post of *Vorspieler* (introductory player) to the King to introduce him 'in the right way to good musical literature'.

On Ludwig's return from Bad Kissingen Wagner presented him with a beautifully written essay 'Über Staat und Religion' (On State and Religion). Ludwig had earlier asked him whether his views on social and political matters had much changed since the publication of his Zurich writings in 1849–51. The essay is a lofty metaphysical disquisition advocating the reconciliation of all discordant elements in church and state in the soul of the king. Ludwig must have liked the general tone of it, particularly as it contained no references to those constitutional and ceremonial duties which he detested. Nietzsche was exalted by the idealism of this document which appeared to him to have sprung from the spirit of Schopenhauer. Never before, he said, had a king been addressed in so dignified and philosophical a manner. Wagner also paid a musical tribute to the king by composing the

Huldigungsmarsch (Allegiance March) for his nineteenth birthday on 25 August. He met a military band of eighty players at Füssen the evening before, the plan being to perform it at Hohenschwangau; the presence there of the Queen Mother, who disliked Wagner, caused it to be abandoned. As always, he took such setbacks philosophically.

The Starnberg idyll ended in September. Wagner moved into 21 Briennerstrasse which the king had generously offered him. The *Nibelungen* reign was about to begin; a formal contract was drawn up between Wagner and the Royal Bavarian Cabinet Treasury for the sale of the *Ring* to Ludwig (who was its third purchaser, Wesendonk having been the first) for 30,000 florins. From 1864 onwards Wagner was to receive from the king about half a million marks in the form of 'presents', fees and help with the rest; in return for these gifts Wagner 'gave' the King the scores of *Die Feen, Das Liebesverbot, Rienzi, Das Rheingold, Die Walküre, Die Meistersinger* and the *Huldigungsmarsch*; the orchestral sketch of *Der fliegende Holländer, Siegfried* Act III, copies of *Götterdämmerung* Acts I and II, and the handwritten text of *Der junge Siegfried*. One of the ten clauses in the contract was that a clean, complete copy of the score of each of the *Ring* operas would be delivered to Julius von Hofmann, the cabinet treasurer, within three years. *Götterdämmerung* was, in fact, completed at Bayreuth on 21 November 1874. Neither the king nor Wagner took this contract seriously; its purpose was to make the project appear plausible to the world at large, to the politicians and press in particular.

On 24 September 1864 Wagner wrote to the king that he proposed to put aside all other work in order to complete the composition of 'my great *Nibelungen* work'. The king was overjoyed and Wagner at once started scoring afresh the second scene of *Siegfried* Act II which he had broken off seven years earlier. A day or two later the *Huldigungsmarsch* was finally performed in the courtyard of the Residenz. This also gave the king great pleasure but not as much as the knowledge that Wagner had resumed work on the *Ring*.

The *Nibelungen* reign was short-lived and from the outset the occasional lightning flash disturbed the sky. Wagner's house in the Briennerstrasse was elegant and spacious; adjoining it was a garden house – ideal, he thought, for the Bülows. Before he could start work in earnest the familiar *mise-en-scène* would have to be created – the soft colours, satins and so forth. Bertha, now an old hand in externalizing Wagner's inner needs, arrived from Vienna bringing with her quantities of tulle, lace, silks and velvets. Off a large room on the first floor, where stood his Erard grand, was a room hung in yellow satin, cynically referred to by Cornelius as 'The Grail'. It was closed to all profane eyes. Here Wagner, robed in costly garments, invoked the mood necessary for creation. Lola Montez's house in the Bärerstrasse where, in her moment of triumph as Countess of Landsfeld, she held court, was of monastic simplicity when compared with the decorative excesses of 'Lolus', as Ludwig II's favourite was beginning to be called. (He was also given the nickname 'Lolotte'.)

At the end of 1864 the king appointed the clerical-conservative Ludwig von der Pfordten as head of his government. Pfordten had been professor of Roman Law in Leipzig and in 1848 was made Minister of Education for Saxony by King Friedrich August II. It was he to whom Wagner had submitted, in that year, his plan for the organization of a German national theatre for Saxony. Pfordten had noticed with disapproval his revolutionary activities and conceived a hearty, ineradicable dislike for him and for his music. 'If only,' he said to the actor Emil Devrient, 'the princes would show the same solidarity as the democrats Wagner's music would never be performed anywhere.' Bismarck described him as a 'worthy and learned but politically foolish German professor'. Wagner's presence in Munich; his influence on the king; the odious and offensive luxury of his personal life; his dangerously extravagant and pointless schemes for a *Nibelungen* opera house and for a new musical academy; the arrival of more and more of his cronies from different parts of Germany; his interference in political matters – all these considerations concentrated Pfordten's narrow mind marvellously on the Wagner problem and determined him to rid Bavaria of this vexatious and pernicious person in the shortest possible time. He needed exactly a year to achieve this aim. Had Ludwig had a prime minister with the musical intelligence to see that Wagner's 'music of the future' was not a lot of humbug, and with the psychological sense to see that the king's friendship with Wagner was the surest way of preventing him from slipping into a mad, hallucinatory world, he would have earned the gratitude of

Wagnerites. As it was, every activity that Wagner undertook, whether good or bad, intelligent or foolish, was scrutinized maliciously and with hostility in the hope that it would provide another nail for his coffin. Munich was a smallish town in which little happened, where women were devout and men faithful; the Catholic Church and the Wittelsbachs were the two leading institutions. The protection of both was the sacred duty of every citizen; to many people Wagner was a dangerous charlatan and cynical adventurer who had ensnared the heart and mind of the young king. Many members of the aristocracy, the ministerial bureaucracy and the clergy were alarmed that this nomadic, revolutionary, Protestant musician should be the confidant of the susceptible king.

The press campaign against Wagner got under way in February 1865 with an anonymous article in the Augsburg *Allgemeine Zeitung* by Oskar von Redwitz, author of the verse novel *Amaranth*. He mentioned the thousands being spent by Wagner on carpets alone out of the purse of his benefactor, his boundless conceit and the arrogant attitude of his hangers-on towards 'Bavarian stupidity' and Munich's 'musical barbarism'. Wagner wrote a dignified rejoinder. He also asked the king whether he still enjoyed his confidence. 'Only one clear word from my heavenly Friend, telling me what I should do! – Should I go? Should I stay? If I go I shall travel to some remote land and never again return to Germany. . . .' The very mention of such a possibility prompted Ludwig to write at once, 'Stay, oh! stay; everything will be wonderful as it was before.' Ludwig had, several weeks earlier, refused to receive Wagner who had, so it was reported by the sneaky Pfistermeister, referred to him casually as *Mein Junge* (my young fellow).

Wagner's great day in Munich was to have been 15 May 1865. This was the date fixed for the première of *Tristan und Isolde*. He had finished it in Lucerne six years before; after seventy-two rehearsals it had been declared unperformable and unsingable in Vienna. Now, with his unique and god-like Friend at his side and, just as important, with the incomparable tenor Ludwig Schnorr von Carolsfeld for whom Ludwig had obtained, from the King of Saxony, three months leave of absence from Dresden, Wagner's ardent wish to see his *Tristan* performed was about to be realized. Bülow was to conduct it and was given, for the occasion, the title of 'Court *Kapellmeister* for special services'. After much discussion it was decided to perform *Tristan* in the large Hoftheater, holding two thousand people, rather than in the cosy Residenztheater. Wagner intended to have only four or five performances to underline the fact that the opera should not be considered as just another addition to the ordinary theatrical repertoire but as a model of the new Wagnerian style. These performances, said Wagner, 'are to be regarded as art-festivals to which I shall invite the friends of my art from far and wide'. Their purpose was to test the reactions of educated people not those of the world at large.

At one of the last rehearsals Bülow, as always on the edge of a nervous breakdown, blurted out a remark which did him and Wagner a lot of harm. He wanted to enlarge the orchestral area and, on being told that this would mean sacrificing about thirty seats in the stalls, said it was of no consequence if there were thirty *Schweinhunde* more or less in the theatre. The Munich newspapers leapt gleefully on this unfortunate remark.

On 15 May, 'Tristan Day', the king and Wagner exchanged ecstatic letters, Ludwig addressing him as 'My one and all – embodiment of my bliss'. He could scarcely wait for the torch to be extinguished, for the day to yield to the night. Then followed a series of misfortunes: Pusinelli informed Wagner that Minna was dying (this was not yet the case); the bailiffs came to his house and demanded 2400 florins in settlement of a bill which he had given a Madame Schabe in Paris five years earlier (she had, at the instance of Malvida von Meysenbug, contributed 3000 francs to the expenses of his Paris concerts); lastly, Malvina Schnorr had suddenly become hoarse and could not sing Isolde.

The première of *Tristan und Isolde* was put off until 10 June. The intervening days were filled up with hours of music-making in the Briennerstrasse; Wagner was anxious to entertain his friends who had hurried to Munich from London, Paris, Vienna and Königsberg, and to persuade them to stay on for the post-poned première. He was bitter about certain absences; Liszt was detained by the Princess in Rome and his most important Zurich friends, the Wesendonks and the Willes, stayed at home on this, 'the most glorious climax' of his life. He had the effrontery to ask Otto Wesendonk, who had bought the rights of the *Ring*, written and unwritten, to return the original score of *Das Rheingold* as he wished to present it to his glorious new benefactor. Otto complied and received from Ludwig a handsome letter of thanks. François Wille visited Wagner a year later at Tribschen with the object of persuading him to use his influence with Ludwig to keep Bavaria neutral in the conflict between Austria and Prussia. There is a delightful photograph, taken in Munich during those days between 15 May and 10 June 1865, of Wagner sitting in the foreground with his dog Pohl and grouped around him his friends and colleagues.

The long-awaited first night arrived. The Hoftheater was packed. The king, simply dressed, sat alone in the royal box with its heavy gilt decorations. Elsewhere in the house sat his grandfather Ludwig for whom Klenze had built this theatre with its Pompeian ceiling and Schwanthaler figures. The romantic beauty of the young king, who was not quite twenty, on that evening (the performance started at six) as he took his place in the box to the sound of fanfares and 'vivats', left the audience breathless. He appeared not to notice his cheering subjects; he looked towards the stage in a state of mystic exultation. His dark blue eyes shone with a gentle lustre and his person glowed with the purest enthusiasm as he waited for Bülow to raise his baton and lead him into the enchanted world of the sublimest musico-theatrical achievement of the nineteenth century. For certain members of the audience that evening it remained the greatest dramatic and artistic experience of their lives. Schnorr von Carolsfeld, who was to die of typhus a few weeks later, sang the title part as it has never, perhaps, been sung since. The total conviction of his acting, his fine head and flowing curly brown hair compensated for the portliness of his build. He proved that *Tristan* was singable and actable.

How many people realized that evening that the event they had just witnessed represented, in the words of Richard Strauss, the culmination of a thousand years of theatrical history, the end of diatonic supremacy and the beginnings of modern music? What could all those courtiers, politicians and aristocrats have thought of that tortured, elusive, 'unmelodic' music? When it was over Wagner, looking very small and wearing a black coat and white trousers, faced the cheering audience between his Tristan and Isolde. He was pale and feverish; after bowing grimly to the public he turned to the Schnorrs, husband and wife, and took each warmly by the hand. Anyone, he said, could write the last act of *Tristan* but only the marvellous Schnorrs could interpret it. As was to be expected the reviews spoke of the 'disharmony' and 'impudence' of the piece. The critic Eduard Schelle wrote, 'The poem is in every possible respect an absurdity and the music, apart from a couple of passages, the refined concoction of an effete, morbid imagination.'

On the other hand, some of the reviews in the Munich newspapers were surprisingly favourable. The *Münchener Neueste Nachrichten* wrote: 'We do not hesitate to affirm that this is a splendid, strange and original work, revealing a deep seriousness, a noble striving, a wonderful energy and a remarkable power of construction. The poet-composer is on the wrong track in his quest for the truth but the search is praiseworthy in itself. It is our duty to exclaim with Dante: we must damn but also deplore and admire.'

Ludwig's soul was too full of ecstasy to remain a minute longer in Munich; a special train took him back to Berg. He penned a couple of lines to Wagner: 'Only, divine one! What bliss! . . . total. In throes of total rapture! *Ertrinken . . . versinken . . . unbewusst – höchste Lust.* Yours forever, beyond the grave.' Wagner, not to be outdone, replied, 'My greatest, my only joy – my king! My friend! who completes me! My triumphant Siegfried! – My holy Parsifal! My victor! My bringer of peace! Oh, my king! It belongs to you; it is your work. It is nothing more to do with me. It was born in pain; no mother ever suffered so much for her child. . . .'

The successful performance of *Tristan und Isolde* was a perfect example of the creative collaboration of king and artist. Three more performances took place; Anton Bruckner came to the third; from that time onwards he was Wagner's disciple. Ludwig felt the stirrings of the Wittelsbach building mania and he wanted to start building the theatre for Wagner's uncompleted *Der Ring des Nibelungen*. A few months earlier he had written to Wagner, 'I have decided to have built a large stone theatre so that the production of the *Ring* may be a perfect one.' Thus encouraged Wagner sent for his old friend Semper from Zurich and introduced him to Ludwig who asked him to design a theatre. The theatre was never built. Semper was scandalously treated by the king, Wagner and, above all, by the king's ministers. During the next four years he came repeatedly to Munich, made plans and models of the proposed theatre, was encouraged, discouraged, lied to – until, at the beginning of 1869, the exasperated Semper took legal action against the Bavarian government. Thus Munich never had its five million florin monumental theatre on the heights above the river Isar which was to have been approached by a processional way over a new bridge. Wagner had to wait a few more years before he had his amphitheatre, sunken orchestra and receding prosceniums.

Another scheme which never saw fulfilment was Wagner's proposed Music School which he outlined in an interesting fifty-page document for the king shortly before the *Tristan* performances. Unlike the French and the Italians the Germans were lacking, said Wagner, in a traditional style suited to presenting the works of their great masters. A typical German style must therefore be developed and this style must be based on *song,* in the broadest sense, which would include acting and physical training. The new school would, by demonstrating how the works of the German masters of the past should be correctly presented, establish a style suited to the needs of contemporary theatre. The scheme was, in short, to train Wagnerian singers to sing Wagnerian music-dramas in the new Wagnerian theatre.

Ludwig's ministers saw to it that these great projects were never realized. The king had no private fortune which meant that his schemes had to be financed out of the Civil List. It had been, for some time, the custom in Bavaria for any surplus funds from the Civil List to be distributed amongst Cabinet officials. This could well have been an unspoken reason for the successful thwarting of several artistic plans of Ludwig and Wagner. Because of this Cabinet obstruction Wagner found himself being drawn against his will into Bavarian politics. The ministers had shown that they were able to block every important initiative taken by Wagner even when it had Ludwig's unqualified support. He had no alternative but to try to persuade Ludwig to replace his present ministers by more amenable ones. His belief that destiny had also entrusted Ludwig's political education to him was encouraged by a Frau Dangl, an old woman who came to him one evening and asked whether he believed in the stars. He, Wagner, was expected to guide and protect the king from whom great things were expected. With these new responsibilities in mind Wagner started a 'Journal' for the political education of the King, later published under the title *Was ist deutsch?* Ludwig had copies of it made for all his ministers. Although of less practical use to Ludwig than Machiavelli's cynical advice to princes these 'thoughts' of Wagner on the nature of kingship and the current ills of Germany may well have encouraged Ludwig's romantic and autocratic tendencies. In 1865, as in 1848, Wagner saw the king as the enlightened leader of his people, setting a shining personal example on the road to regeneration. The princes, said Wagner, have let Jews, Junkers and Frenchmen come between themselves and their subjects. The German spirit is seen at its best in the works of Bach where the 'beautiful and noble' seeks no advantage for itself. Examples of the pernicious are the Paris 'spectacular' operas and the 'French-Jewish-German democracy', which is alien to Germany and destructive of what is noble.

The king, longing to know still more about Wagner, his life and thoughts, wrote saying, 'It would give me unspeakable joy were you to let me have a detailed account of the song of your spirit (*Geistesgesang*) and of the external events of your life.' Wagner started to dictate to Cosima his thousand-page auto-biography. By now she was behaving as the mistress of 21 Brien-nerstrasse, running the household, dealing with his correspon-dence and deciding who should be admitted to his presence. She had placed herself totally at his service. She and the king, between them, did not do his character much good. He was for them the Master, the greatest genius of all time. She wrote out in her own hand, for Ludwig, copies of all Wagner's writings during his first Paris, Zurich and Dresden periods. She also gave Ludwig a cushion on which she had embroidered symbols from Wagner's operas – the Dutchman's ship, Tannhäuser's staff, Lohengrin's swan, Siegfried's sword, etc. Wagner's friends noticed with disapproval the deleterious effects of Cosima's influence. She encouraged him to make sweeping, unpleasant judgments on his former friends; his manners deteriorated; his irresponsible *bonhomie* was stifled by this new Priestess of the Grail; she gave him bad advice in the exceedingly difficult position in which he found himself, his enemies waiting to pounce upon his smallest indiscretion.

The events leading to Wagner's fall came in quick succession. In October 1845 Ludwig agreed to let Wagner have 40,000 florins as part of a new contract of employment. Pfistermeister disapproved strongly and even the king had reservations about giving him a lump sum which he would certainly dissipate. When Wagner was informed that the 40,000 florins were at his disposal Cosima went, accompanied by her eldest daughter and a governess, to collect the money from the Treasury. Instead of giving her the money in notes the churlish officials pointed at a pile of sacks containing small silver coins. They had reckoned without her sang-froid and aristocratic deportment instilled into her by her Russian governesses. She sent the governess to find two cabs and herself loaded the sacks into them. 'I depended,' she wrote to Ludwig when describing this incident, 'on a certain sense of honour which never allows a lady to be made a public spectacle.'

The story of the sacks of silver, despite Cosima acquitting herself with such aplomb, spread quickly around Munich. Wagner was now referred to contemptuously as 'Lolus' or 'Lolotte' and in Munich society there was increasing interest about the exact nature of his relations with Cosima. The king's loyalty to him, however, could not be shaken. His enemies then enlisted the help of old Ludwig I, now eighty years old; he wrote his grandson a letter, full of 'coarse rebukes', advising him to drop Wagner. Ludwig's reaction was to invite Wagner to Hohenschwangau where they passed a delirious week together. Military musicians were brought from Munich and posted on the turrets of the castle; they answered each other across the depths with notes from *Lohengrin*. Both had to communicate their ecstasy to paper, Wagner to his 'Brown Book' and Ludwig to Cosima. They greeted each other in prose or verse several times a day. 'I now,' wrote Wagner, 'realize the great profundity and beauty of Parsifal's love for me ... he is myself, in a younger, lovelier re-birth: altogether me, and only so much of himself as to be beautiful and powerful.' Ludwig wrote to Cosima,

It is impossible for me to bear this bliss alone. I must pour it out to a heart that knows and understands me. . . . Oh, he is divine, divine! My mission is to live, fight and suffer for him when he needs it for his salvation. How happy I am that the Beloved One has found pleasure in this rock-bound castle and its surroundings! It was here that I wandered joyfully as a boy through woods and meadows, always with his picture in my heart and mind. On the smooth surface of the Alp See I read the *Ring*. And now to have the One I longed for with me, to be able to spend the day with him – what unmerited happiness for me! Now the profane world must open its eyes and understand our relationship in spite of all scandalous intrigues.

These effusions make it clear how dangerous for Ludwig would be the sudden removal of this object of his adoration. During the coming years, of more or less permanent separation from 'the Friend', Ludwig invoked his name and his works to help him fight the lower impulses of his nature. In 1886, several months before his death, he wrote in his diary, 'Three years since the death of Richard Wagner: swore by his imperishable name and before the image of the Great King, never again (sensual kisses).'

When they returned to Munich trouble awaited them. Wagner's enemies had been laying snares, hoping to elicit from him some indiscretion. On 26 November the *Volkbote* (People's Messenger) published a story which accused Wagner of intriguing for the dismissal of two members of the Cabinet secretariat, Pfistermeister and Hofmann, referred to by Wagner and Ludwig as 'Mime' and 'Fafner', in order to appropriate to himself their salaries. Egged on by Cosima he fell into the trap and wrote a furiously angry, indiscreet 'anonymous' article for the *Neueste Nachrichten* (Latest News) in which he attacked members of the Cabinet secretariat, thereby exposing himself to the charges of interfering in Bavarian politics. Von der Pfordten had his chance at last; he wrote Ludwig a bold letter:

Your Majesty must choose between the love and respect of your faithful people and the friendship of Richard Wagner. This man who has the impudence to assert that members of the Cabinet, whose fidelity has been proven, do not enjoy the slightest respect amongst the Bavarian people, is himself despised by every section of the community where the throne can and must find its support – despised not only for his democratic leanings, which the democrats themselves do not take seriously, but for his ingratitude and treachery towards friends and benefactors, his overweening and debauched luxury and extravagance and the shamelessness with which he exploits the undeserved favour of your Majesty. This is the view not only of the nobility and clergy but also of the respectable middle classes and of the workers who painfully earn their daily bread by the sweat of their brow whilst arrogant strangers revel in royal generosity and, by way of thanks, vilify and ridicule the Bavarian people.

Von der Pfordten was backed by all his fellow ministers, the Queen Mother, Prince Karl, the King's great uncle, the Archbishop of Munich and many members of the nobility. The Cabinet, after a hurriedly convened meeting, threatened to resign; there was talk of a possible revolution in Bavaria. Ludwig, not wishing to share his grandfather's fate, gave way and Lutz, the second Cabinet Secretary, was asked to request Wagner to leave Bavaria.

Wagner's special mental mechanism helped him through the crisis; during those stormy days, instead of neurotically pacing his silk-lined study, he was calmly immersed in scoring *Siegfried* Act II and confident of his unshakable position with the king.

At 5 in the morning on 10 December 1865 Wagner left Munich. He looked grey and broken; his features were pale and distraught as he climbed into the train with his servant Franz and his dog Pohl. Cosima, Cornelius and Porges were at the station to see him off. Ludwig wrote to him before he left: 'Beloved, ardently loved friend! Words cannot describe the pain which is ravaging my soul . . . write to us often and at length, we beseech you . . . never misjudge me, never for a second; for me that would mean the tortures of Hell. Heil! to the beloved Friend! May his creations prosper. . . .'

The enforced separation of these two friends did not do Wagner any serious harm; for Ludwig it was the premature and permanent crushing of his spirit.

CHAPTER TEN
Tribschen and Cosima
1866–70

WAGNER WAS DETERMINED never to return to Munich unless it were to mete out punishment to the hated 'Pfi' and 'Pfo', his nicknames for Pfistermeister and Pfordten. He now detested the place, overrun he decided, by Jesuits and Jews. His thoughts turned to Nuremberg as an appropriate site for the special Wagnerian festival theatre. At the beginning of 1866 he was absorbed in *Die Meistersinger* which he had abandoned two years before in Penzing; he again took up the compositional sketch at the point in Act 1 where Beckmesser, having smothered the board with chalk marks, stuck his head out of the box, asking Walther, 'Seid ihr nun fertig?' (Have you finished?).

After leaving Cosima and his friends on the Munich railway platform that grim December morning Wagner had gone first to Vevey and then on to Geneva where he took a country house outside the town – Les Artichauts; its condition was dilapidated but the view across the country of Mont Blanc, which he saw from the piano, was wonderful. He no doubt remembered the last time when he was in that part of the world – as a patient in Dr Vaillant's water clinic at Mornex near Mont Blanc. A fire in one of the rooms in Les Artichauts led him to continue his search for a suitable residence in the south of France; he had in mind somewhere between Avignon and the Pyrenees. He travelled to Lyons, Toulon, Hyeres and Marseilles. In Marseilles he received a telegram from Pusinelli in Dresden, 'Ton épouse morte la nuit passée sans maladie précédente, ni agonie. Que faire?' The telegram had reached him after considerable delay and it was impossible for him to go to the funeral. He wrote to Pusinelli that the

215

news had induced in him a complete stupor, 'in which I sit brooding apathetically, not knowing what to do next. I assume that you have made the same sort of provision for my poor wife's remains and caused the same honour to be shown to her in my name as I would have done had she passed away happily at my side.'

Wagner's reaction to the news of Minna's death was sincere and unaffected, although she had never understood or appreciated his work. Indeed she had recently told a friend that Wagner was played out as a composer; his work had become a trickle of tortured compositions, unlike Meyerbeer who had left chests of manuscripts behind him.

Back at Les Artichauts Wagner finished scoring Act I of *Die Meistersinger*. Cosima and her daughter Daniela joined him on 8 March. At the end of the month she returned to Munich, Wagner accompanying her as far as Romanshorn on Lake Constance. As they travelled along Lake Lucerne they saw a charming little house raised up on a promontory above the lake. It was called Tribschen. After putting Cosima on the steamer at Romanshorn Wagner returned to Lucerne to take a closer look at Tribschen. Although it was in a state of disrepair he decided, there and then, to take it from the owner, a Colonel Am Rheyn. The king sent 5000 francs as a year's rent in advance. Wagner moved into Tribschen on 15 April. Here he was to spend the next six, very happy, years of his life during which he finished *Die Meistersinger* and *Siegfried*, composed *Götterdämmerung* and the *Siegfried Idyll* wrote books on Beethoven, conducting and the destiny of opera. It was here that Cosima became his wife after bearing him two more children – Eva (who later married the writer and 'philosopher' Houston Stewart Chamberlain) and his son Siegfried.

Tribschen is today a Wagner museum; anyone who has seen this charming little house, looking oddly high for its size, and the incomparable view over the Vierwaldstättersee, will nod with approval at Wagner's enthusiastic description to Cosima of the boats on the smooth, still surface of the lake, each encircled with a silver glow ... of the cows in the surrounding meadows, the lazy jingle of their bells linking day and night. 'I would give all the bells of Rome to hear this.' Ludwig accepted Wagner's decision to rent Tribschen with good grace although he would rather have installed him in one of his hunting lodges. He was obliged, reluctantly, to turn his attention to political matters although his thoughts were with Wagner. At the end of April Ludwig sent him an urgent telegram: 'This evening inspired and transported by God-sent tones from *Tristan* and *Rheingold*. Burning desire for news of the Only One, the fount of all rapture . . . united with the longed-for one is to live in a world of bliss. Without him hideous torture. . . .' Wagner sent the 'sublime protector of my life' one of his immensely long letters giving him the benefit of his ideas on the present political situation which was developing fast. Bismarck's stealthy and ruthless plan to create a new German empire under a Hohenzollern emperor was the basis of his strategy at this time. His first move was to be, in June 1866, the provocation of a war between Austria and Prussia. Bavaria would hardly be able to avoid becoming enmeshed in such a situation.

What should be the policy of Bavaria towards the Prussian bully from the north? Instinctively the feelings of Ludwig, his ministers and his people were with Austria. The reasons for this sympathy are obvious – cultural, religious, geographical and dynastic. Ludwig disliked Prussia; he could not forgive his mother for being a Hohenzollern princess. What was the attitude of the Friend and Only One to this menacing colossus from the north? Wagner had had in his Dresden days high hopes that King Friedrich Wilhelm IV of Prussia might have honoured his early operas with his patronage but he did nothing of the kind. The Jews, Meyerbeer and Mendelssohn, had insinuated their way into important musical positions and, of all the German cities, Berlin and Leipzig were unwaveringly hostile to Wagner's music. Furthermore, Wagner had no use for German political nationalism especially if it emanated from Prussia. In his letter to Ludwig of 29 April 1866 he warned him that Bismarck was an arrogant Junker cynically deceiving his weak-minded king and causing him to play a dishonourable game. He forsaw the collapse of

. . . my Germany – what then is the use of my life, my works, my labours? to what end the divine love of my sublime redeemer who has saved me and my words for the world? The ideals of my art stand or fall, my works live or die with Germany. The downfall of the German princes will mean the Jewish-Germanic masses getting the upper hand. . . . I must witness [these horrors] in silence since how can a mere 'composer of operas' understand politics!? However, my celestial Friend, himself the most endowed of all the princes, has been placed by the genius of Germany, as if deliberately for its own salvation, at the head of the only well preserved dynastic German state. . . .

Two months later Wagner had changed his mind about Bismarck who became for him, just before the Austrian defeat at König-gratz and the Bavarian defeat at Kissingen, Germany's only hope.

Wagner's impractical advice, as the German political crisis deepened, could not have been of much help to the bemused young king. In the middle of May, just after Cosima had arrived at Tribschen with her three daughters, Daniela, Blandine and Isolde, and Wagner was starting to compose *Die Meistersinger* Act II, Ludwig sent a telegram saying that he was thinking of abdicating, 'if it is the wish and will of the Dear One'. Wagner answered counselling patience for another six months. Ludwig's abdication threats became more frequent as time went on and Wagner showed considerable psychological skill in dissuading him from taking such a step. He was convinced that Ludwig had the makings of a great ruler; Bismarck himself respected his political judgment. The trouble was, according to Wagner, that his deplorable upbringing had turned him against everything associated with matters of state and against all classes of persons who belonged in some way to the constitutional and social order: the royal family, the aristocracy, the court, the army, the priests, the mob, the government all filled him with nausea. 'There is only one way', Wagner told the Prussian politician and publicist, Constantin Frantz, who came to have the same sort of influence on his political, as had Schopenhauer on his philosophical, ideas, 'to turn this contempt into a sympathetic interest and that is through me, my work and my art, which are for him the only real world, everything else being ludicrous nonsense.' Wagner might have been equal to this extraordinarily difficult task if he had seen Ludwig, like a psychiatrist his patient, several times a week; as it was he did what he could through his letters in which he played, with great skill, on the king's ideas and emotions, and tried to keep before his eyes the noble nature of his royal calling and to emphasize that only as a king, conscientiously carrying out his functions, would he be able to help the Wagnerian ideal.

When war between Prussia and Austria was almost certain and the Bavarian government had ordered the mobilization of the army Ludwig decided to escape to Tribschen. He sent his young aide-de-camp, Prince Paul von Thurn und Taxis, in advance and, on the morning of 22 May, Wagner's fifty-third birthday, after giving assistant cabinet secretary Lutz an audience and sending Wagner a birthday telegram, he galloped from Berg to Biessenhofen, took the express to Lindau and crossed the Bodensee by steamer to Rorschach. At Tribschen he announced himself as 'Walter von Stolzing'. Wagner was astonished to see him. He gave him the sensible advice to open the Bavarian parliament in person when he got back. Ludwig's flying visit to the Dear One, at this grave hour in Bavaria's history, shocked all Munich. His reception in parliament was 'ice-cold' and the press was 'scandalous', he reported to Cosima whom the newspapers had named the 'carrier-pigeon', because of her journeys to and from Wagner's residences. Ludwig was not abashed by his sullen reception; 'inspired and strengthened by those ecstatic days' he proposed to review the troops and attend the Corpus Christi procession.

As the political situation worsened Wagner hurriedly drew up a 'Political Programme' which reflected the views of his new hero, Constantin Frantz: Bavaria, under the leadership of his celestial Friend, must save Germany; Prussia and Austria had, by taking up arms against each other, forfeited their right to remain members of the German Federation. The King of Bavaria, as head of the oldest German state, should convene a congress, at Bamberg or Nuremberg, of all the other German princes. He would be the leader of this third force which, based upon a strong army, would hold the balance between Prussia and Austria and dictate to the two renegade states the terms upon which they might rejoin the Federation. This document shows, at least, that Wagner was not a strong upholder of Bavarian particularism; his mystic belief in the German *Volk* and *Reich* was too great for that. He was, when not diverted by other matters, in the midst of weaving music around his 'Meistersinger' poem, that apotheosis of German virtues.

Ludwig had neither the resolution nor the political interest to carry out the part which Wagner had assigned to him. In any case events were moving too fast. War between Prussia and Austria broke out on 14 June; a few days before that François Wille, as Bismarck's unofficial envoy, called on Wagner at

Tribschen and asked him to use his influence with Ludwig to prevent Bavaria siding with Austria in the coming war. Wagner's reply was, 'I have yet to decide what is in Germany's best interest and that will only be after we are rid of Bismarck and other rotten imitations of the unGerman spirit. I shall not, in any circumstances, advise the j.K.v.B. [young King of Bavaria] to follow the policy you recommend.'

Pfordten and his colleagues had let Bavaria drift into the Austrian camp. Wagner suddenly changed his mind. 'God has settled the fate of the German Federation,' he wrote to August Röckel, '. . . if you wish to carry on in politics stick firm to Bismarck and Prussia. God knows there's nothing else.' 'A Bavarian', remarked Bismarck, 'is halfway between an Austrian and a human being.' Ludwig, having handed over the command of his troops at Bamberg to his great-uncle Karl, retired with Paul von Thurn und Taxis to the Roseninsel (island of roses) on the Starnbergsee where they went for night rides, played games and let off fireworks. After the Bavarian defeat at Kissingen on 10 July Bismarck treated the humiliated country with statesmanlike magnanimity by asking for only a few Franconian villages and an indemnity of thirty million florins. When peace had been declared Ludwig, oddly enough, made a triumphal tour of his kingdom and was everywhere acclaimed with patriotic rapture. The Bavarians resembled the Austrians in being as proud of their defeats as of their victories.

One result of this war was the resignation of Wagner's two *bête noires* – 'Pfi' and 'Pfo' – Pfistermeister and Pfordten; the latter was succeeded, as chief minister, by Prince Hohenlohe-Schillings-fürst who did not take Wagner as seriously as had the stick-in-the-mud 'Pfo' and would not have objected to his taking up quarters once again in 21 Briennerstrasse. Wagner's ideas had now changed. He was determined never again to live in Munich, no matter how many 'Wagner-Theatres and Wagner-Strassen' they named after him. There were several reasons for this change of heart. 'Pfi' and 'Pfo' had now met their deserts; these 'diplomatic lackeys' had, in his view, been replaced by 'honest men'. His presence was no longer needed in that quarter. His feelings of self-importance, assiduously inflated by the king and Cosima, were enraged by the lampoons about him in the newspapers which his presence in Munich encouraged. In the quietness and beauty of Tribschen he could write and compose in peace; during the few months that he had been there he had finished the orchestral sketch of *Die Meistersinger* Act II, had started that of Act III and had written the words and the music of Walther's *Preislied* (prize song). What is more he could keep Ludwig at a safe distance; brilliantly as he managed to sustain it, this exalted friendship was exhausting. The king was not all that clever or educated and Wagner must, at times, have found his company annihilatingly boring; the king's letters consisted largely of 'sacred' ejaculations taken from Wagner texts and he did not have the humour and sophistication of Wagner on his better days. Furthermore, Wagner had quietly decided that Munich was not to be the place for his festival theatre and school of song; his experiences there had been too frightful to bear any repetition. In July 1866 he was urging the king to transfer his residence to Bayreuth and the government to Nuremberg – far from the loutish Munich rabble worked upon by treacherous priests. 'In Nuremberg, the town of the Meistersinger, my king will breathe the pure Franconian air, the same Franconia where my "Walther" lives and Hans "Sach", the Saxon [i.e. Wagner] will there crown his "Walther" [i.e. Ludwig] in Nuremberg.' Five months earlier Wagner confided to Bülow that he hoped the king would give him a wing of the Residenz in Bayreuth; at that time he was dictating to Cosima the passage in his autobiography where he describes his pleasant impressions upon seeing Bayreuth, on his way from Prague to Nuremberg in July 1835, 'lovingly bathed in the evening sunshine'. At that time he witnessed, in Nuremberg, a street brawl which became his model for *Die Meistersinger* Act II, *Prügelszene* (beating-up scene).

Wagner's proposal that the king move with his government to Franconia was an astute psychological red herring, designed to turn his thoughts away from abdication. Cosima had received from him a heart-breaking letter. Ludwig feared that Bavaria would, after his defeat, be a vassal state under Prussia and he a phantom king – that he was on his way to becoming one was not really Bismarck's fault. 'I am driven to tell you that it is utterly impossible for me to live any longer separated from him who is everything to me . . . so long as I am king I cannot be united with him . . . prepare the beloved one for my resolution to lay down the crown. . . . I cannot any longer endure these torments of hell . . . my place is with him; destiny calls me to his side. . . .

As Wagner had made up his mind not to live in Munich it was all the more necessary for Bülow to be there. Munich's main usefulness was that it provided opportunities for the production of his new works and of 'model' performances, under Bülow, of his old ones. The authority and status of the unpopular Bülow – he was suspected by many of being a Prussian spy – had to be defined and safeguarded.

The first thing was to get Bülow back to Munich. In June 1866 he had resigned as *Vorspieler* to the king, the entertaining press campaign against the 'compliant Herr Hans de Bülow and Madame Hans, better known as the "carrier pigeon",' having driven him quite demented. The *Volksbote* reminded its readers of Cosima's visit to the treasury to collect 40,000 florins. 'What are 40,000 florins? Madame Hans should now be hailing more cabs; Richard Wagner is being sued for another 26,000 florins. Where is the "carrier pigeon" now? She is with her "friend" (or what?) in Lucerne.' The humorous magazine *Punsch* published a 'Programme for a Grand Future – Musical Procession', the 'tableaux' to include 'a herd of *Schweinhunde* driven in pairs by Dr Hans von Bülow, twenty holders of bills of exchange with lighted candles and the staff of the Royal Treasury, followed immediately by St Cosima holding the master-key'.

The three conspirators (as indeed they were) drafted a statement for Ludwig to sign; it read as a full vindication of the 'besmirched' honour of Wagner, Cosima and Bülow. Although Ludwig signed it he began to feel uneasy that some deception was being practised on him and that he might have been compromised by this declaration which no one in Munich took seriously. 'I cannot and will not believe that there is any truth in this unhappy rumour. If Wagner's relations with Frau von Bülow exceed the bounds of friendship; if this is a case of adultery – then woe!' Wagner was in a difficult position; his inclination was to come out into the open about his relationship with Cosima. This might have led to an irreparable breach with the king and to the end of his artistic schemes. Bülow agreed about this and had, in addition, his own reasons for wishing to keep up appearances. His father-in-law, now the pious Abbé Liszt living in Rome, would disapprove and it would give sadistic satisfaction to his journalistic tantalizers in Munich. It was decided, then, to keep up the charade. Wagner and Cosima thus manoeuvred themselves into many tight corners out of which they had to lie their way brazenly. This came naturally to Cosima, the high priestess of Wagnerism, in whose cause all means were justified. With Wagner it was different; he once told August Röckel, 'The moment I dissimulate or lie my whole magic disappears; I know this instinctively – which is why I cannot.' He lied over and over again to Ludwig – probably unnecessarily – to cover up his liaison with this formidable woman.

The vulnerability of Wagner and Cosima, caused by their illicit association, is illustrated by the Malvina Schnorr episode. She was his Isolde on that great first night in June the previous year. She had adored her husband, eleven or twelve years younger than her; after his tragically early death she took to spiritualism and communed with him. During these 'conversations' he ascribed his death to the exhaustion of singing Tristan; she then saw it as her divine mission to help Wagner atone for Schnorr's death by uniting himself in some mystic way with her. When he repulsed her she turned her wrath on Cosima, his 'unclean spirit', whom she proceeded to denounce to Ludwig as an adulteress and Wagner's mistress. Wagner had, once again, to deny what he knew was true.

Bülow divided his time between Tribschen and Basel where he gave recitals and piano lessons. He was in Tribschen in February on the day that Cosima gave birth to Wagner's second daughter Eva. At her bedside he said, 'Je pardonne,' to which she replied, 'Il ne faut pas pardonner, il faut comprendre.' In April 1867 he was back in Munich as *Hofkapellmeister* 'extraordinary', director-designate of the projected musical academy and as holder of the Grand Cross of the Bavarian Order of St Michael! Ludwig was engaged to be married; he ordered the preparation of 'model' performances of *Lohengrin* and *Tannhäuser* for the coming summer. Semper was to proceed with the model of the festival theatre and *Die Meistersinger* was to be performed in October in time for the wedding festivities of himself and his cousin, the Duchess Sophie Charlotte of Bavaria. Wagner wrote in his 'Annals', on 21 January 1867, 'Parsifal betrothed', which a telegram from Ludwig confirmed the next day: 'Walther informs his dear Sachs that he has found his faithful Eva, Siegfried his Brünnhilde.' Although the king was beginning, to his pain, to notice the growing discrepancy between Wagner the man and Wagner the artist he had not yet started to dislike the former. He told his fiancée, to her surprise, that 'the God of my life is Richard Wagner'. To Cosima he wrote: 'My love for her [Sophie] is deep and loyal but the Friend will never cease to be dear to me beyond all others.' Ludwig, sensing perhaps that, with Wagner in Switzerland and the romantic bond between them nearly broken despite their passionate protestations, his marriage to Sophie was his last link with happiness and reality, ordered the event to be celebrated throughout his kingdom. There were balls, banquets and masquerades; medals were struck of Sophie and engravings distributed of the affianced pair; Lohengrin crossed the Starnbergsee in his boat, the *Tristan*, at all times of the day and night to visit his Elsa at her home in Possenhofen. The bridal carriage was built at the cost of one million florins. And then, on 11 October 1867, as suddenly as it was announced, Ludwig broke off the engagement 'by mutual consent'. Liszt, who had arrived in Munich a few days earlier, saw the royal pair at a performance of *Tannhäuser* and commented that 'Les ardeurs matrimoniales de sa Majesté semblent fort tempérées.' In the early days of the engagement Wagner met Sophie at her mother's house in circumstances of the strictest secrecy, the rest of her family strongly disapproving of him. Wagner complimented Ludwig on her beauty and her many other virtues, 'Oh, Parsifal! How I must love you, my trusted hero!' Later he congratulated him, with equal warmth, on his courage in extricating himself from this fatal commitment. Ludwig was very relieved at having averted the danger of matrimony. 'Had something occurred at Versailles where he first became intimate with Hornig?', one of his biographers has asked. Hornig, who was the other 'Richard' and the subject of compromising references in Ludwig's diaries, had a long reign as Ludwig's favourite – he made him Master of the Horse – and shared with him the lonely, lunatic grandeur of his new chalets, hunting lodges, castles and palaces in the Swan-country. He dismissed him in 1883, the year of Wagner's death.

Whether Ludwig's brusque termination of his engagement to the hapless Sophie (within a year she married the Duc d'Alençon, a grandson of Louis-Philippe) did or did not precipitate his later oddness or madness, is anyone's guess. As far as his relations with Wagner are concerned his behaviour during the next few years was admirable in its restraint and dignity. Their correspondence often shows Wagner in a deplorable light – importunate, disingenuous, self-pitying and unreasonable; the big lie about Cosima got steadily bigger, having the same corrupting effect on him as the possession of the 'ring' has on his beloved Siegfried. The years 1865–70 show Wagner at his least attractive; their saddest features are the trickery of the trusting Ludwig and the aggressive self-righteousness of Wagner himself.

After the birth of Eva in April 1867 Cosima and Bülow left Tribschen and returned to Munich. Bülow insisted that appearances be kept up. Wagner and Cosima were disconsolate at having to part. Wagner confided to his 'Brown Book' that he had never been so miserable. 'I yearn for a severe illness and death. I cannot, will not, go on. If only it would all end!' Ludwig wanted Wagner to celebrate his birthday, on 22 May, with him at Starnberg. Although he preferred to stay at Tribschen and work on *Die Meistersinger* Cosima warned him in a telegram that it would be unwise not to comply with the royal wish. To Munich therefore he went; the king had rented for him the Villa Prestele near Starnberg. No sooner had he moved in than the king went off to visit the Wartburg – no doubt to get some ideas for the forthcoming performance of *Tannhäuser*. Upon returning he burst in on Wagner late at night, his head not full only of *Tannhäuser* but also of *Lohengrin*. He was determined to have model performances of both, rehearsed by Bülow and supervised by Wagner. The *Lohengrin* rehearsal led to a serious disagreement: Wagner had chosen, for the title part, Joseph Tichatschek, his old Dresden comrade-in-arms, now sixty and no longer looking the part of the radiantly youthful knight of the Grail. Ludwig was appalled when he saw this travesty of his beloved Lohengrin and, without consulting Wagner, ordered him to be replaced forthwith. Wagner, very angry, left the Villa Prestele and returned to Tribschen. A few days later came a contrite letter from the king: 'I kiss the hand which slapped me.'

This episode indicates yet again the fundamental dissimilarities in the attitudes of the king and Wagner to the staging of his operas; for Ludwig the show was more important than the song. From now on Wagner thought more and more seriously about a theatre of his own although it was not until April 1871 that he paid his first visit to Bayreuth, that charming old margravian capital on the Red Main, which had been in his thoughts on and off for several years.

Wagner's visitors remarked on the comfort and happiness of life at Tribschen. His handsome stipend from the king and the growing demand for his works in Germany, France and Italy enabled him to indulge his seignorial propensities. The six-year lease did not deter him from spending lavishly; he rebuilt and refurnished the house with the inevitable assistance of Bertha Goldwag, the Penzing milliner. Nietzsche's sister, Elisabeth Förster-Nietzsche, thought the house had been furnished by some Parisian interior decorators who had been 'disagreeably lavish with the pink satin and cupids'. The irrepressible decorators were none other than Wagner and Bertha. Cosima may, with her more austere taste, have later toned down the boudoir atmosphere of silks and satins which did not altogether harmonize with the external simplicity of the house. On this tiny isthmus the dogs romped and the peacocks strutted amongst the tall poplars. There was an aviary with golden pheasants and other rare birds. Wagner laid out a park and kitchen garden, had eight servants and a horse and carriage. In this 'Isle of the Blessed', as Nietzsche called it, he devoted most of the second half of 1867 to working on *Die Meistersinger*; the score was finished at eight in the evening on 24 October. His creative serenity was disturbed, however, by the unhappy and complex Cosima situation, his pathological hatred of Munich and the exhausting and unpredictable course of his friendship with the king, now becoming, with the birth of the Bayreuth idea, the object of a double deception.

On 16 November 1868 Cosima took an irrevocable step, after her four-year 'secret' liaison with Wagner. She moved, with her daughters Isolde and Eva, into Tribschen and started to keep a diary whose recent publication has provided us with what is probably the last important source of information about the remaining fifteen years of Wagner's life. From now on Cosima took Wagner's destiny in hand, bringing stability into his work, pushing into the background his socialistic and revolutionary notions and encouraging nationalistic, xenophobic and anti-Semitic influences, although Jews like Tausig, Mottl, Porges and later Neumann and Levi continued to remain, to Cosima's mild displeasure, within his intimate circle of friends. On 25 August 1870 Wagner and Cosima were married in the Protestant church in Lucerne; the witnesses were Malvida von Meysenbug and his young assistant Hans Richter.

Wagner and Cosima looked an unusual pair as they took the air together on their little property or walked or drove to Lucerne on shopping expeditions. He wore a Flemish painter's costume – a black velvet coat, black satin knee-breeches, black silk stockings, a colourful satin cravat, a shirt heavily ornamented with lace and a velvet beret. Cosima wore long cashmere gowns, overhung with lace, and carried a wide hat trimmed with flowers.[1] Cosima's stern, motherly control did not suppress his occasional bouts of high spirits and naughtiness. When Judith Gautier and her husband, Catulle Mendes, visited him in July 1869 he entertained them with his pranks: he stood on his hands on the terrace, scrambled up trees and climbed up the walls of the house. Many years earlier, after he had fled from Leipzig to Zurich, he had one evening, when in a jovial, inebriated mood, gone round the house of his host taking all the doors off their hinges.

Ludwig had asked Wagner to let him have a detailed picture of his daily round at Tribschen. Wagner was very pleased to oblige and gave him, in February 1869, an agreeable description of life there:

The rule is: up early, wash in cold water, a simple breakfast, a glance at the newspaper which I only read more closely if it contains news about the King of Bavaria [for a long time the only means of obtaining news about the Noble One!] . . . at ten I settle down to the score [of *Siegfried*]; this gives me three really enjoyable and rewarding morning hours. At one o'clock Jacob (the husband of Vreneli) summons me to luncheon; I then leave my desk in the green study . . . take a simple meal at which my dogs are generally present; after that I take coffee in the drawing-room and another quick look at the papers, followed either by a short sleep or an interlude at the piano. At three I put on my large intimidating Wotan hat and embark on my regular walk accompanied by Russ and Koss – Falstaff with his pages! – which invariably, in all weathers, takes us to Lucerne. There I collect the post and browse in an antiquarian book store . . . at five I am back at Tribschen, rest for quarter of an hour, and then return to the score if there are not letters to be answered; after having worked until eight I take a light supper and tea in the small drawing-room on the first floor which is reserved for the friend during her summer visits [Cosima was,

[1] The writer possesses the bread-basket which she and Wagner sometimes took with them to Lucerne.

in fact, permanently residing there] and I end the evening reading, preferably Schiller, Goethe or Shakespeare – although occasionally Homer, Calderon or something unusual and scientific like Winckelmann. At eleven I go to bed; you may ask whether I have a good night's sleep? Alas, this is not always the case. . . .

The great event of the previous year was the première of *Die Meistersinger* which took place in Munich on 21 June 1868. Wagner had worked immensely hard rehearsing players and singers. His friends and enemies had come from all over Europe to be present on this occasion. At the final dress rehearsal in the presence of Ludwig and one hundred guests he made a short speech expressing his belief that this production of *Die Meistersinger* would lead to a rebirth of the German theatre. The première itself was one of the greatest triumphs in Wagner's career. During the prelude he was summoned to sit next to the king; after the second and third acts he acknowledged the applause, at the king's request, from the royal box itself – an unparalleled breach of etiquette. A local newspaper reported the universal astonishment caused by this mark of royal favour. The audience looked nervously up at the ceiling to see whether it would collapse in indignation. 'Wagner, the heretic and exile, whom, two years ago, not even the royal grace could protect from the vicious hatred of the upper and lower rabble of our artistic metropolis, has been rehabilitated in an indescribable fashion,' wrote one newspaper. Other newspapers reacted with vicious sarcasm to this mark of royal favour.

After the full dress rehearsal the king wrote to Wagner: 'I had indeed expected much but that it could be so sublime I did not even dare to dream. I was so thrilled, so transported to another world that I could not join in the profane hand-clapping signs of approval. This is for me an experience that nothing can erase, something permanent, inspiring and quickening for my whole life, only to be compared with that which I felt after *Tristan*. . . .' Wagner penned some hurried lines in return. 'I knew it! He understands me! It was impossible that he would not clearly perceive, beneath the popular humour that plays upon the surface, the deep melancholy, the lamentation, the anguished cry of imprisoned poetry whose irresistable magic power triumphs over baseness thus leading to regeneration and a new birth. . . .' For Hanslick, on the other hand, *Die Meistersinger* was an interesting musical disease. He bestowed especial praise on Franz Betz, who sang Sachs, because 'the untold trouble which he took was not worthwhile and the part is thankless. It consists of numerous monologues and dialogues which are unspeakably boring for the listeners'. The work, nevertheless, established itself in European repertoires with remarkable speed even though the subtle interplay of its bourgeois-democrat and nationalistic elements have not always, to the disadvantage of the former, been appreciated by directors.

An early enthusiastic admirer of *Die Meistersinger* was Friedrich Nietzsche, Wagner's junior by thirty-one years. They met in Leipzig at the Brockhaus's a few months after the *Meistersinger* première. It represented for Nietzsche that special 'German merriment' found in Luther, Beethoven and Wagner, not understood by other nations and not even by contemporary Germans – 'a bright, golden, glowing mixture of simplicity, the deep look of love, reflection and boisterousness, which Wagner has poured out as the most precious drink to those who have suffered in life but who return to it with the smile of the healed'. A few months later, on 22 May 1869, on Wagner's birthday, he thanked him for the 'best and highest moments' of his life which were tied to the name of Wagner. Now started that unreal and perplexing friendship which was to end, after a few years of intensity and excitement, in Nietzsche's disillusionment and madness.

Wagner's relations with Ludwig became cooler in 1869 and 1870. The king refused to receive him until his family affairs had been respectably settled. Bülow, who had in July 1869 agreed to a divorce, left Munich the following month for Florence after conducting at the Hoftheater a final performance of *Tristan und Isolde* with Vogl and his wife singing the title parts. Ludwig was deprived now of the society of Wagner and of Bülow, Wagner's ablest and loyalist collaborator. With the plans for a Nibelungentheater in abeyance, he was resolved, nevertheless, to see *Das Rheingold* and *Die Walküre*, the first two parts of the tetralogy, onto the stage. In August he ordered the rehearsals of *Das Rheingold* to begin. Wagner fumed from Tribschen that they should be taking place without his permission and without his presence. At his instigation Richter, the conductor, and Betz, who sang the part of Wotan, both withdrew after the general rehearsal on the ground of 'technical inadequacies'. Ludwig, who saw

Wagner's hand behind these machinations, was furious at this challenge to his authority and spoke about 'the abominable intrigues of Wagner and his theatre rabble'. 'J'en ai assez', he wrote to Pfistermeister. Richter was dismissed for impertinence and replaced by Franz Wüllner, a competent but inexperienced musician. Wagner, who had come to Munich to have Richter reinstated and to reassert his own authority over the rehearsals, now that he knew the king was set on a performance of *Das Rheingold*, returned in high dudgeon to Tribschen. There he drafted Wüllner a belligerent letter: 'Hands off my score! That's my advice to you; if not, you can go to Hell!' The première took place without Wagner on 22 September 1869.

The following year, on 26 June 1870, at Ludwig's insistence in the face of Wagner's opposition, a highly successful première of *Die Walküre* took place in Munich with Wüllner conducting. Wagner had written to the king a few days earlier: 'Once again I beseech you, have it produced for yourself alone, but do not let the public in.' Wagner's objections to these Munich performances were bound up with his reactions to the scurrilous campaign waged against him by the Munich newspapers, who had intensified their attacks after his 'presumption' in acknowledging applause from the royal box after the première of *Die Meistersinger* on 21 June 1868. Their baiting made him furiously, impotently angry; he could not deny their taunts about the adulterous 'Madame Hans' and the complaisant 'Monsieur de Bülow'. Wagner did not object, on principle, to individual performances of the *Ring* operas or to concert performances of extracts from them. In certain moods he spoke of them as desirable publicity for the cycle as a whole. It was rather the Cosima entanglement that had induced in him a pathological hatred of Munich which, in its turn, led his thoughts in the direction of a theatre of his own at Bayreuth.

CHAPTER ELEVEN

Bayreuth
1871–8

ON 19 JULY 1870 France declared war on Prussia. Wagner found himself, for once, caught up in the mood of the nation. Germany was no longer for him a geographical expression or a philosophical or poetic idea, to be carried about in the hearts of artists and dreamers, but the virile triumphant fatherland. Prussia under Bismarck was the natural leader destined to bring about the reunification of Germany. Cosima, most gratified, echoed these sentiments, so much more desirable than his earlier socialistic and international leanings. It is difficult to understand why she should have been so fiercely pro-German. Perhaps Bülow had something to do with it; for him there were only three great men in the nineteenth century: Napoleon, Bismarck and Wagner.

At the time of the Austro-Prussian War Wagner, influenced by his reading of Constantin Frantz, advocated that Bavaria take the lead in convening a meeting of the German princes and that Prussia and Austria be expelled from the Federation for breaking the rule that member states do not take up arms against each other. Two years later, in a letter to Ludwig, Wagner complained that Bavaria had failed, as arbitrator, to save the Federation. 'This was because the Bavarian prime minister [Hohenlohe-Schillingsfürst] was hand in glove with Prussia; the ignominious phoney war which he waged and the consequent enfeeblement and humiliation of Bavaria have demoralized the country. Everyone is now turning to Prussia if only to be associated with a strong government.' The only way now for Bavaria to preserve its independence was by an alliance with Prussia.

On 2 September 1870, eight days after the marriage of Wagner and Cosima, the French capitulated at Sedan. Wagner's excitement knew no bounds; egged on by Cosima he perpetrated one piece of chauvinism, musical and literary, after the other. A few years earlier in 1863 he was ridiculing the idea of a 'German Fatherland' in a poem of that name. Was it, he asked, Nibelheim (the home of the Nibelungs) or a place where the Jews gave themselves airs, where mediocrity and vulgarity thrive? Now, in November 1870, the month that Ludwig signed the document requesting the King of Prussia to accept the imperial crown, he wrote, during the siege of Paris, *A Capitulation: A Comedy in the Antique Manner*. In it he mocked the defeated French, the beleaguered Parisians and, less obviously, the Germans who capitulated to the trivialities of French operettas. He asked Richter, without revealing that he was the author, to turn it into a 'parody of an Offenbachian parody'. (It was turned down by a Berlin theatre and no more was heard of this little piece until Wagner published it in the first edition of his collected writings in 1873.) The following month, in the early hours of Christmas morning 1870, Cosima had her famous birthday surprise: fifteen musicians, carefully positioned on the staircase, with Wagner conducting, played her the *Siegfried Idyll*, that exquisite little symphonic birthday poem, celebrating her virtues as wife and mother.

At the beginning of 1871 Wagner's new patriotic fervour took over once more. He wrote 'An das deutsche Heer vor Paris' (To the German Army before Paris), five patriotic stanzas in the style of Beckmesser glorifying the Germans as a race of conquerors. In January the German Empire was proclaimed in the Hall of Mirrors at Versailles, Wilhelm 1 was crowned as Emperor and Wagner composed his *Kaisermarsch*. He had wanted to write, on the occasion of the return of the German troops to Berlin, either a 'Funeral symphony for the fallen' or a triumphal march for a military band and voices. Both suggestions were tartly rejected by the director of Prussian military music; he therefore wrote the *Kaisermarsch* for the concert hall – a stirring and delicate piece of music.

In March 1871 Wagner officially communicated to Ludwig his plan for a German national theatre at which his works would be performed under his sole direction. Although the old opera house in Bayreuth was the theatre which he had in mind he did not reveal this to the king. Ludwig's comment on this proposed national festival theatre, to his cabinet secretary Düfflipp, was, 'This plan of Wagner's displeases me very much.' Nevertheless, in his letters to Wagner he applauded the scheme, repeating approvingly the arguments which Wagner had himself put forward in support of it.

On 15 April 1871 Wagner and Cosima set out for Germany – an 'Empire' since the Versailles proclamation. Cosima had uneasy feelings about showing herself, for the first time to the world, as Wagner's wife. Siegfried was ill and her eyes hurt so much that she thought she might be going blind. There was nothing, however, to stop Wagner's new fanaticism about a festival theatre in Bayreuth. In Augsburg they met Düfflipp who told them that the king wished to stage the first two acts of *Siegfried* as he had been informed that the third act was not yet finished. Wagner had, in fact, completed the full orchestral score of *Siegfried* on 9 February. In 1857 he had stopped work on *Siegfried* after completing the composition of the first two acts and was only to resume it in September 1864, seven years later, after he had come to Munich and settled in the Briennerstrasse. Wagner told Düfflipp that he would rather burn his *Siegfried* and go begging than agree to the king's suggestion.

This brings us once again to the question: was Wagner deliberately deceiving the king? The answer is that he probably was; he had finished scoring *Siegfried* Act III at the beginning of the year. He had developed a pathological hatred of Munich and was determined never again to allow his new operas to be torn from him and staged in that city. Had Ludwig known that *Siegfried* was completed he would certainly have insisted, as the legal owner of the *Ring* scores, on its speedy production. Ever since he had read the public edition of the *Ring* poem in 1863 with Wagner's foreword, in which he asked rhetorically after the prince who would enable these operas to be fittingly staged, Ludwig had yearned to see them performed. They symbolized for him the ideal co-operation of prince and artist who would together bring about a revolution in the artistic life of the nation. It was for this reason that Ludwig brought Wagner to Munich in May 1864, paid his debts, set him up in the Briennerstrasse with a handsome salary, commissioned Gottfried Semper to design a festival theatre embodying Wagner's requirements for an amphitheatre form and an invisible orchestra. He had ordered the management of the royal court theatre to spare no expense and to comply fully with Wagner's wishes to ensure impeccable performances of *Tristan und Isolde* and *Die Meistersinger*. Wagner himself later said that these Munich performances should be taken by other theatres as their models, as they were the most perfect productions that his works had attained. And yet, Wagner, on 12 May 1871, in breach of his agreement with the Bavarian government and of his colossal moral obligations to Ludwig, publicly proclaimed from Leipzig the first Bayreuth festival for 1873.

For Ludwig Wagner's move meant the end of their partnership in the cause of German artistic regeneration. He continued to write affectionate letters and to take a polite interest in the new scheme, which he was later to save, but the joyous, trusting, passionate idealism had left their friendship. Ludwig now turned to building as a means of satisfying his thwarted theatrical impulses; after Lindehof, an elegant rococo folly, came Neuschwanstein in 1871, a Romanesque phantasmagoria springing out of the rock. He peopled this fortress, high up in the mountain, with scenes and figures from Wagner's operas, in this strange way keeping in touch with the old friend whom he was seldom to see again.

It appears that the principal, or only, reason for Wagner's sullen fury with Munich was the Cosima entanglement. The newspaper taunts about the whereabouts of 'Madame Hans de Bülow', their sustained mockery of his sybaritic tastes, the successful attempt to drive him out of Munich and the impossibility of Cosima later showing herself there whilst still married to Bülow, filled him with an inextinguishable hatred for the place. Ludwig hated Munich because he hated all cities where he was stared at by the populace. He had hoped that, by making it the centre of Wagnerian drama, his frequent and enforced periods there would become less painful. His patronage of Wagner, who always encouraged him to take seriously his constitutional duties, was the one stabilizing element in his life; as this friendship weakened his ties with artistic reality became more and more tenuous and, without a powerful and educated mind any longer to guide him, he drifted irretrievably into a world of hopeless, vulgar and morbid imaginings.

Wagner, on the other hand, was entering the last heroic phase of his life. For the sake of an ideal – the proper performances of his operas – he was prepared, as he approached the age of sixty, to leave his enchanting house at Tribschen, to jeopardize his allowance from the king and to wear himself out in the pursuit of his goal. His admirers watched, stupefied, as the impossible became possible in the hands of this formidably energetic little man.

After their meeting with Düfflipp in Augsburg Wagner and Cosima went on to Bayreuth. His presence in the little town, Cosima tells us, caused a great stir amongst the Bayreuth population. The Wagners looked at the rococo court theatre of the margraves of Bayreuth; Wagner found the stage too small and altogether unsuited to his purposes. He liked the town and the surrounding countryside, however, and he decided, then and there, to move to Bayreuth, build a festival theatre and prepare for the first festival with a performance of the *Ring*.

After brief visits to Leipzig and Dresden Wagner and Cosima arrived in Berlin. Cosima was full of forebodings; she feared Wagner might be assassinated by a Jew or doublecrossed by Jesuits. She was also shocked to hear Bismarck, Wagner's new hero, being discussed irreverently. He was said to possess, 'more luck than intelligence – no character'. One of Wagner's reasons for going to Berlin was to enlist both the support of the Kaiser and of Bismarck for Bayreuth. Ostensibly he went there to give an address on the 'Destiny of Opera' to the Academy of the Arts; the real purpose, however, was to confer with Karl Tausig and Marie von Schleinitz, Cosima's old friend, on how to organize support for Bayreuth. Tausig was appointed organizer of the festival enterprise; aged thirty, and looking desperately ill (he was shortly to die of typhus), he was planning a special Berlin Wagner-*Verein* (Wagner association) with its own orchestra which would introduce Berliners to the master's works. Wagner chose to forget the disappointments and mortifications which he had received in Berlin in the past; he now saw Berlin and Bayreuth as the twin centres of a politically and artistically regenerated Germany. This was doubtless the point of view which he put forward to Bismarck who invited him for the evening of 3 May. Bismarck was *en famille*; he received Wagner with great courtesy. Cosima noted in her diary the same day that Wagner had returned highly satisfied after this historic meeting. 'R. is absolutely delighted by his genuine, unforced kindness, no trace of reticence, a light voice, the most delightful communicativeness, emanating trust and sympathy. But, says R., we can only observe one another, each in his own sphere . . . to win his support for my cause – that I would not be able to do.' He wrote afterwards to Düfflipp, 'The expenses of my enterprise will have to be borne by private persons.' Thus originated the *Patronatscheine* (patrons' vouchers), upon which the financing of Bayreuth was originally based.

Before leaving Berlin Wagner conducted at a charity concert in the presence of the Kaiser and Empress Augusta. He began with the *Kaisermarsch* followed by Beethoven's Fifth Symphony, the *Lohengrin* prelude, Wotan's farewell and the fire music from *Die Walküre* and, in response to the applause, a repetition of the *Kaisermarsch*. The Kaiser declared that he had never before heard such perfect music.

Wagner chose to make the first public proclamation of the Bayreuth festivals from Leipzig, his birthplace, on 12 May. The first festival was earmarked for 1873; he had only just started writing the compositional sketch for *Götterdämmerung* Act II and the full orchestral score was not to be finished until November 1874. This timetable is a good example of his invigorating optimism. Two days earlier the Franco-Prussian War officially ended with the Treaty of Frankfurt; France ceded Alsace-Lorraine and paid reparations of five million francs. Wagner announced that benefactors and enthusiasts, who had raised money for Bayreuth, would 'receive the titles and privileges of patrons of the stage-festivals in Bayreuth, whereas the running of the enterprise is left entirely to my own knowledge and my own efforts'. A few days later, on 26 May, Ludwig wrote to him, 'Your plan to have the *Nibelungen* work performed in Bayreuth is divine (*Gottvoll*)!'

They were back in Tribschen on 16 May and Cosima confided to her diary, 'It is uniquely blissful to be in his world once more.' They were not destined to enjoy much longer their lakeside tranquillity; during the next twelve months Wagner achieved the prodigious feat of both writing the compositional sketches of *Götterdämmerung* Acts II and III and doing all the preparatory work for the first Bayreuth festival. His invaluable associate in helping him both realize the scheme and overcome hideous subsequent difficulties was the Bayreuth banker and president of the town council, Friedrich Feustel. After finishing the compositional sketch of *Götterdämmerung* Act II and sketching the *Siegfried* funeral music for Act III, Wagner wrote to Feustel, who was a friend of his sister Ottilie Brockhaus, formally acquainting him with his festival plans. He had chosen Bayreuth, he told him, as the site for his festival because it had no spa visitors, lacked a large theatre and was, above all, in Bavaria, the kingdom of his royal benefactor. He asked to be given a plot of land on a suitable spot for the erection of his theatre; he mentioned, at the same time, that he desired for himself a strip of meadow connecting the Schlossgarten (the palace garden) to the road which lead to the Eremitage, the eighteenth-century baroque country house outside the town built by Frederick the Great's sister, Wilhelmine. Here he would, and later indeed did, build a house for himself and his family. Since his liaison with Cosima Wagner had become a real *Familienvater* with two step-daughters, Daniela and Blandine, and his own three children, Isolde, Eva and Siegfried.

The Bayreuth town councillors responded to Wagner's proposal with remarkable enthusiasm; they were a superior, imaginative and generous group of men. After they had agreed to place a piece of land at his disposal Wagner went to Bayreuth, on 14 December, to inspect the site 'for the construction of his national theatre', as it was described in the resolution of the town council. From Bayreuth he went on to Mannheim where he conducted a concert of works by himself, Mozart and Beethoven in aid of the newly-founded Mannheim Richard Wagner-*Verein*. As he arrived at the station all the members of the *Verein* greeted him with a resounding *Hoch*. The death of Tausig in July had been a grievous blow to the Bayreuth scheme; this prodigious young Jewish pianist, thought by some to have died through overtaxing his musical memory, who took no exception to Wagner's anti-Semitism but who had thrown himself wholeheartedly into the Wagnerian cause, had been largely responsible for organizing the *Patronat-Verein*. Wagner had estimated the cost of the theatre and of the performances at 300,000 thalers and it was decided to issue 1000 *Patronatscheine*, each costing 300 thalers; the performances were to take place in the completed theatre for two months in the summer of 1873. He compared the death of Tausig with that of Schnorr von Carolsfeld; a malevolent fate took from him those devoted helpers and interpreters of his art at the moment that he most needed them. A new helper now providentially appeared –

Emil Heckel, a Mannheim music dealer and founder of the Wagner-*Vereine* which still flourish in Germany today.[1] These *Vereine* consisted of members who could not individually afford 300 thalers for a *Patronatscheine*; instead, they clubbed together to buy one or more.

Wagner was in Mannheim, with Cosima and Nietzsche, to celebrate the founding of the first of the new Wagner-*Vereine* which he was later to regard with mixed feelings. He found himself, before long, being expected to give concerts for these proliferating *Vereine*. This was a waste of time and detrimental to his health. Later, when it turned out that the revenue they brought in was quite inadequate to cover the larger deficit after the 1876 festival, he cursed them and pressed for their liquidation saying that their only usefulness was to enable people to see his operas without paying. On the other hand he was gratified on finding the drawing-room ceiling at Wahnfried covered with the coats-of-arms of all those German towns which had Wagner-*Vereine* – a surprise birthday present from Cosima. In these inspiring days Wagner told Heckel that he entertained the highest expectations of the German national spirit with which he was again to become bitterly disenchanted. In those days Wagner's relations with Nietzsche were at their most cordial. After hearing the *Siegfried Idyll* played by a small orchestra of thirty-six players at Mannheim Nietzsche declared that everything other than music was unreal to him. This was what he meant by the word 'music' when using it as the symbol of Dionysius. 'I have concluded an alliance with Wagner,' he wrote to his friend, and fellow philologist, Erwin Rohde; the two of them were to be partners in the renewal of German culture. He sent Cosima a pre-publication copy of *Die Geburt der Tragödie* (Birth of Tragedy) specially printed on yellow paper; he regarded this book as his own humble tribute to Wagner's art.

Wagner returned to Bayreuth at the beginning of February and founded the festival committee consisting of Feustel, Theodor Muncker, the mayor of Bayreuth and Käfferlein, a lawyer; they started at once with the issue of patrons' vouchers. He also bought the plot of land, on which he had set his heart, for himself. He was orchestrating *Götterdämmerung* Act III and beginning to have

[1] There are now about forty-two Wagner-*Vereine* in the cities of Western Germany.

his doubts about placing too much reliance on the German national spirit for his great undertaking. He wrote to Pusinelli, 'We must not expect too much from the Germans ... if it's a little local merrymaking that's another matter; but a splendid, imaginative conception – if its not commanded from above, à la Bismarck etc. – will come to nothing. . . . I know just how much to expect from the glorious German nation.'

At the end of April 1872 Wagner, Cosima and their five children said good-bye to Tribschen. Nietzsche paid his twenty-third, and last, visit as their belongings were being put into packing cases. 'Tribschen,' he wrote, 'is no more; as we wandered amongst the debris, emotion hung in the air and in the clouds; the dog would not eat; the servants were continuously sobbing. We packed the books, letters and manuscripts – it was all so disheartening. What do these three years I have spent near Tribschen mean to me? Without them what would I be?' They moved with the children and their dog into the Hotel Fantaisie in the village of Donndorf, west of Bayreuth. Immediately Wagner and Cosima went to Vienna for a concert of the Vienna Wagner-*Verein*, where he was enthusiastically received by an audience of two thousand.

At 11 in the morning on 22 May 1872, on Wagner's fifty-ninth birthday, the foundation stone of the theatre was laid. On this great day it poured and poured with rain. It had been his hope that Liszt, who was in Weimar, would attend the ceremony thus bringing to an end the long period of coolness between them. Wagner sent him an emotional and, as Cosima thought, 'magnificently worded' letter: 'You came into my life as the greatest person ... you gradually withdrew from me ... in place of you, your innermost being came towards me and fulfilled my yearning to know you were near me ... you were the first person to ennoble me through his love ... to a second, higher life [i.e. Cosima] I am now wedded and can do what I could not alone have done. You have thus been everything to me whereas there was so little that I could give to you. . . .' The Princess, her indignation about Cosima's adultery aggravated by her apostasy,[1] imposed her will on the feeble Liszt. He did not come to the ceremony, although Weimar is only a short distance from Bayreuth, but entrusted a Frau von Meyendorff with a warmly worded congratulatory letter for Wagner.

[1] In October 1872 Cosima became a Protestant.

Cosima's elaborate birthday 'surprises' for Wagner, as 22 May came round again, became part of the ritual of their somewhat self-dramatized lives. On this occasion, she notes in her diary, she gave him the simplest presents as he himself was arranging the great celebration. In spite of the pouring rain hundreds of people trudged ankle deep in mud up the festival hill to witness the ceremony. Ludwig sent a telegram addressed to the 'composer-poet Richard Wagner . . . all hail and good fortune (*Heil und Segen*) to the great undertaking for the coming year. Today I am united with you more than ever in spirit.' To the strains of the *Huldigungsmarsch*, played by a military band, the stone and, in a separate casket, Ludwig's telegram and a short poem by Wagner, were lowered into place. Wagner struck three blows with a hammer, 'Be blessed, my stone, stand long and hold firm!' As he turned round he was deathly pale with tears in his eyes. The night before he had dreamt, he told Cosima, that he had seen his son Fidi (Siegfried) with his face covered in scars. Neither knew what significance to attach to this. Because of the rain the proceedings were transferred to the eighteenth-century opera house which still had the biggest stage in Germany. Wagner drove there with Nietzsche and some other friends.

When, on that day in May in the year 1872 [wrote Nietzsche, whose disenchantment was soon to appear] the foundation stone was laid on the heights of Bayreuth in pelting rain and under a dark sky, Wagner drove back to the town with some of us. He was silent and appeared to be giving himself a long inward look that it is beyond the power of words to describe. He entered this day the sixtieth year of his life; everything he had done until now was a preparation for this moment . . . what his inward eye saw on that day – what he was, what he is, what he will be – we, who are nearest to him, can perceive this to a certain degree; and only outwards from this Wagnerian look can we, ourselves, understand his great deed and, by understanding it, stand security for its fruitfulness.[1]

In spite of partly claiming to understand Wagner's inner vision Nietzsche dissociated himself from the 'great deed' when, the following year, it ran into financial trouble.

In the opera house Wagner delivered the speech intended, had the weather permitted it, for the foundation stone ceremony. He described the simple building about to rise on the hill; it would,

[1] *Richard Wagner in Bayreuth.*

as no theatre had ever done before, bring home to the audience the full meaning of every word and sound and gesture. They were to be given, within the limits of contemporary artistic possibilities, the most perfect examples of theatrical art. Although the undertaking had been referred to as a 'National Theatre' this was not correct. Where was the nation who would build such a theatre? He said to his distinguished and devoted audience,

I had to turn to you, the friends of my particular art, of my ideals and labours, as my collaborators. In this almost personal setting we are laying a stone upon which to build the as yet chimerical edifice of all our most noble German hopes. If we call it provisional it is so in the sense that, for many centuries, the external manifestation of the German spirit is that it builds from within: the eternal God dwells inside it, even before the temple in his honour has been built.

Later in the afternoon the guests reassembled in the opera house to hear Wagner conduct the Ninth Symphony which had been, since his childhood, a vital element in his musical life. 'We're giving no concert,' said Wagner cheerfully, 'we're simply making music and showing the world how to play Beethoven. If anyone criticizes us he can go to Hell!' The most serious men had tears in their eyes wrote Cosima. She hoped that, with the opening ceremonies over, Wagner would be able to get into a peaceful, creative mood for the orchestral sketch of *Götterdämmerung* Act III which he resumed, after a two-month interval, on 15 July, and completed a week later. He played the final phrases to Cosima: 'I do not know', she told her diary, 'what has thrilled me most – the sublimity of the music or the sublimity of the achievement. I feel as if *my* own goal has been reached and I can now shut my eyes.'

Towards the end of 1872 Wagner and Cosima set out on a grand tour of Germany to spy out operatic talent for Bayreuth. Before that they visited Liszt in Weimar, from 2–6 September, at his charming little house in the Hofgarten (now the Liszt Museum). The old atmosphere was, to a certain extent, re-captured although both Wagner and Cosima complained of his '*Seelenmüdigkeit*' (spiritual lassitude). The Princess, alcohol, drugs, social climbing and his new religious activities had all been doing their work, leaving him morose and enervated. Cosima found his long silences unnerving and she was relieved when he took to the keyboard and played Chopin's Preludes, Isolde's 'Liebestod', 'Am stillen Herd' (*Die Meistersinger*) and his own Mephisto Waltz. A few weeks later, just after the Wagner family had left the Fantaisie and moved into a house in the Dammallee (number 7), Liszt paid a return visit on the eve of Cosima's reception into the Protestant Church. He had been staying with Cardinal Hohenlohe and had had an uncomfortable journey to Bayreuth, changing trains five times. He reported that the Grand Duke of Weimar was unfriendly to Bayreuth ('Je ne donnerai pas le sou pour Bayreuth'); Cosima's comment was to produce the recently arrived statutes of the New York Wagner-*Verein*.

'He is weary, weary,' wrote Cosima about her father in her diary. He was unhappy and restless, wanting to bestow his unstinted admiration upon Wagner's genius but tormented by that evil woman in Rome who insisted that he escape from Wagner's influence, which she considered artistically and morally pernicious. Cosima's sympathetic attention to Liszt led to neglecting Wagner for one whole evening. He had one of his frequent outbursts of jealousy, always touched off by the relationship of Liszt and Cosima. 'It is wrong of him, it seems to be, to attack me so frequently on this subject . . . for the sake of peace I can't help wishing that my father would not come here again.'

Wagner needed Cosima's constant attention if he was not to break down under the colossal burden which he had voluntarily assumed. It was soon clear that the *Patronatscheine* were dangerously undersubscribed and that other ways of raising money would have to be explored before commitments were made to builders, machinists, decorators, designers and so on. The tour upon which they embarked at the beginning of November 1872 in search of singers presupposed that the theatre would be built and the *Ring* operas staged. When he brooded about the impossibility of the whole undertaking Cosima reminded him that it was permissible for the creator of *Tannhäuser, Lohengrin, Die Meistersinger, Tristan* and the *Nibelungen* to undertake the impossible. 'God knows', said Wagner, 'whether I shall succeed. It is my calling, like Goethe's Egmont, to set an example.' Their tour took them in five weeks to Würzburg, Frankfurt, Darmstadt, Mannheim, Stuttgart, Strasbourg, Karlsruhe, Wiesbaden, Mainz, Cologne, Düsseldorf, Hanover, Bremen, Magdeburg, Dessau and Leipzig. He returned to Bayreuth profoundly depressed; he had found one solitary female singer and the one admirable production he saw was of Gluck's *Orfeo* in 'little Dessau'. He saw now, more clearly than ever before, how lamentably retrograde was the German theatre; with his usual industry he listed its failings in an article, 'A Glance at the German Operatic Stage of Today', bitterly ironical in tone. He was accustomed to seeing his own operas mutilated; the incompetence of the conductors and producers, whether staging Mozart or Meyerbeer, had exceeded his worst expectations; no one understood how his own music-dramas differed from the usual 'operas'; none of the singers or actors realized that the continuous flow of melody and action was essential to his works.

After returning to Bayreuth on 15 December the first signs of Wagner's heart ailment appeared. The year ended with Cosima acutely anxious about his health and their own personal finances – quite apart from those of the festival. 'I can only follow him, suffer with him, unable to help.'

The state of the festival finances was decidedly serious; by the beginning of 1873 barely 200 of the 1300 vouchers, needed before operations could be started, had been subscribed. Wagner was told by Feustel and Muncker that he would have to conduct a series of concerts in Germany to help the Bayreuth fund. He reckoned that he would have to give about 200 concerts at about 1000 thalers a concert if he was to raise a respectable sum. The prospect appalled him. There appeared to be no alternative; the building orders must now be placed or the whole scheme cancelled.

The German princelings had, as usual, failed Wagner miserably, his theory being that they hated him for having survived their failure to help him in the past. Although the King of Württemberg did not take up a single voucher the Sultan of Turkey took ten and the Khedive of Egypt sent £500. Wagner and Cosima decided to concentrate their money-raising efforts on Berlin and Hamburg. The valiant couple set off again to continue the desperate fight to realize an artistic vision for the greater glory of an indifferent country. In Berlin, in January 1873, Wagner read the poem of *Götterdämmerung* to a mixed but select company in the house of von Schleinitz. Princes, field-marshals, ambassadors, university professors, painters and Bismarck's banker Bleichröder were present. Cosima admitted to being unable to assess the impression which the reading had made. Wagner was apparently a magnificent reader; when he read aloud he lost most traces of his Saxon accent. He took his readings, whether of his own works or of Shakespeare's, very seriously; chatter and unpunctuality were not tolerated. 'If only someone could describe him at these moments,' wrote Cosima; 'without any pathos, yet the effect thrilling – his countenance irradiated; his eyes sublimely rapt; his hand magical, whether in repose or in movement; his voice quiet, pure soul which reaches into the depths and into the outer distances.' Cosima was not the only person who commented on the beauty and majesty of Wagner's readings. He read his poems not only as a poet but as an actor. He had lived every instance of the lives of each of his characters and knew, better than any actor, how they should declaim, or sing, their lines. Ernest Newman has said that Wagner was unique in the history of art in that his operas had been created by the simultaneous functioning within him of the composer's, poet's, dramatist's, conductor's, scenic designer's, singer's and mime's imagination. Such a combination had never happened in a single individual before. He was, said Newman, 'a far better actor than any of his actors, a far better singer than any of his singers in everything but tone, a far better conductor than any of his conductors'. He was therefore doomed to permanent dissatisfaction whenever he saw his works performed. The best he could hope for was that, by casting the spell of his personality on each individual singer, instrumentalist and stage-hand, by explaining in the minutest detail, in action and by writing, exactly what he wanted, there would be a performance, within the limitations of the available talent which went some way towards his ideal.

The personal fascination exerted by Wagner on his contemporaries, men and women, has been the subject of many memoirs. This fascination was at its most powerful when he was in an intimate gathering of the 'friends of his art'. His unfailing kindness to aspiring younger musicians and his seriousness in matters concerning his art went hand in hand with an irresistible wit and levity, sometimes bordering on coarseness about himself, his pretentious fellow artists and the characters in his music-dramas. On these occasions he sometimes upset the well-bred Cosima and her father Liszt who always took himself so seriously. Before the reading of *Götterdämmerung* in Berlin Marie von Schleinitz, reports Cosima in her diary, asked him beforehand to forbear, in his introductory remarks, from mentioning certain 'details' such as copulation and pregnancy 'for the sake of the prudes'. However excited he got, whether in enthusiasm or in anger, his large head was always still and his features reposed, his clear blue eyes fixed searchingly on members of the company or on some inner vision.

After concerts in Berlin, Hamburg and Schwerin Wagner returned, exhausted and disheartened to Bayreuth. He had collected a few thousand thalers and promises to subscribe to *Patronatscheine*. Once again he had found little understanding for his art and he was unimpressed at being a box-office draw amongst the rich parvenu class that had sprung up in Berlin, the same sort of people who had admired Meyerbeer in the days of the July Monarchy in Paris. In Bayreuth Wagner, frail and tired, inspected with Cosima the work that had been done on their new house; he approved, said Cosima, of the proportions of the whole and of the layout of the rooms. He had bought the land at the beginning of the previous year when he had given Muncker, who was in charge of operations, his own detailed plans for the house and garden. The house would be approached from the street (now the Richard-Wagner-Strasse) along an avenue of chestnut trees; at the back of the house would be the main garden which abutted onto the garden of the Residenz (Neues Schloss); there would be a large circular lawn dotted, in the Victorian style, with flower-beds, but also broken up with plane trees and catalpas, a flowering tree of which Wagner was very fond. They stood at the site of their joint sepulchre, something they both liked doing. The good Muncker recoiled when Wagner insisted on talking to him in detail about his sepulchre but was reassured, says Cosima, when told that we should 'with cheerful calm view the prospect of eternal peace'.

One February evening in 1873 Wagner and Cosima read together the German edition of Darwin's *The Origin of Species*; the original edition had been published in 1859. Darwin, said Wagner, was simply, without perhaps realizing it, developing Schopenhauer's 'Idea'; Laplace had done the same thing with Kant. With Bayreuth still desperately short of money Cosima feared that they would, before long, be called away on another concert tour; in the meantime Wagner continued the dictation of his autobiography; entertained Nietzsche, who was appalled at the apparent hopelessness of his struggle; wrote 'Zum Vortrag der neunten Symphonie Beethovens' (The Rendering of Beethoven's Ninth Symphony), a brilliant exposition of the correct interpretation of that piece; and worked on the eighth volume of his collected works. Cosima's fears were realized; the festival committee had high hopes of subscriptions from Cologne so there Wagner and Cosima went to give another concert; on the way back they stopped at Eisleben where Wagner, aged eight, had gone to school after his step-father's death and stayed with Geyer's younger brother, a goldsmith.

Despite Wagner's herculean fund-raising efforts things were getting steadily worse for Bayreuth. He tried, in his usual way, to forget them by immersing himself in the scoring of *Götterdämmerung*; at the beginning of May he scored the glorious opening chords in the prelude of Brunnhilde's 'Weltbegrüssung' (Greeting to the World). Cosima, in the meantime, was secretly preparing the most elaborate celebrations for his sixtieth birthday; on 22 May 1873, in the royal opera house, he was treated to a series of imaginative birthday surprises: performances of two of his juvenile compositions, the Concert overture in C major and his Magdeburg New Year Cantata, Peter Cornelius having turned the latter into a sort of visual and verbal pastiche which he called a '*Künstlerweihe*' (consecration of an artist) and in which the painter Genelli turned the young Wagner's thoughts in the direction of music-drama; and a passing repertory company played Geyer's 'Der bethlehemitische Kindermord'.

The festival committee now saw to it that Wagner concentrated his mind on financial matters. The funds in hand were barely enough to complete the shell of the building; of the 300,000 thalers needed, 130,000 had been subscribed and that only after the most intensive efforts from Wagner, his influential supporters and the Wagner-*Vereine*. If work on the theatre was to coninue, and essential machinery and scenery ordered, they would need a large loan; the loan would have to be guaranteed and the guarantor would have to be the king. Unfortunately Ludwig's own building mania was now at its height and he instructed Düfflipp to inform Wagner that nothing was to be allowed to direct attention from the furtherance of his 'own plans', these being the building of Neuschwanstein. This cheerless news did not stop Wagner organizing, at the beginning of August, a *Hebefest* (hoisting celebration) for the completion of the timber structure of the theatre. Of all their close friends Liszt, alone, came to the ceremony. They and the children climbed up the scaffolding, Cosima having, she tells us, 'the most wonderful thoughts that, for the first time ever, a theatre has been built for a single idea and for a single work [i.e. the *Ring*]. As the *Tannhäuser* march was played *not* for noble knights (or for people dressed up as such) but the noble workmen, as the final blows of their hammers resounded, I felt that this march had received at last its true consecration.'

Before this ceremony Wagner had written a pamphlet, 'Das Bühnenfestspielhaus zu Bayreuth' (Festival Theatre at Bayreuth), in which he further developed his ideas about the sunken orchestra, the second proscenium and other novel features of the building; he attached to it six architectural plans and elevations. His purpose was to encourage his supporters to come to Bayreuth for the *Hebefeier*[1] and to acquaint the public in general with the progress that had been made. He sent Bismarck a copy of this pamphlet, with an accompanying letter asking discreetly for help. Bismarck never answered. At the end of the month Wagner was compelled to write to the patrons of Bayreuth with the news that the festival could not, for financial reasons, take place before the summer of 1875. He wrote to Ludwig complaining about the manners of the German princes who preferred to put their money into Jewish or Jesuit undertakings. In January 1874 Düfflipp informed Wagner by telegram that the King had refused his request for a guarantee; instead he had been awarded, with Brahms, the Maximilian Order for services to music. Before looking elsewhere for help Wagner finished the orchestral score of *Götterdämmerung* Act I.

The Bayreuth festival project was now facing ruin. He comforted Cosima with his aphorisms. 'We must be careful, clever, truthful and superior . . . how pleasant it is to be abandoned by everybody!' It soon turned out that Ludwig had not totally abandoned him. Possibly because he had heard that Wagner was now appealing to the Kaiser for help he wrote to him, on 25 January, a letter in the old tone. 'No, no and again no! It shall not end thus; help must be given! Our plan must not fail!'

---

[1] When the rafters are in position, the event is celebrated by sticking a pole surmounted by a maple wreath, with many flowing ribbons, on top of the roof. Speeches are made and beer and wine are distributed amongst the guests and workmen.

Wagner replied, 'Oh, my gracious king. Just take a look at all the German princes and then you will realize that you are one on whom the German spirit pins its hope.' He told the loyal Heckel in Mannheim that he knew the appeal to the Kaiser would fail. 'My cause requires a "wise fool".' No time was lost in drawing up an agreement between the Bayreuth festival committee and the Bavarian court secretariat. The committee received a loan of 100,000 thalers on condition that all monies received for *Patronats-cheine* be paid immediately into the royal *Kabinettskasse*. The exact amount drawn from the royal treasury was 216,152 marks and forty-two pfennigs which, in due course, was paid back in its entirety by Wagner and his heirs out of festival funds.

With the occupation of the Wagners of the Villa Wahnfried on 28 April 1874, to the building of which Ludwig had contributed 25,000 thalers, a new cultural phase may be said to have started. The king's guarantee had ensured the realization of the *Ring* in Bayreuth; this, in its turn, established that curious religion or philosophy which came to be known as 'Wagnerism'. In Wahnfried 'Wagnerism' was to have a temple and in Cosima the temple was to have a priestess who, as the 'Keeper of the Grail' (*Die Hüterin der Grales*), 'interpreted' to the world the Master's recorded outpourings on matters concerning every aspect of human thought and action. For the next few years, at any rate until Wagner's death in 1883, Wahnfried was essentially a home for Wagner and Cosima and their five children where he had musical evenings with his friends and followers and rehearsed his singers and entertained festival guests. Some would disagree that Wahnfried was, in its early days, a harmless family residence where children played and music was made. Over the entrance Wagner had engraved an explanation in verse of the name he had given his neo-Roman villa:

> Hier, wo mein Wähnen Frieden fand –
> WAHNFRIED
> Sei dieses Haus von mir benannt.[1]

Wahn is not easily translatable into English; it savours of illusion, phantom, madness and fantasy. *Wahnfried*, therefore, means peace

[1] 'Here, where my torment found peace, let this house be named by me Peace from Torment.'

from these particular forms of *Wahn*. Left-wing Wagnerites have said that Wagner's new found freedom from *Wahn* meant the end of all his earlier, healthy democratic beliefs and that he was surrendering to Cosima's aristocratic convictions about man's fundamental inequality. The most welcome visitor at Wahnfried was soon to be the Comte de Gobineau, author of 'Essai sur l'inégalité des races humaines', which culminates in an apotheosis of the German race.[1] It is true that Wagner's Zurich dream, or *Wahn*, of the people flocking, free of charge, to see the *Ring* in a makeshift wooden structure on the banks of the Rhine, to be torn down when the performance was over, had now turned into a more exclusive concept. The left-wing argument goes that the Franco-Prussian War released in Wagner a tasteless, brutal nationalism which found its way into the Bayreuth 'programme'; he now derided the idea of 'so-called human progress; 'genius' was now the one and only form of progress. Wahnfried became the temple of the 'Bayreuth Idea', the new art religion which extolled 'inequality'. Everything now served the cause of this new religion: his autobiography, his appellation the *Meister*, the publication of his collected works, the founding of a journal, *Die Bayreuthe Blätter* to serve as his mouthpiece, and the establishment of Wagner-*Vereine*. 'Art and Inequality', 'Art and Religion' are the new themes of Wagner the theoretician. All this is to take Wagner's theoretical effusions much too seriously; in fact his observations on life in his later 'elitist' days are more entertaining in their eccentricity than in his egalitarian period. For real Wagnerian 'truths' we should turn to the theatre on the festival hill rather than to the Villa Wahnfried.

Whanfried could have been the home of any reasonably well-off, German *Bildungsbürger* (educated citizen), i.e. of middle-class extraction who, through exceptional intelligence and ability, could claim to be accepted by all classes. There was no trace, as Wagner was at pains to tell Ludwig, of that suggestive, scented luxury of silks and satins which his enemies professed to see in his new home. Dozens of lithographs have familiarized us with the large bow-windowed drawing-room opening on to the garden where Wagner, wearing his velvet hat, read his poems or Liszt

---

[1] Arthur de Gobineau (1816–82), writer and diplomat, described the Aryans as a 'master race'. His morality of strength influenced Nietzsche. Wagner found his French 'devilish difficult' to listen to.

played the piano to a small group of musical and artistic friends. Wagner's vast reading was reflected in the three thousand books which lined the walls, above which were portraits of Goethe, Beethoven, Liszt, Ludwig, Cosima, his mother, Geyer and others who had, in some way, left their mark on his life. (This room was destroyed in an air-raid on 5 April 1945.)

Ludwig thirsted for more details of Wagner's private life, which was a good deal more wholesome than his own. The 25,000 thalers which he had given Wagner for his house was his only outright gift in cash; all his other advances were later repaid. Wagner reported to him that, after breakfasting with Cosima, he worked from ten to one. His study on the first floor was an austere little room, its only decoration being a portrait of Cosima by Lenbach.[1] If he felt well enough, or had not been put out by disagreeable business matters, he would join the children for lunch. Coffee was taken in the garden at which time he glanced at the *Bayreuther Tagblatt*, the only newspaper allowed in the house, or discussed with Cosima some topic of current interest. After a short rest he went to the drawing-room where he and Cosima dealt with their correspondence. In the afternoon he went for a walk or for a drive with the children to the Eremitage or the Fantaisie. At seven in the evening he had a light meal with the children. At eight he and Cosima read in the drawing-room or he saw the members of what he called the *Nibelungenkanzlei* (*Nibelung* Chancellery) who corrected his proofs and copied out parts and whom he was training to become future Wagnerian musicians.

Wagner disposed of his time with great care which partly explains his ability to deal with such a variety of day-to-day matters. In April 1874, the month he moved into Wahnfried, he finished the orchestral score of *Götterdämmerung* Act II and started to rehearse the singers. From now onwards he was continuously occupied – scoring *Götterdämmerung*, supervising the building of the theatre, ordering machinery, costumes, and stage scenery, engaging and training instrumentalists and singers, rehearsing those singers taking leading parts, and going on concert tours. On 21 November 1874 he finished the orchestral score of *Götterdämmerung* Act III, thus completing the tetralogy of *Der Ring des Nibelungen*. Cosima, instead of rejoicing, spent the night in sorrow.

[1] Franz von Lenbach (1836–1904) was the most successful portrait-painter of his day.

He had abused her for preferring, so he said, to show him some trivial letter from her father rather than rejoice with him that the great work was finished. Too distressed to explain that she did not know that he had finished the score she rushed to her bedroom and confided her anguish to her diary.

> ... I am sobbing as I write this. And so I have been deprived of the highest joy ... that I have dedicated my life in suffering to this work has not earned me the right to celebrate its completion with joy. So I celebrate it in pain, bless the sublime and wonderful work with my tears and thank the stern God who has decreed that this completion be expiated by my pain. To whom can I speak? To whom can I confide this pain? With R. I can only stay silent; I confide it to these pages and may they teach my Siegfried to harbour no anger, no hatred, but only infinite pity for that most wretched creature, man. ...

And so she went on. All was soon made up, however, and a contrite Wagner composed for her birthday a tender little *Kinderkatechismus* (Children's Catechism) in praise of the name 'Cosima' which was performed on Christmas Day 1874 in the hall at Wahnfried.

The first half of 1875 was largely filled with concert tours which Wagner came to hate more and more. The festival committee urgently needed money to finance rehearsals and other matters which were specifically excluded from the king's guarantee. Wagner and Cosima went, accordingly, to Vienna, Budapest, Leipzig, Hanover, Brunswick and Berlin. On 1 July the piano rehearsals with individual singers started. Hans Richter had been rehearsing singers that he had discovered on a theatrical inspection tour of Germany the previous year. Wagner had also, during his latest fund-raising tour, been looking for singers. The motley crowd assembled at Bayreuth. Wagner told them to be proud that they were working for an ideal and not being paid for their labours apart from their travelling and maintenance expenses. Their parts had been carefully written out by the enthusiastic members of the *Nibelungenkanzlei* – Joseph Rubinstein, Anton Seidl and others. From 2–12 August there were orchestral rehearsals under Richter in which the singers also took part. The orchestra numbered 115, with sixty-four strings; the players came from many of the important German opera houses and the leader was the great violoinist August Wilhelmj. Work on the building was finished. As Richter conducted in the sunken orchestral pit

Wagner sat at a small table near the prompter's desk; his score was lit by a green-shaded paraffin lamp. From here he issued instructions to the players and singers, excitedly waving his arms and legs – a scene recorded by the painter Adolf Menzel in a well-known drawing. The rehearsal over, Wagner and his team repaired to Angermann's beer house where he delighted his artists with his charm and vivacity. He managed, by force of personality and by his technical mastery of every production detail, to unite and uplift his cast, the most divisive member of which was the truculent tenor, Albert Niemann, who had not changed since the Paris *Tannhäuser* in 1861.

The rehearsals went so well that Wagner was able to announce that the festival would take place the following summer in 1876. Hermann Levi, the conductor, wrote to his father saying that he had heard the rehearsals of *Siegfried* and *Götterdämmerung*. 'I am old enough now not to become any wiser and I am telling you that there will take place in Bayreuth next year a radical change of direction in our artistic life.'

Franz Jauner, the Vienna opera director, blackmailed Wagner into going to Vienna for six weeks at the end of 1875 to rehearse new productions of *Tannhäuser* and *Lohengrin*. He threatened otherwise not to release Amalie Materna who was to sing Brünn-hilde. In Vienna he met the baritone Angelo Neumann who later became the great Wagnerian impresario. Wagner left Vienna in disgust, nauseated by the vicious hostility of the press. As money was still needed he went to Berlin in March 1876 to supervise the production of the Berlin première of *Tristan*, at which Albert Niemann sang the title part. The net receipts of the première amounting to 5000 thalers went, on the Kaiser's instructions, to the Bayreuth festival fund.

Wagner's carefully worked out timetable for 1876 allowed for three full rehearsals: 3–12 June, 14–26 July, 29 July to 4 August. How he managed, despite daily vicissitudes of greater and lesser importance – the sudden pregnancy of Sieglinde, the death of a player, or the disappearance of Fafner's neck[1] somewhere between London and Bayreuth – to hold together his heterogeneous army of singers, players, machinists and designers cannot be satis-factorily explained. It can only be repeated that Wagner was a

[1] Fafner, the dragon in the *Ring*, was made in London and sent to Bayreuth in parts.

genius, born to command, with a magnificent mind and able to achieve the impossible. Cosima's diaries, with their catalogue of daily crises, make his achievement appear all the more remarkable. They also support the theory that, by starting Bayreuth, he signed his own death-warrant; he seldom had a good night and his attacks of cramp about the heart became more and more frequent.

Wagner prepared to receive a flush of royal personages. For Ludwig he had arranged, from 6–9 August, a full-dress private performance. The king, true to form, arrived in Bayreuth in circumstances of the strictest secrecy. 'To be obliged to welcome those dreadful princesses in Bayreuth and listen to their prattle, instead of immersing myself in your sublime work, is something that I could never bring myself to do. I am coming to feast myself on your mighty work, to refresh myself in heart and soul and not be gaped at by the inquisitive multitude.' At one in the morning on 6 August the special train stopped at a signal station near the Rollwenzelei Inn between the town and the Eremitage. The king stepped out of the railway coach and silently offered his hand to Wagner who was waiting for him. This was their first meeting since the Munich première of *Die Meistersinger* in June 1868. A royal carriage took them to the Eremitage where they talked until after three in the morning. After the rehearsal of *Götterdämmerung* the king left as he had come; in the middle of the night he got into the train at the signal station near the Rollwenzelei Inn and was taken back to Hohenschwangau from where he wrote to Wagner in ecstasy. What he had seen and heard in the theatre had exceeded by far his wildest expectations:

Great, incomparable friend, precious to me above all things . . . I was so deeply moved, that you may have wondered at my silence. . . . You are the God-man who cannot fail, who cannot err . . . the true artist who, by God's grace, has brought down from Heaven the holy flame to inspire, ennoble and redeem us on earth . . . the more I think about this miraculous work of art the more overcome I am with awe and with growing admiration for the titanic spirit that created so divine and glorious a work . . . only you, with your glowing and triumphant light, can melt away those crusts of ice which petrify those many pains which we suffer in our hearts and minds.

No sooner had Ludwig gone than the Kaiser arrived on 12 August, the day before the start of the first cycle. Wagner had to leave a rehearsal to greet him at the station where an enormous crowd had gathered. The Kaiser's first words to Wagner were, 'I never thought that you would bring it off!' After the formalities of the reception Wagner's irrepressibility came to the surface; he got into his carriage and, like a little boy, shouted 'hurrahs' and waved his hat at the crowd. The first two operas in the cycle were perhaps as much as the old and unmusical Kaiser could manage; after *Die Walküre* he went off to attend military manoeuvres.

'It is probable', wrote Wagner later, looking back on the 1876 festival, 'that no artist has ever before been so honoured. He has been known to wait upon emperors and princes but none can remember when emperors and princes ever came to him.' Amongst the other emperors and princes who came to Bayreuth in August 1876 were the Emperor Dom Pedro II of Brazil, to whom he had sent from Zurich copies of his works bound in red, the King of Württemberg and dozens of grand-dukes and princes. The distinguished commoners included Nietzsche, who was suffering from splitting headaches and fled to the neighbouring woods after a couple of acts, Bruckner, Tchaikovsky and the Wesendonks; they had been driven out of Zurich by the strength of anti-German feeling after the Franco-Prussian War and had since lived in Dresden. Before the curtain rose on *Das Rheingold* Wagner wrote 'A final request to my dear companions: *Clarity*! The big notes come on their own; the little notes and the text are the main thing – never speak to the public; only to each other; in monologues look up or down, never straight ahead. My last wish – remain good to me, you dear ones!' Richter conducted; the stage scenery was done by the brothers Brückner to the designs of Joseph Hoffman; Franz Betz was Wotan; Karl Hill was Alberich; and Lilli Lehmann was Woglinde. In the other operas in the first cycle Niemann was Siegmund; Amalie Materna was Brünnhilde; Georg Unger was Siegfried; and Wagner's niece Johanna was the first Norn. At the end of *Götterdämmerung* Wagner appeared on the stage before a wildly cheering audience. He told them that now at last they had a national German art and that it was up to them if they wished it to thrive. At a banquet the next day for 700 guests he turned suddenly, in the middle of his speech, towards Liszt. 'Here is the man ... without whom you would perhaps never have heard a note of mine – my dear friend Franz Liszt.' His arms wide open he descended the steps and embraced him.

Between the first two cycles of the *Ring* Karl Marx wrote to Engels from Karlsbad about the mass movement to the 'Bayreuth fools' festival of the town musician Wagner'. Judith Gautier came from Paris to the second cycle and started a tender romance with Wagner, thirty years older than her. Ludwig returned for the third cycle, arriving and leaving with his usual discretion. He had agreed to receive members of the festival committee before the first performance; after that he would speak to no one except Wagner, preferring, like a good Wagnerite, to spend the long intervals mugging up the text for the following act.

In her diary Cosima breathed a sigh when it was all over; nobody had ever believed that the programme would be kept; although many had gone, Wahnfried was still full of guests – 'many English people, including a Reverend, very Jesuitical, who declared himself enchanted'.

The festival was over; Wagner was triumphant and exhausted. He had achieved one of the greatest artistic feats in history. During these fifteen hours of music he had attempted to describe the whole world of emotional and intellectual experience. People began to take sides for and against him in earnest; he became the object of idolatry and loathing, one of the most controversial composers of all time. Arguments about his greatness and wickedness have generally arisen from the *Ring* which he conceived in Dresden in the late summer of 1848. Out of his reading of Jacob Grimm's *Deutsche Mythologie* and of various Nordic sagas he fashioned this wonderful creation of sound which reaches into forbidden depths of the psyche, exposes our deeply repressed instincts, and outrages our morality with its uninhibited sensuality and many other things besides. The literature about the *Ring* is enormous and many great men, musicians and writers, have described its effect upon them. Wagner had told Ludwig that it had been his wish to humanize the world of Germanic and Nordic sagas, to address them to the German soul. He believed that he had, with his poem of the *Ring*, given the German nation a work which would be cherished in the future. It was now his task, through music-drama, to convey the human and psychic truthfulness of the ancient Germanic myths. 'The world's last and highest glory lives in my heart and soul; the old German world – ash tree (*Weltesche*), the wonderful tree of the Norns will, through me, spread a mighty, vaulted foliage which shall embrace all feeling human hearts.' How Wagner breathed life into these misty Nordic figures has been the subject of many a thick volume and learned monograph during the last century. He perceived intuitively the humanity and the relations to each other of these archetypal figures with their psycho-sexual problems. Nietzsche, in *Richard Wagner in Bayreuth*, written in 1876 when he was on the threshold of going mad and turning against Wagner, understood the meaning of the *Ring*. 'And now ask yourselves . . . was this composed for you? Have you the courage to point with your hand to the stars in this great constellation of beauty and purity and to say: it is our life that Wagner has put thus beneath the stars?' For Gerhard Hauptmann in 1911 the *Ring* was a subterranean geyser, pouring forth out of the depths of the earth an unknown glowing substance which purges the human soul of the dross of a few thousand years. For Thomas Mann, Bernard Shaw[1] and for dozens of other writers and poets the *Ring* has different and fascinating meanings.

Wagner's intention was to give three more cycles of the *Ring* in 1877. He wanted now to escape from Bayreuth and refresh himself in the Italian sun. On 14 September he, Cosima, four of their children and a governess set off for Italy; he planned a long, expensive holiday paid for out of his fee of $5000 for the *American Centennial March*, commissioned on the centenary of the Declaration of Independence and written by him in February 1876. His holiday mood was spoilt by the grim news about the festival deficit of 120,000 marks which reached him in Sorrento in November. After visiting Naples, Rome, Florence and Bologna they returned to Bayreuth towards the end of December 1876. As there seemed to be no way out of the financial impasse Wagner, after conferences with Düfflipp and exhortations to the *Patronat-Verein*, turned, as he had done in the past to restore his spiritual equilibrium, to creative work. On 25 January he told Cosima, 'I am starting *Parzifal* and I shall not leave him until he is finished' – whereupon she laughed with joy. He changed the spelling to *Parsifal* because he had been told that *fal parsi* was Persian for the Foolish Pure One which he turned round into the Pure Fool. He recast the prose sketch which he had done for Ludwig in August 1865, started on the poem and, on 19 April,

[1] In *The Perfect Wagnerite* 1898, Shaw interpreted the *Ring* as a scathing denunciation of the capitalist order.

presented Cosima with the complete text of *Parsifal* Acts I–III. 'In the evening R. read me the third act of *Parsifal* and gave me the poem which is, for me, the highest comfort in the misery of our existence.'

Wagner could not proceed with the composition of *Parsifal* until some way out of the latest financial crisis had been found. Düfflipp said that Ludwig could do nothing about the festival deficit. 'I have for years made no secret of the fact that, by reason of his Majesty's building activities, the demands on the funds of the royal treasury are such as to preclude completely their employment for any other purpose.' Wagner decided to go to London for the third time, his previous visits having been in 1839 and 1855, and give eight concerts in the Albert Hall. He and Cosima arrived in London on 30 April.

Owing to the incompetence of the London theatre agents who did not realize that one third – two thousand! – of the seats belonged to subscribers and could not be sold to the public, the financial rewards were very small. All he received was £700.

In Bayreuth Wagner had had misgivings about the financial wisdom of the London concerts. He remembered the miserable rewards of his four months in London in 1855 and how Bülow was swindled out of £1500 by a crooked English agent. But Feustel and his other friends insisted that he go; Hodge and Essex had promised a clear profit of £500 for each of twenty concerts before packed houses of 10,000 people and an initial allowance of £1500. He could expect to return triumphantly with £10,000, liquidate the deficit and save Bayreuth. Anxious to show his friends that it was not 'indolence or love of ease' which caused him to hesitate, he decided in the end to go and he took with him Richter, Wilhelmj and a few Bayreuth artists. His fears were justified; the agents were unable to keep any. of their promises.

'Hodge and Essex (the agents) are very nice people,' says Cosima, 'but quite inexperienced, and all Israel is working against us.' Nevertheless, she said, were she to live in a large town she would certainly like it to be London where the fog gives everything a ghostly fascination. She and Wagner went by train from Charing Cross to Greenwich where they had a 'Fish Dinner'. They returned by steamer; the damp, misty weather and the giant shipyards along the Thames were enough for Wagner to tell her that this was the fulfilment of Alberich's dream: 'Nibelheim, world dominion, activity, work, everywhere the pressure of steam and fog'.

Wagner and Cosima were earnest, indefatigable sightseers: the Beefeaters at the Tower of London; breakfast in the aquarium; the prints and drawings in the British Museum; the Hogarths and Reynolds's in the National Gallery; a flower show at the Crystal Palace; a parliamentary debate; a service at Westminster Abbey which ended with the organist playing 'Elizabeth's Prayer' out of Tannhäuser, and Hampton Court – these are some of the episodes which she mentions in her diary. They could not indulge in these agreeable activities for long; there were rehearsals every day with the singers and the large orchestra and London's hunters of artistic big game were hot on their heels. Wagner's reception was altogether different from that of his last London visit in 1855 when he spent most of his time alone, cold and hungry, in his room in Portland Terrace; his only friends then were the musicians, Sainton and Lüders, whom he now saw again and they reminisced together about those Philharmonic concerts. Wagner and Cosima stayed at 12 Orme Square, off Bayswater Road, in the comfortable house of Edward Dannreuther, the musicologist and Wagnerian propagandist. It was a pleasant walk for Wagner across Kensington Gardens to the Albert Hall. They dined with Browning and met George Eliot who was described by Cosima as 'the well-known poet' and who made upon her 'a noble and pleasant impression'.[1] Wagner was painted by Sir Hubert Herkomer, the fashionable painter of German birth, and photographed by Elliot and Fry, the well-known photographers. Cosima tells us in her diary that she sat for Burne-Jones who went to one of Wagner's concerts, 'an extraordinary thing for Edward to do', said his wife, as he disliked Wagner's music. Seven years later, in 1884, Burne-Jones went to a concert performance of Parsifal in the Albert Hall and was pleased to find that Wagner had successfully struck the 'Celtic' vein in the Grail Legend which he himself was attempting to express in his paintings. Cosima also lunched with Millais, another 'Pararaphaelite' painter.

Wagner travelled by train to Windsor where he was received

[1] One evening Wagner read 'the Lewes' (i.e. George Eliot and G. H. Lewes) the poem of 'Parsifal'.

by the Queen and Prince Leopold, Duke of Albany, who claimed to have seen his dog Rus in Lucerne. Although Windsor Castle impressed him he found that the decorations of the rooms were unsuited to the style of the building. 'Even the beautiful Van Dycks, the magnificent Holbein and the magic Rembrandt are out of place!' At one of his concerts Wagner met the Prince of Wales; he reminded him of his mother's remark, back in 1855, that all Italian singers in London were German and that he should therefore have no difficulty in staging his operas in London.

The eight London concerts were a great success: the *Ring* numbers – Wotan's *Abschied* (Farewell), Siegfried's forging songs and his farewell to Brünnhilde, the Ride of the Walküre – were rapturously applauded, although Hill (Wotan) and Unger (Siegfried) both lost their voices. The £700 raised by the London adventure represented one tenth of the Bayreuth deficit. As Wagner got into the train at Victoria he shouted to his friends, 'All is lost except our honour.' He had already written to Feustel from London asking him to send out an appeal from the festival council for subscriptions; he would himself head the list with a subscription of 3000 marks which he later raised to 10,000 marks. Should this fail he would sell his plot of land in Bayreuth, emigrate with his family to America and never again return to Germany.

The day after leaving England Wagner and Cosima arrived at the Villa Diana in Bad Ems where their children joined them. His health in London had been bad and this, said certain critics, had showed itself in his conducting. He hoped that a month in this famous spa would restore his health and calm his nerves. The shadow of the festival deficit was, however, always present. Before going to London he had been negotiating with the Leipzig theatre and had very nearly come to an agreement whereby, for a down payment of 10,000 marks and a ten per cent royalty for each performance, Leipzig would have the sole North German rights in the *Ring* – likewise Munich for Southern Germany and Vienna for Austria. It came to nothing mainly because of the doubts which August Forster, the cautious director of the Leipzig theatre, had about the whole scheme. Before six months were out Angelo Neumann, Forster's successor, was to revive this agreement in a dramatic form. But now the shadows over Bayreuth were deepening; three courses of action – the

London concerts, the new appeal to subscribers and the negotiations with Leipzig – had all failed to find the urgently needed money. Wagner and Cosima provided 50,000 marks out of their own resources to pay the more insistent Bayreuth creditors. It was not, as he saw it, the *Ring* that was a failure but Bayreuth. 'My work', he wrote to Feustel, 'will be performed everywhere and will draw numerous spectators but no one will come to Bayreuth. . . . I can only blame the place in as far as it was I who chose it. And yet I had a great idea: I wanted, with the help of the nation, to create something quite new and independent in a place which would acquire significance through this creation – a kind of artistic Washington. I expected too much from our higher society. . . .'

The king, on hearing from Düfflipp about Wagner's plans to settle in America, beseeched him in the name of the love and friendship which had bound them to each other for so many years to give up this dreadful idea; it would be an indelible stain on the German nation if his great spirit were to withdraw from its midst. All the same he was not prepared to do anything to save the 'Bayreuth Idea'; he even rejected a plan, worked out by his intendant Perfall, which provided for a repetition of the *Ring* in Bayreuth the following year with the singers and players being supplied by the Munich theatre; he ordered instead that the *Ring* be performed in Munich. This appeared to confirm what Wagner had said earlier – that his works would survive but not in Bayreuth. Undaunted as usual he made a spirited speech to the delegates of all the Wagner-*Vereine* who had assembled in Bayreuth on 15 September to hear the worst. They gathered round him in a half-circle on the stage of the Festspielhaus. The only response he said, sarcastically, to the recent appeal for funds had been that a Herr Plüddemann's aunt in Kolberg had sent 100 marks. There would be no repetition of the *Ring* in 1878; he then presented the delegates with a detailed plan for the establishment of a music school in Bayreuth where singers, players and conductors would be properly trained to give model performances of all his works – not only of his works but 'of all good dramatic works in a distinctively German style'. All that came of this plan was the founding of the journal, the *Bayreuther Blätter*, which was intended to be a monthly bulletin from the music school to the Wagner-*Vereine*. The first number, edited by the devoted Wagnerian, Hans von Wolzogen, appeared in February 1878; unable to be the mouthpiece of the music school that never was, it took on the character of a Wagnerian house journal. 'All these plans leave me with the sad feeling that R. is being diverted from his creative work,' wrote Cosima in her diary. No sooner had she written this than he started on the composition of *Parsifal* Act 1. 'May Heaven bless him and his work.' On 25 September 1877 he began the orchestral sketch of Act 1.

A letter from Cosima to the king in January 1878, sent without Wagner's knowledge and enclosing Feustel's note to her about the impending catastrophe, had the effect required. Munich came, once again, to the rescue of Bayreuth with a loan at five per cent interest to cover the deficit. Under a new agreement the Munich theatre would be allowed to stage *Parsifal* and Wagner received a ten per cent royalty on the Munich performances of all his works. 'The great thing now,' Wagner wrote to Feustel, 'is that I may turn myself to my work with a cheerful serenity; when it is disturbed and troubled the good spirits fly away from us strange geniuses.'

Wagner in 1862, by Augener.
Courtesy, Richard Wagner Museum, Bayreuth.

Richard and Cosima during the Tribschen period.
Courtesy, The Bettmann Archive.

Wagner with his collaborators in Munich, 1865.
Hans von Bülow is in the back row immediately behind Wagner.
Courtesy, Richard Wagner Museum, Bayreuth.

King Ludwig II of Bavaria.
Courtesy, Richard Wagner
Museum, Bayreuth.

Franz Betz as Wotan.
Courtesy, Richard Wagner
Museum, Bayreuth.

Ludwig and Malvina Schnorr von
Carolsfeld as the first Tristan and
Isolde, 1865. Courtesy, Richard
Wagner Museum, Bayreuth.

Minna Lamment, Lilli and Marie Lehmann as the Rhine Maidens, 1876.
Courtesy, Richard Wagner Museum, Bayreuth.

Wilhelmine Schröder-Dev-
rient, the first great Wagnerian singer, by F. Hanfstaengl.
Courtesy, Richard Wagner
Museum, Bayreuth.

Wagner at home in the Villa Wahnfrie

The Villa Wahnfried.
Courtesy, Richard Wagner Museum, Bayreuth.

CHAPTER TWELVE
The Final Years
1878–83

MOST of the year 1878 working on the music for
ever composed anything as fantastic as this; it's
the time,' he told Cosima in January – and con-
.... to the *Bayreuther Blätter*. He conducted, through
the mediation of the Bayreuth hairdresser Bernhard Schnappauf,
a clandestine correspondence with Judith Gautier in which,
recalling her kisses and caresses during the second *Ring* cycle, he,
the ageing man, implored the young and beautiful Frenchwoman
to inspire him, from afar, for the composition of his great work –
'*mein Weltabschiedswerk*' – with which he would take leave of the
world. 'Aidez-moi!... je me sens aimé, et j'aime. Enfin, je fais la
musique au *Parsifal*....' In these letters he asked her to send him
some silks, scents and bath essences and, her loving assurances
having done their work, Wagner, tired of the correspondence,
asked Cosima to continue it. Instead of fleeing to her diary for
consolation in her grief at her husband's infidelity she winked an
eye at this instance of senile susceptibility and wrote a French
prose translation of *Parsifal* for Judith – who knew Chinese but
not German! – to turn into a poem. It goes, perhaps without
saying, that Wagner needed all these satins and scents as aids for
the composition of the music for Kundry's seduction of Parsifal
in Klingsor's magic garden rather than for the unveiling of the
grail by the suffering Amfortas in 'Monsalvat'.

The poem of 'Parsifal' was printed in December 1877 and
Nietzsche was one of the first to receive a copy. Next day, he gave
to his friend Reinhart von Seydlitz, his impressions after a first
reading. 'More Liszt than Wagner; the spirit of the counter-

reformation; it is too Christian and narrow for me, accustomed to the Greeks and universal humanism . . . the language reads like a translation of a foreign tongue. But the situation and their sequences – is not this the highest form of poetry? Is it not a last challenge to music?' Wagner and Nietzsche had met for the last time in Sorrento in October 1876; Wagner was escaping from the Bayreuth weather and the post-festival troubles and Nietzsche was trying to regain some strength, in the company of the elderly and earnest Malvida von Meysenbug, after those excruciating headaches and eyeaches which had driven him from the *Ring* rehearsals into the Bavarian woods where he wrote the first of his scathing judgments of Bayreuth. They went together for an evening walk along the coast; Wagner spoke of his revived interest in *Parsifal* which he had last worked on twelve years before. His apparent conversion to Christianity displeased Nietzsche who was now an anti-Christian. Nietzsche's later hysterical hatred of Wagner, culminating in *Der Fall Wagner* (The Case of Wagner) in 1888, was focused on Wagner's supposedly false, new-found piety as exemplified in *Parsifal*. He accused Wagner of saying that the public, satiated with Nordic mythology, wanted to see something Christian; he also accused him of cynically trimming his sails to this prevailing wind. It is difficult to reconcile this with Wagner's proprietary attitude to *Parsifal* which he would not allow to be performed anywhere than in Bayreuth. He told Ludwig,

I have had to deliver my ideally conceived works to vulgar, unprincipled theatres and their publics and I must now consider carefully how to protect this last and most sacred of my works from a similar fate . . . I am calling *Parsifal* a *Bühnenweihspiel* (stage-dedication-drama) and to it I shall dedicate one special stage and that can only be in my own festival theatre in Bayreuth. There, and there alone, shall *Parsifal* in future ages be performed: it shall never be offered in other theatres to the public for their amusement. . . .

Nietzsche, on his way to becoming the Antichrist, had been disturbed and repelled by the turn that German political and cultural thought had taken since the victories of 1871. He found it lacking in 'decency and self-respect' that the Kaiser, Bismarck and the German generals should publicly flaunt their Christianity whilst being 'anti-Christian in their deeds'. Wagner's offence was all the greater – corrupted by snobbery and ambition he was prostituting his talents to turn out a Christian music-drama. Such accusations were unjust; Wagner displayed throughout his career a shining integrity as far as his art was concerned. It was the subject-matter of *Parsifal* that had made him artistically Christian-minded. Although the story goes that Nietzsche broke with Wagner because he turned Christian in *Parsifal* this cannot be seriously entertained as the principal cause of their breach. In *Der Fall Wagner* Nietzsche called him the artist of decadence – 'is Wagner a man at all? Is he not rather a disease? Everything he touches he makes morbid. He has made music morbid. . . . *Parsifal* is a work of cunning, of revenge, of secret poison-brewing, hostile to the prerequisites of life. The preaching of chastity is an incitement to unnaturalness: I despise anyone who does not regard *Parsifal* as an outrage against morality.' And yet, in the same year as *Der Fall Wagner*, he told his admirer, the unsuccessful composer Peter Gast, of the effect on him of the *Parsifal* prelude.

The other day I listened for the first time (in Monte Carlo of all places!) to the prelude to *Parsifal*. When I see you again I shall tell you precisely what impression it made on me. Apart from all irrelevant questions such as what purpose this music serves, or should serve, has Wagner ever done anything better aesthetically? It shows the highest kind of psychological perception and sureness of expression and communication; every shade of feeling is conveyed epigrammatically. It has a clarity of musical description that reminds us of a shield of exquisite workmanship; and, finally, there is a sublimity of feeling, an event of the soul at the very heart of music, that does Wagner the highest honour. This synthesis of states attains a critical rigour, a 'loftiness', and is imbued with an awareness and a penetration of vision that cuts through the soul like a knife – a compassion for all that he sees and judges. The like of this can be found in Dante and nowhere else. Can any painter have ever painted such a sorrowful view of love as does Wagner in the last notes of his prelude?

It is fairly clear, then, that *Parsifal* had little to do with Nietzsche's perplexingly vehement reaction to Wagner after 1876. Cosima's view was that his headaches during the *Ring* rehearsals were at the bottom of it all. Later followers of Nietzsche, led by his sister Elisabeth Förster-Nietzsche,[1] who falsified his letters of

---

[1] She suppressed references to his illness which later developed into madness.

this period, were at pains to show that his disillusionment with Wagner was based on sound, Dionysian, artistic principles. Wagnerites have seen in it the earliest symptoms of his brain disease brought on by syphilis. The truth lies between these two assertions. The young Nietzsche, like his contemporary Ludwig, had succumbed to the charm and genius of the older man (both were over thirty years younger than Wagner).

Nietzsche saw himself as Wagner's partner in the task of German cultural revival. The days which he spent at Tribschen were the happiest in his life, the nearest he ever came to having a home with a father and mother. Wagner was born in the same year as his father Ludwig Nietzsche, a Lutheran pastor, who went mad and died of softening of the brain at the age of thirty-six. Nietzsche spent the rest of his unhappy childhood in exclusively feminine company – his mother, sister, grandmother and maiden aunts – until he entered the old boarding school of Pforta where he did well in religion, German literature and classics. He was appointed professor of classical philology at Basel in 1869 at the age of twenty-four; he taught there for ten years until his health broke down and he became a prey to migraine headaches and vomiting fits. Were these attacks brought on by genuine medical causes or were they psychosomatic, brought on by the realization that, if he was to save his soul from 'this old robber', he must break away from the two people he most loved? (Nietzsche was, in his own way, 'in love' with Cosima, harbouring for her a secret Oedipal passion.) Wagner ruthlessly directed and re-directed the intellectual labours of his young admirer towards himself; he forced him to rewrite parts of his first book, *The Birth of Tragedy*, with its antithetical conceptions of the Apollonian and Dionysian influences in Greek art, because it barely mentioned Wagnerian drama as a significant new cultural force.

Nietzsche gradually became aware that his friendship with Wagner was inimical to his own intellectual independence. He continued to like Wagner's music but increasingly questioned his personality and opinions, coming ultimately to the conclusion that a violent, total and dramatic break with Wagner – the man and his music – was essential for his own future as a writer and philosopher. The King of Bavaria, the other 'madman', was more balanced; he accepted, without bitterness, the ending of his early dream of an artistic 'alliance' with Wagner and he never let his disapproval of his behaviour affect his admiration of him as an artist. It is uncertain how much these two famous admirers knew about music. Ludwig was able to endure two whole *Ring* cycles whilst Nietzsche fled to the woods after a single act. His own jejune musical compositions, of which he thought highly, his praise of the worthless music of his disciple Peter Gast, his later preference for light music, suggest that he was hardly capable of making useful comments on the *Ring*. Thomas Mann said that, with the founding of Bayreuth, Utopia had arrived – 'and Nietzsche fled'. Nietzsche fled because he was 'mixed up' and jealous. He was jealous that the Bayreuth scheme had not failed. At Tribschen he had had Wagner all to himself; in Bayreuth he saw him at the rehearsals as a 'magician of souls', controlling, with consummate brilliance, the huge ensemble of singers, players and machinists, and delighting them with his wit and ebullience, with his tenderness and his anger, continuously keeping an eye on the smallest details.

Edouard Schuré, a French Wagnerite, who was present at these rehearsals, said that during the short pauses Wagner's mirth knew no bounds. He said that Nietzsche's pride was hurt at Wagner's obvious superiority. The touchy, self-conscious young professor felt left out; at Wahnfried Wagner could not draw him out of his morose silences. Nietzsche may, by then, have planned the break and his headaches and vomiting fits were simply signs of his mental anguish at having to take such a step.

Nietzsche was, as a writer, more interesting than Wagner and the form and content of his pronouncements generally have more to commend them. Wagner, in his letters, conversation and occasional writings was responding to the different movements of the day. Unlike Nietzsche he is not to be judged in his writings but in his music. After 1876 Nietzsche apparently decided that Wagner was 'dangerous', that Bayreuth was becoming a centre of 'cultural philistinism', a symbol of 'the extirpation of the German spirit in favour of the German Reich', the Holy City of anti-Semitic 'Christian' chauvinism. Other writers, taking Nietzsche's cue, have suggested that Wagner, the moment he set foot in Bayreuth, became snobbish, hypocritical and nationalistic; the establishment of a 'Bayreuth Church', with its Wagner theology, his new title of *Meister*, and the 'conventional' Christian drama *Parsifal* were indications of this new direction. When he sent Nietzsche the poem of 'Parsifal', he inscribed it 'From Richard Wagner, Higher Ecclesiastical Councillor' (*Ober-Kirchenrat*). Nietzsche was not amused by this piece of friendly flippancy.

The successful foundation of Bayreuth, the founding of the *Bayreuther Blätter* and the steady flow of admirers and disciples to Wahnfried caused Wagner's utterances to take on an infallible and prophetic quality. Towards the end of his life he came to express himself, with evident enjoyment, more and more on matters outside his own practical experience. His growing number of adherents were anxious to have the *Meister*'s views on the British, the Jews, socialism, life after death, the origins of man, love, literature and the machine age. His biographer, Glasenapp, prepared a Wagner-*Lexikon*, to be presented to him on his seventieth birthday, which quoted his views on a large number of subjects, alphabetically arranged.

In May 1881 Wagner met Arthur de Gobineau in Bayreuth. For four weeks they discussed subjects like race, blood and regeneration. These talks inspired some of Wagner's contributions to the *Bayreuther Blätter*. Regeneration was the idea that dominated his thinking towards the end of his life. In *Parsifal* it found sublime expression; in his writings it took many quaint and curious turns. The human race, he said, had been degenerating for thousands of years through eating the wrong food and through lacking the guidance of the Schopenhauerian philosophy. 'Our blood is vitiated by the mixing of the hero-blood of the noblest races with that of onetime cannibals [i.e. Jews], now trained to be the skilled business leaders of society.' He was still convinced that man was fundamentally good although the wrong diet and fatal blood crossings had done their worst. 'The Jewish race', he wrote to Ludwig, 'is the born enemy of pure humanity and everything that is noble in it; it is certain that we Germans will go under before them and perhaps I am the last German who knew how to stand up, as an art-loving man, against the Judaism that is already getting control of everything.' He agreed with de Gobineau that superior race can be irreparably tainted by mingling with inferior races and he saw, in the contamination of the Aryan idealist by the Semitic realist, one of the most serious causes of the decline of modern society. This decadence was, however, essentially a moral decadence. To recover his health modern European man must regenerate himself physically and morally: physically by the practice of vegetarianism and the practice of a healthy racial hygiene and morally by returning to the principle of pure Christianity via Wagnerian music-drama. He was prepared to accept, and indeed to welcome, a socialist state provided that it entered into binding agreements with the vegetarian, anti-vivisection and temperance societies.

All these wayward effusions were at once forgotten and forgiven by the true friends of the man and his art. The Frenchman Gabriel Monod, who had been at the 1876 *Ring* rehearsals, had this to say about Wagner:

On everyone who comes near him he exercises an irresistible fascination, not only by reason of his musical genius, or the originality of his intellect, or the variety of his learning, but above all by the energy of temperament and will that emanates from every fibre of him. You feel you are in the presence of a force of nature, unleashing itself with almost reckless violence. After seeing him at close quarters, at one moment irresponsibly gay, pouring forth a torrent of jokes and laughter, at another vehement, respecting neither titles nor powers nor friendships, always letting himself be carried away by the first thing that comes into his head, you find yourself unable to be too hard upon him for his lapses of taste, of tact, of delicacy: if you are a Jew you are inclined to forgive him his pamphlet on Judaism in music, if a Frenchman his farce on the capitulation of Paris, if a German all the insults he has heaped on Germany ... you take him as he is, full of faults – no doubt because he is full of genius – and incontestably a superior being, one of the greatest and most extraordinary men our century has produced.

Hand in hand with his writings went the composition of *Parsifal*, the search for health in the Italian sun and tedious business worries connected with the festival and the performing rights of his works. Wagner completed the score of *Parsifal* in Palermo on 13 January 1882; shortly afterwards Schott paid him 100,000 marks for the publishing rights, the highest sum ever paid by a German music publisher. The day before its completion Auguste Renoir called at his hotel and left a letter; Judith Gautier, and other mutual Paris friends, had entreated Renoir not to leave Palermo without sketching Wagner. He called again next day, when Wagner was putting the finishing touches to *Parsifal*, to be told by Paul von Joukowsky, a rich young Russian painter and friend of Henry James who had met Wagner in Naples two years before, that the *Meister* was in a state of nervous tension and unable to eat. Wagner overheard the conversation and came forward to greet Renoir in a black velvet gown with thick padded satin sleeves. 'He is', said Renoir, 'very handsome and charming, offers me his hand, invites me to come in and sit down and then proceeds to talk quite meaninglessly in French and German, punctuated by many an Ah! and Oh!...' The sketch was done the following day during a thirty-five minute sitting. Wagner's comment on this rather grim sketch was that he looked like a Protestant pastor.

By the end of 1879 Wagner's health had become so bad that it was essential for him to get away, once more, from the cold, damp Bayreuth climate. In January 1880 he and his family moved into the Villa Angri at Posilippo near Naples. He had almost come to the end of dictating his autobiography to Cosima; it was to end on 3 May 1864, 'the moment', he wrote to Ludwig, 'when our complete alliance was wrested from fate'. Meanwhile Cosima's diary was in full swing. 'She is keeping for our son an exceptionally detailed diary in which she records every day the state of my health, my work and my occasional utterances.' He was disgusted with Germany and awaited calmly the advent of socialism.

I am repelled by this new Germany. Is this what you call an Empire? Can Berlin ever be an imperial capital? The whole thing is a pure joke, perpetrated from above and will soon be answered from below [he told Ludwig]. My exhaustion is complete... all these useless efforts to find means to set up a permanent foundation in Bayreuth are frustrated by the wretched condition of the German 'nation'. I am furious and determined to put an end to the whole thing... the reports about the performances of my works [in German theatres] fill me with uneasiness; I would like to withdraw permission for them to be performed anywhere and I am still thinking seriously about emigrating to America as I would there have the means of buying back all previously granted performing rights. For many other reasons besides, in particular my total despair about Germany, I am refusing to give up this project.

One of Wagner's new friends at this time was Paul von Joukowsky. This artistocratic young Russian painter had a studio near the Villa Angri and spoke German as his native language. He immediately fell a victim to Wagner's fascination and remained with him, as far as he was able, until his death. He lived through the final stages of the instrumentation of *Parsifal* and Wagner gave him the job of designing the scenery and costumes. He wrote,

No one who has not known Wagner in the intimacy of his home can have any idea of the goodness of his nature, of his childlike lovableness ... whoever has known Wagner as intimately as I have done can see how a hero-cult develops; it is, simply, faith in those beings to whom the impossible is possible. His nature was demonic through and through; the powers dwelling in him possessed him utterly. His need to give artistic shape to things, his willing and wishing, his loving and hating, the ideas springing up inside him, all these took complete control of him; for him, artistic creation and literary expression meant liberation from the oppressive abundance of his being; no one who has not known him can have any idea of the breadth of the horizons which his talk opened out to his listeners ... born to command, as few other men have been, endowed with a force that could either construct or destroy, possessed with a thirst for superhuman beauty, he had to struggle for three quarters of his life against every sort of want, ill health, distress and the complete failure of those nearest him to understand him.[1]

This was Joukowsky's description of Wagner when he was ill and approaching seventy and had barely three more years to live. They went together to Amalfi and there Wagner found at the Moorish Palazzo Rufolo, occupied by an Englishman, the realization of Klingsor's palace and garden. Joukowsky at once made some sketches for *Parsifal* Act II. Later they went on to Siena; Wagner was so impressed by the beauty of the domed interior of the cathedral that he was on the point of tears. Once again, Joukowsky did some sketches which were later used as the model for the Bayreuth Temple of the Grail.

In the summer of 1880 Wagner refused to sign a petition to the Reichstag against the Jews and their increasing power in Germany. Since the failure of the anti-vivisection campaign he had lost interest in petitions. It was organized by Bernhard Förster, one of the leaders of the German anti-Semitic movement, who later, in 1885, married Nietzsche's sister Elisabeth. They founded a Teutonic colony in Paraguay, Nueva Germania. It did not flourish; the colonists thought themselves swindled by the

---

[1] This quotation, given by Ernest Newman, had never before been published.

Försters; Förster killed himself and Elisabeth returned to Germany. She tried, first of all, to re-establish her husband's reputation; his departure for Paraguay had been hastened by an episode in which he had insulted and manhandled Jewish bus passengers. This proving too much for her, she decided to become instead the guardian of her brother's reputation; she changed her name to Förster-Nietzsche and started on her thorough campaign of acquisition and falsification of Nietzsche material; she was anxious to show both that Nietzsche's judgment had not been clouded by illness and that Wagner himself was largely responsible for the rift between them.

Another reason for Wagner's refusal to sign Förster's petition was that several of his most important and devoted collaborators were Jews. Angelo Neumann, who was himself a Jew and later, with his travelling theatre, spread Wagner's fame throughout the world, was now preparing the Berlin première of the *Ring*. Anti-Jewish agitation was particularly strong in Berlin; Wagner feared that the success of the *Ring* might be imperilled if he was thought to have signed the Förster petition. He wrote to Neumann reassuringly that 'I have nothing whatsoever to do with the present "anti-Semitic" movement; an article from my hand shortly to appear in the *Bayreuther Blätter* will show *intellectuals* the futility of trying to associate my name with such a movement.' Another Jew, Hermann Levi, who conducted the Bayreuth première of *Parsifal* was, as Munich *Kapellmeister*, conducting Wagner operas to packed houses. In spite of being frequently provoked by Wagner about his racial origins he wrote to his father in these terms:

He is the best and noblest person. That our contemporaries misunderstand and slander him is natural; it is the practice of the world to besmirch that which shines; Goethe had to suffer a similar fate. Posterity will one day, however, recognize that Wagner is just as great a person as an artist, a fact which those close to him already know. Even his fight against what he called 'Judaism' in music and in modern literature was inspired by the highest motives. The fact that he is quite free from any petty dislike of Jews, unlike 'Land-junkers' or Protestant hypocrites, is shown by his behaviour to myself and to Joseph Rubinstein and earlier to Tausig whom he tenderly loved.

Joseph Rubinstein had been living with the Wagners in Bayreuth and in Italy; he finished the piano score of *Parsifal* in the Hotel des Palmes at Palermo just before Wagner had completed the full score. Another of his young visitors at Posilippo was the twenty-six-year-old Engelbert Humperdinck who, later at Bayreuth, wrote out the *Parsifal* parts for the singers and won brief fame by adding some bars of his own to the score to allow more time for the cumbersome machinery to do its work during the collapse of Klingsor's castle. He was in Italy on a Felix Mendelssohn travelling music scholarship.

To the première of *Parsifal* on 26 July 1882 came many of Wagner's old friends with three important exceptions – Bülow, Nietzsche and Ludwig. To the latter he penned one of his short extempore poems accusing him of disdaining the refreshment of the Grail. Nietzsche would only come at Wagner's pressing invitation although, as a member of the *Patronat-Verein*, he was entitled to a seat for one of the first two performances. 'I assuredly will not go', he told his sister, to whom he gave his voucher, 'unless Wagner invites me personally and treats me as the most honoured of his guests.' Nietzsche was obviously most anxious to hear the music for a work which he was, from now on, to vilify in strident, hysterical language. For Nietzsche *Parsifal* was a heinous betrayal of the spirit of those halcyon Tribschen days. His views were largely responsible for misunderstandings about *Parsifal* which held sway for at least two generations; *Parsifal* came to be regarded as a new ersatz religion with the ecclesiastical ritual transferred to the stage; the Bayreuth Festspielhaus was the equivalent of the Mormon tabernacle or the First Church of Christ Scientists, and the faithful were Wagnerites rather than latter-day saints or Christian scientists. This approach to *Parsifal*, which Wagner in certain ways unwittingly encouraged, is erroneous and damaging because it ignores the fact that *Parsifal* is an integral part of Wagner's *oeuvre*, the final expression of a coherent and developing artist in a philosophy of life which, step by step, achieved a higher degree of sublimation. Wagner diverted the public's awareness of the organic relationship of *Parsifal* to the rest of his art by treating it as something special, as a 'stage-dedication-drama', thus laying the foundation stone for a 'dedicatory cult' in which orthodox Wagnerites delighted to luxuriate. The practice of not clapping at the end of the last act, intended as a special sign of respect in 1883, the year of Wagner's death, was turned into a hallowed tradition. Finally, *Parsifal* could not, until the copyright expired thirty years after

Wagner's death, be performed anywhere other than at Bayreuth.

In the summer of 1845 when Wagner went with Minna, his dog and his parrot to take the waters at Marienbad he took as part of his holiday reading Wolfram von Eschenbach's *Parzival*. Twelve years later, on Good Friday in April 1857, at the Villa Wesendonk, memories of the poem came flooding back to him and, inspired by thoughts of Good Friday, he sketched the whole three-act drama. 'I'm especially fond', he told Mathilde Wesendonk, 'of a creation of mine – a wonderfully, demoniacal woman (the ambassadress of the Grail), who daily becomes more vivid and riveting. If I were ever to complete this poem I would have achieved something really original. But I simply cannot see how long I shall live to carry out all my plans.' The idea of *Parsifal*, therefore, had been occupying him intermittently for over thirty-five years. The need to overcome the tragic egocentricity which, in *Tristan und Isolde*, led to individual self-destruction and, in the *Ring* (as the will to power), destroyed a whole world, found expression in *Die Meistersinger* in the clear-sighted, temperate renunciation by Hans Sachs. In *Parsifal* it becomes the theme of an allegorical action: the 'pure fool' (*der reine Tor*), through learning compassion (*durch Mitleid wissend*), steps onto the stage, replaces the Wagnerian redemptresses – Senta, Elisabeth, Brünnhilde, Isolde – and heals the wound of life's tragic conflict. In January 1849 Wagner had written a detailed fifty-page draft of a musical drama 'Jesus of Nazareth', in which Jesus appeared as a social revolutionary. He and Barabbas together planned a Jewish uprising against Rome but Jesus, yearning for death, chooses the path of self-destruction. Although rejecting 'Jesus of Nazareth' as the subject of an opera Wagner continued to look for a moral hero; in May 1856, in Zurich, he wrote a prose sketch of *Die Sieger* with the twin themes of abstinence and renunciation. In *Tristan* Wagner thought seriously of leading Parzifal, in search of the Grail, to his hero who lay on his deathbed consumed by passion; he recognized in the ailing Amfortas the Tristan of Act III, 'with an unimaginable climax'. In his essay 'Die Nibelungen' (1849) he had described the Grail as a 'spiritualization of the *Nibelung* hoard'.

It is important not to be misled by the 'Christian' symbolism in *Parsifal* – Wagner, in his last music-drama, is thinking in symbols and archetypal images; the Grail and the Spear, the two vital symbols of the drama, are also heathen sexual symbols and in *Parsifal* they symbolize the ideal unity between love and masculine energy. In *Religion und Kunst* (Religion and Art) (1880) Wagner had written, 'One could say that, when religious forms become artificial, it is reserved to art to rescue the quintessence of religion. This is done by apprehending certain mythical symbols, which religion expects us to take literally, grasping their allegorical (or archetypal) value and then, by means of an ideal representation, reveal the hidden depths of the truth of these symbols.' In this famous sentence, which was embedded in verbiage about Jews, vivisection and vegetarianism, Wagner gives us the secret of the enduring appeal of his art. He objectifies the archetypal elements in the unconscious life of the soul; the revelation of these spiritual depths through the Wagnerian art has nothing to do with any Christian or other religion. Through the continuous struggle for redemption, which achieves its triumphant conclusion in the 'redemption of the redeemer' (Parsifal), mankind marches upwards towards God to form a regenerative alliance of human and divine, a religion freed from all artificial confessional restraints. Wagner's dramas are all, in a sense (not only *Parsifal*) 'stage-dedication-dramas' because they reveal to us, in poetic-musical works of art, the primeval drama of the clash of divine and human wills which underlies all tangible, visible phenomena. The continuous revelation of these archetypal Wagnerian truths continues to be the artistic and cultural mission of Bayreuth.

For Thomas Mann one aspect of Wagner's genius shows itself most unmistakably in *Parsifal*. In *The Sufferings and Greatness of Richard Wagner* (1933) he wrote,

Wagner is in all his works entirely himself; every beat can only be his and bears the ineffaceable imprint of his style. And yet every work is at the same time something quite special, a stylistic world in itself, the result of an objective inner sensibility which counter-balances and neutralizes all purely personal views and prejudices. The greatest miracle in this respect is perhaps *Parsifal*, the work of a man of seventy, which achieves the limit by way of comprehending and expressing remote, eerie and holy worlds. It is, despite the achievement of *Tristan*, the most extreme amongst Wagner's works and surpasses, in its spiritual and stylistic adaptive ability, what we have come to expect of him. It is a work full of sounds which linger in our consciousness in constantly disquieting curiosity and enchantment.

275

The little town of Bayreuth in July 1882 was thinking less about the cosmic, redemptive and regenerative effects of the music-dramas of its extraordinary new citizen than about how to accommodate and amuse the festival visitors. There were to be sixteen performances of *Parsifal*, all but two open to the general public. The streets were better lit than in 1876; the shops were full of souvenirs – 'Siegfried' pens, 'Parsifal' cigars and a sparkling wine called 'Klingsor's magic potion' – and the large restaurant, next to the Festspielhaus, which held 1500 people had been greatly improved. Wagner had, before the opening of the festival, dissolved the *Patronat-Verein*; it had shown itself unable to finance the 1882 *Parsifal* production; henceforth the festivals would have to be supported by the general public. It had always been his wish that those interested in his art, but otherwise impecunious, should have free admission to his operas; in May 1882 he founded a special stipendiary fund for the poorer Wagnerites; it should, in his words, 'provide the means not only for free entry but also for travel and accommodation for those with meagre resources who are generally the worthiest and most deserving of Germany's sons'.

The *Parsifal* preparations had been a great strain for Wagner; during and after the festival he had several severe attacks of cramp in his chest and asthma. At the final performance of *Parsifal* on 29 August 1882 Wagner slipped into the orchestra, took the baton from Levi and, unknown to the audience, conducted from the 23rd bar of the transformation music of Act III to the end. At the end of the opera the public, according to Levi, broke into wild applause which defied any description, calling repeatedly for Wagner who refused to appear. From the conductor's stand beneath the stage he addressed the singers, players and staff, thanking them for all their efforts in his inimitably witty and charming way. 'You have accomplished everything; up there it was the perfection of dramatic art and down here a continuous symphony.' He expressed the hope that they would all meet again next year to which they all replied with a resounding 'Ja!' Everyone, said Levi, was on the point of tears. 'It was an unforgettable moment.' The festival was also a financial success; 8200 tickets were sold, bringing in 240,000 marks; Wagner was already planning twenty performances for 1883.

A few days before the last performance of *Parsifal* Cosima's daughter Blandine von Bülow married Count Biagio Gravina, son of the Sicilian Prince of Ramacca; they had become engaged at Palermo. Bülow did not come; he had himself married, a few days earlier, the actress Marie Schanzer. As soon as the festival was over Wagner's one thought was to hurry back to Italy with his family and Joukowsky. They arrived in Venice in the middle of September 1882 and installed themselves in eighteen rooms on the first floor of the sixteenth-century Palazzo Vendramin on the Grand Canal. One of the first things they heard was that de Gobineau had had a stroke when entering a railway carriage in Turin and died the same day. Wagner lived quietly in the Palazzo Vendramin; as was to be expected he draped his study liberally with silks and satins and sprayed them with heavy scents. He went for an occasional ride in a gondola with Cosima; he sat in the little French garden at the back of the Palazzo; he read, with irritation, Nietzsche's latest book, *Die fröhliche Wissenschaft* (The Gay Science) and with interest Hermann Oldenberg's *Buddha*. He wrote for the *Bayreuther Blätter* an article, 'The stage-dedication-festival in Bayreuth'; in it he deplored the difficulties with the transformation scenery and the interruption of the scene through the drawing of the curtain. On a more general note he said that *Parsifal* had, in its presentation, come very near his conception of it as a flight from the world. 'Who can, his whole life long, in full alertness, look at this world of lies, fraud, hypocrisy, legalized murder and thieving, without having, from time to time, to avert one's gaze from it all? Where then do we look? Generally into the depths of death.'

The even tenor of life in the Palazzo Vendramin was soon disturbed by the arrival of Liszt who installed himself there and wrote a piano piece, 'La lugubre gondola'. 'Wherever he goes he is surrounded the whole time,' Wagner wrote to Ludwig, 'by a motley crowd of acquaintances who dig him up and then drag him off on an endless round of matinées, dinners and soirées so that we never see him, living as we do remote from everything and thrown entirely upon ourselves.' During the brief moments they had together Wagner and Liszt discussed the idea of a one-act symphony which Wagner was thinking of composing. The cramps in his chest became worse and more frequent and Wagner was given doses of valerian and opium. On 11 February 1883 he started to write an essay, 'Das Weibliche' (The Feminine), giving his views on polygamy, monogamy and fidelity. The next evening he read aloud from Fouqué's fairy story *Undine*, whilst Joukowsky sketched him, and he later played the song of the Rhine-maidens as the curtain falls on *Das Rheingold*. On 13 February he sent a message asking to be excused from luncheon; he was at grips with his cramp pains. The maid heard him groaning; he rang the bell violently and asked for 'my doctor and my wife'. He had had a heart attack and died in Cosima's arms at half-past three that afternoon. His unfinished essay, 'Das Weibliche' lay on his desk. 'Notwithstanding, the emancipation of woman can only proceed in circumstances of ecstatic convulsions. Love – tragedy. . . .' With the word *Tragik* the pen ran off the paper.

Wagner's body was embalmed, a death mask made by the sculptor Augusto Benvenuti, and, on 16 February, he began the long journey to Bayreuth. Cosima had cut off her long hair and placed it on his heart; for twenty-four hours she had clung to his body. D'Annunzio is thought to have followed the coffin as the cortège proceeded along the Grand Canal towards the railway station. Cosima sat in a small compartment alone with the coffin; by the time the train arrived at Bayreuth, shortly before midnight on the seventeenth, she was so thin, after four days of fasting, that her wedding rings had fallen off her fingers. The coffin spent the night of the seventeenth at the station under a guard of honour; next day, on Sunday, 18 February, after tributes had been paid by Muncker and Feustel, and a regimental band had played Siegfried's 'Trauermarsch', the funeral procession set out for Wahnfried. The streets of Bayreuth were packed and silent and a black flag hung from every house; the coffin, on which lay two wreaths – both from the king – was carried on an open hearse drawn by four horses. At Wahnfried twelve of Wagner's friends and associates carried the coffin to the tomb in the garden and later, in the presence of Cosima, it was lowered into the vault.

When Ludwig first heard the news of Wagner's death all he was able to say was 'Terrible! frightful! Let me be alone.' A few days later, after his court secretary Bürkel had returned from the funeral ceremonies at Bayreuth and reported the stir which Wagner's death had caused in Germany and abroad, the king exclaimed: 'This artist who is now mourned by the whole world, it was I who first understood him; it was I who rescued him for the world.'

CHAPTER THIRTEEN
Epilogue

In August 1976 the centenary of Bayreuth was celebrated with a new production of the Boulez-Chéreau *Ring*. The audiences were surprised at what they saw: Siegfried looked on indifferently as Nothung, his sword, was forged in a blast-furnace; in *Götterdämmerung* he fidgeted, chain-smoked and wore a dinner-jacket; the Walküre warrior-maidens erotically fondled the naked corpses of the slain heroes; Wotan, in a frock-coat, looked a crooked Victorian entrepreneur; the Rhine-maidens, if not whores, were sluttish factory girls; the final immolation scene, when Brünnhilde and her horse Grane leapt into the flames of Siegfried's funeral pyre, was witnessed by a group of surly dockers.

These were some of the features of this controversial anniversary *Ring* produced by the young Frenchman Patrice Chéreau and conducted by Pierre Boulez. The indignation was great; each performance was loudly booed and soon afterwards an association was formed with the aim of 'exposing' the fallacies of this production by showing it to be a hideous travesty of the *Ring* as conceived by Wagner and an insult to the Master's memory.

Another event in the summer of 1976 was the publication of the first volume of Cosima's '*Tagebücher*' (Diaries); the second volume followed a year later. Cosima opened her diary on 1 January 1869, six weeks after she had moved openly into Tribschen with her daughters Isolde and Eva, and she ended it in Venice on 12 February 1883, the evening before Wagner died. Her diaries had a strange history; written for Siegfried (who never read them) and for her other children they found their way into the possession of her daughter, Eva Chamberlain, who bequeathed them to the town of Bayreuth with the condition that they would not be published within thirty years of her death which occurred in 1942. These twenty-one note-books, consisting of five thousand closely written pages were deposited, after Eva's death, with the Bavarian State Bank in Munich. In 1974, after two years of legal complications, the diaries were brought, under police protection, from Munich to Bayreuth.

Cosima's diaries are, in the words of their editors, 'the fervid jottings of a wife totally absorbed in her husband's mission and who has no wish to bequeath to posterity anything other than this great passion of her life'. Apart from providing a fascinating account of the most trivial happenings in Wagner's everyday life they also correct posterity's picture of their author. Wagner did not need humanizing but Cosima did. When he died she was forty-five years old; Bülow telegraphed her, 'Soeur, il faut vivre,' and she lived another forty-seven years. During their relatively short thirteen-year marriage Wagner and Cosima became known as *das hohe Paar* (the sublime couple); as a widow and as the *Herrin von Bayreuth* she became *die hohe Frau*, revered and feared by all. In 1906 she suffered a kind of physical collapse when staying with Prince Ernst zu Hohenlohe-Langenburg; she then handed over the running of the festival to her son Siegfried and lived thereafter, for the next twenty-three years, the life of an invalid. Although illegitimate and an adulteress she laid stress on good breeding and social connections. The festivals, under her direction, became a meeting-place for the international aristocracy and beau-monde. It would be a mistake, however, to associate her too closely with the anti-Semitic ideology of the *Bayreuther Blätter* under Hans von Wolzogen and with the nationalistic views of her son-in-law, Houston Stewart Chamberlain, who married Eva in 1908, two years after Cosima's physical collapse. Her diaries show that she was not opiniated, but that she did her dutiful best to assimilate Wagner's theories on Jews, art, politics and all else besides.

After Wagner's death she displayed her remarkable practical ability. 'I am,' she wrote, 'only destined for painstaking industriousness and I cannot take the smallest matter lightly. When I see so many people relying upon their impulses and inspiration I regard myself as being quite inartistic and Philistine.' At first she remained withdrawn, nursing her grief. Her own position was not clear; Wagner had left no will and certain influential nationalistic Wagnerites distrusted his French, cosmopolitan widow and tried to persuade Liszt and Bülow to rescue the festival from Hermann Levi's Semitism. When Cosima learned that the uncertainty about the succession was beginning to demoralize the artists and was leading to slipshod singing and acting she intervened. At first her artistic intervention took a discreet form; she had erected on the stage a small wooden partition behind which she sat during the performances. Out of the darkness she dispatched to the performers a flow of comments on small pieces of paper about every aspect of the performance, pointing out when they had deviated from the Master's instructions. Instead of provoking opposition this established her authority in the Festspielhaus and in 1886 she was officially in charge of the whole Bayreuth organization.

Cosima's reign was naturally conservative. Richter, Levi and Mottl, and, after 1896, her son Siegfried, were her conductors and close collaborators. Her greatest sorrow since Wagner's death was in 1914 when *Parsifal* passed out of copyright and the Reichstag could not be prevailed upon to pass a 'Lex *Parsifal*' reserving to Bayreuth the sole right to perform it. Although many expressed doubts about her understanding of both music and drama her management of the festival was very successful. Her aim was to institutionalize and to stabilize Bayreuth. She introduced into the repertoire all Wagner's operas written since, and including, *Der fliegende Holländer*. In 1891 she ordered a new production of *Tannhäuser* and released a live pack of hounds in the hunting scene in the first act. Although her treatment of the Venusberg scene was too full of Greek mythological allusions for certain tastes the dramatic power of her production had a profound impact on audiences that year.

Siegfried Wagner assumed control of the festival in 1906. It had earlier been settled that the Bayreuth inheritance would be divided equally between him and his mother (Cosima later bequeathed her half share to Siegfried). Under Cosima the Bayreuth festival became an established event even if it was also an international rendezvous for snobs as was thought by certain earnest Wagnerites. The programmes acquired their permanent character; each year *Parsifal*, the *Ring* and one additional opera were performed. Siegfried was also a composer of operas with whimsical titles. Debussy heard him, in 1903, conduct extracts from his *Herzog Wildfang*; his comment was that it sounded like a piece of homework by a pupil of Richard Wagner, who did not think its author would go far. Siegfried was a result of the self-dramatizing propensities of his parents, *das hohe Paar*. His birth, on 6 June 1869, took place as his father was composing the music for *Siegfried* Act III. It was more a 'coup-de-théâtre' than an ordinary human birth, an event to meet the needs of the new Wagnerian 'dynastic' legend which was beginning to blend with that of the *Ring*. Siegfried was fourteen when his father died; from then on his life was run by his mother and by his four older sisters and half-sisters. Urged by Eva Chamberlain to marry and thus prevent the Bayreuth inheritance from falling into the hands of the son of her hated sister, Isolde Beidler, he chose in 1915, as his bride, the eighteen-year-old Winifred Williams, an English orphan and ward of Karl Klindworth. He was twenty-eight years her senior.

Siegfried was dapper, polite and uncommital. He had assimilated his parents' 'reactionary' views on politics and culture. He took no interest in the music of his great contemporaries – Richard Strauss, Ravel, Bartók, de Falla, Berg – most of whom he considered to be dangerous examples of cultural Bolshevism. Although he was a competent conductor, many thought that he, the son of Wagner and grandson of Liszt, did not take much interest in music. He had at first wanted to be an architect; it was the architectural and visual aspects of the operas that he most enjoyed. He designed the sets for the 1911 and 1914 productions of *Die Meistersinger* and *Der fliegende Holländer*. Then came the Great War 1914–18; the Festspielhaus remained shut during and after the war; it only reopened in 1924 after Siegfried and Winifred had gone on a fund-raising tour of America.

Siegfried died in 1930, a couple of months after his mother. He had bequeathed the entire Bayreuth estate to his wife, provided she never remarried. Winifred found herself the new *Herrin von Bayreuth*. This English orphan was brought up by her ancient guardians in the Wagner cult; they took her, aged seventeen, to Bayreuth where she fell for the ailing, middle-aged Siegfried. She married him the following year and moved into Wahnfried where a hard training awaited her at the hands of Cosima, now nearly eighty, and her new, unattractive and highly critical sisters-in-law, Eva Chamberlain and Daniela Thode. In a short time she became a hard, efficient and dominating wife, mother and business partner. Were it not for her exceptional abilities Bayreuth would probably not have survived the nearly simultaneous deaths of Cosima and Siegfried in 1930. Winifred Wagner, recognizing that her talents were essentially administrative, had no pretensions to being her own artistic director. The dazzling success of the 1930 festival had been due to the presence of Toscanini who conducted *Tristan und Isolde* and *Tannhaüser*. She saw the absurdity of appealing for funds from America and trying to attract international audiences whilst at the same time propagating an official reactionary ideology directed against Jewish artistic decadence and cultural Bolshevism. The death in 1927 of Houston Stewart Chamberlain, Wahnfried's evil intellectual genius, of some unpleasant lingering illness, paved the way for a more liberal outlook. She realized that Bayreuth, if it were not to become a cultural backwater, would have to bring in conductors, singers, set designers and instrumentalists from Berlin, the capital of German music. She accordingly invited the conductor Furtwängler, the intendant of the Berlin opera Heinz Tietjen and the set designer Emil Pretorius to Bayreuth.

Winifred Wagner was one of the early admirers of Adolf Hitler. He was a guest at Wahnfried in October 1923, a month before the unsuccessful *Bürgerbräuputsch* in Munich and she sent him presents of food and stationery during his term of imprisonment in Landsberg. (He was said to have written *Mein Kampf* on paper supplied to him by Winifred.) The German film director, Syberberg, made a television film in 1976, the Bayreuth centenary year. In it seventy-nine-year-old Winifred Wagner spoke for over five hours about her life in Bayreuth and her friendship with Hitler. Looking at times aristocratic, at times like a cunning old peasant woman, Winifred had this to say about her friend Adolf – or 'Wolf':

He played the piano nicely. In his youth he composed an opera. He loved the children ... he treated women with the greatest civility ... although a vegetarian he occasionally ate *Leberknödelsuppe*. He hated discussing politics and talked passionately about stage problems. He had a deep love for, and knowledge of, Wagner's music which he tried, despite the inconveniences of his profession [!] to hear regularly. When he telephoned he always announced himself as *Kapellmeister* Wolf.[1]

[1] When Winifred asked him why he liked to be called 'Wolf', he replied, 'Because it sounds to delightfully Jewish!'

She disregarded the more sinister aspects of Hitler's character. 'We had a human, personal and confidential relationship based upon our admiration and love for Richard Wagner.'

As a mother Winifred was cold and impersonal; Hitler gave more affection to her children, particularly Wieland and Wolfgang, than she did. At Wahnfried he talked to them until the early hours of the morning about the future of Bayreuth. He let Wieland off military service and visited the wounded Wolfgang in hospital. He was a musician 'manqué' and hoped, vicariously, to realize his operatic dreams through Wagner's grandsons.

Hitler's friendship with Winifred benefited Bayreuth during the National-Socialist era. It kept the festivals free from official interference and witch-hunts; Winifred was able to run them much as she liked. During the 1939–45 war the festivals, which continued at Hitler's instructions for the benefit of troops going to or returning from the front, were largely financed by contributions from the *Kraft durch Freude* (Strength Through Joy) organization. The conventional and uninteresting productions of Tietjen and Pretorius aroused the contemptuous anger of Wieland Wagner who saw in them a debasement of his grandfather's art.

At the end of the war Bayreuth was badly bombed and a direct hit on Wahnfried destroyed the drawing-room on the garden front. Winifred, as a member of the Nazi Party, was in disgrace; not until 1949, after a series of convictions and appeals in various courts, was she 'denazified'. She transferred to Wieland and Wolfgang the authority to manage the festivals. Wieland spent the early years after the war on Lake Constance reading Freud and Jung who both left their mark on the new Bayreuth theatrical style. The tendency was for the scenery to be reduced to its barest essentials and for the characters to appear as archetypal symbols of a subconscious reality. In 1966 Wieland died, aged forty-nine, leaving his brother Wolfgang in sole charge of the festivals.

Wieland's stark, stylized productions ran into the inevitable critical storm; one of his purposes was to rid Wagner's operas of the near fatal effects of the embraces of the Third Reich. This was best done by emphasizing their timelessness and truth. He saw no reason why he should abide by his grandfather's stage instructions; Wagner was, as a producer, a child of his time and he accepted, willingly or unwillingly, contemporary theatrical styles and techniques. Wieland wished to liberate Wagner's mythological works from what he called the 'impotent pseudo-naturalism' of his own and later periods. 'Only the re-creative spiritual act can replace a scheme of scenery and action which has become sterile after a hundred years . . . we must not shrink from returning to the womb – the origins of the work.'[1]

Wieland's productions and modern Wagner criticism had the effect of opening the eyes and minds of people of different generations throughout the world to new splendours and profundities in the Wagnerian drama. It has been the lot of Wieland's brother Wolfgang to lead the dramas out of the womb and to encourage us to look at the *Ring* as a description of the history of ideas in the nineteenth century. Bayreuth is entering a new phase of 'realism'. In July 1835, when he was writing the music for *Das Liebesverbot*, Wagner passed through Bayreuth for the first time on his way from Prague to southern Germany. At odd times during the next forty years his thoughts returned to this little town in the Franconian Alps. Although he finally built a theatre there in which his works could be properly performed he was, up to the day of his death, depressed and doubtful about the future of the festivals. The very popularity of his operas was a threat to Bayreuth. Bernard Shaw, writing in 1889 in the *English Illustrated Magazine*, seemed to bear out his fears: 'The sooner we devote our money and energy to making Wagner's music live in England instead of expensively embalming its corpse in Bavaria the better for English art in all its branches.' The felicitous outcome has been that Wagner's art flourishes today not only in Bavaria but throughout the world. It is, however, only in Bayreuth where Wagner can be most fully experienced – in the plain and practical theatre on the festival hill, in walks and refreshments during the long opera intervals in the Festspielhaus gardens where his bust sternly presides, and now in Wahnfried, which, as the new Richard Wagner Museum, opened its doors for the first time to the public in the centenary year. There the Wagnerite relives his hero's life, the phases of which unfold in room after room, each packed with pictures, scores, letters, photographs, costumes and curios. The large drawing-room, where Wagner and Cosima held their soirées, has been rebuilt; his library, rescued from destruction, is again on the bookshelves

[1] *Denkmalschutz für Wagner?*

and his Erard piano, given to him in Paris in 1858 and strummed on by G.I.s in 1945, is back in its former place.

In this room visitors are treated to taped excerpts of Wagner's music-dramas. It is not quite the same as being in the presence of the *Meister* himself who, in his velvet cap and satin tunics, played, sang, recited and talked inexhaustibly and irrepressibly to his wife and Liszt; to his conductors, singers and other collaborators; to holders of *Patronatscheine* and members of Wagner-*Vereine*; to the festival visitors, whether kings or commoners, who came from far and wide to pay homage to this 'god-man who in truth cannot fail nor err', as Ludwig exclaimed on leaving Bayreuth after the *Götterdämmerung* rehearsals. Wagner's visitors, no doubt, echoed his further words of gratitude, penned after returning to Hohenschwangau, 'Fortunate century that saw this spirit arise in its midst! How future generations will envy us the incomparable privilege of being your contemporaries.'

Important Dates in
Wagner's Life

Historical Events

1813

10 Oct. Birth of Verdi

16–19 Oct. Battle of the Nations

Wagner's Personal History

1813

22 May Wagner born in Leipzig

1814

Aug. Wagner's mother marries Geyer

Family move to Dresden

1817

Weber *Hofkapellmeister* in Dresden

1819

Publication of Schopenhauer's
Die Welt als Wille und Vorstellung

1821

Première of *Der Freischütz* in
Berlin

1821

Sept. Death of Geyer

Historical Events	Wagner's Personal History
	1822
	Dec. Enrols at the Kreuzschule in Dresden
1824	
Mar. Première of Beethoven's Ninth Symphony in Vienna	
1826	
June Death in London of Carl Maria von Weber	
1827	**1827**
26 Mar. Death of Beethoven in Vienna	*Leubald und Adelaïde* Wagner is confirmed Family return to Leipzig
1828 19 Nov. Death of Schubert in Vienna	**1828** Harmony lessons and 'experiences' Schröder-Devrient
1830	**1830**
July 'Bourgeois' Revolution in France	Meets Schumann in Leipzig
	Dec. Performance of Overture in B major in Leipzig
	1831
	Gambles; studies counterpoint with Weinlig Symphony in C major In Vienna and Prague *Die Hochzeit*

288

Historical Events **Wagner's Personal History**

1832

Mar.   Death of Goethe in Weimar

1833	1833

7 May   Brahms born in Hamburg

Jan.   Poem of *Die Feen*
Chorus manager in Würzburg

1834

Jan.   Score of *Die Feen* completed
June   Prose sketch of *Das Liebesverbot*

July   Meets Minna Planer in Bad Lauchstädt

Oct.   Musical manager in Magdeburg

1836

29 Mar.   Première in Magdeburg of *Das Liebesverbot*

24 Nov.   Marries Minna in Königsberg

1837

Apr.   Musical manager in Königsberg

July   Prose draft of *Rienzi*

Aug.   Musical manager in Riga

1839

July   Flight from creditors in Riga

Historical Events	Wagner's Personal History
	Aug. With Minna and Robber in London
	Sept. Arrival in Paris; start of 2½ year stay
	1840
	Jan. *Faust* overture
	Nov. Completion of score of *Rienzi*
	1841
	Mar. Meets Liszt in Paris. Writes musical articles for Dresden newspaper
	May Original version of *Der fliegende Holländer*
	June *Rienzi* accepted by Dresden court theatre
	Nov. Completion of score of *Der fliegende Holländer*
	Dec. Draft of *Die Sarazenin*
1842	**1842**
Liszt appointed *Hofkapellmeister* in Weimar	Reads 'Tannhäuser' and 'Lohengrin' legends
	7 Apr. Wagner and Minna leave Paris for Dresden
	June Prose draft of *Tannhäuser*
	20 Oct. Première of *Rienzi*

Historical Events **Wagner's Personal History**

1843

2 Jan.   Première of *Der fliegende Holländer*

1844

Dec.   Weber's remains arrive in Dresden from London. Wagner organizes ceremony

1845

25 Aug.   Birth of future King Ludwig II of Bavaria

1845

July   Prose sketch of *Die Meistersinger*

19 Oct.   Première of *Tannhäuser*

Nov.   Reads poem of 'Lohengrin' to members of the *Engelklub*

1847

Nov.   Death of Mendelssohn in Leipzig

1848

Communist Manifesto

Feb. Fall of the 'July' Monarchy in Paris

May   National parliamentary assembly in Frankfurt

1848

Jan. Death of his mother in Leipzig

Apr.   *Lohengrin* score completed. Meets the revolutionary Bakunin

Oct.   Prose sketch of the later *Der Ring des Nibelungen*

Dec. Reads poem 'Siegfrieds Tod' to circle of friends

Historical Events	Wagner's Personal History
	1849
	Jan. 'Jesus of Nazareth'
	Feb. Start of close friendship with Liszt
	May Dresden uprising. Warrant for Wagner's arrest. Flees from Germany; crosses Lake Constance in steamer and arrives in Zurich
	Sept. Minna, with dog and parrot, in Zurich
	1850
	Feb. Wagner in Paris
	Mar. Jessie Laussot adventure
	28 Aug. Première of *Lohengrin* in Weimar in Wagner's absence
	Sept. First idea of a *Ring* festival
1851	1851
	Jan. *Oper und Drama*
	May Prose sketch of *Der junge Siegfried*
	Aug. *Eine Mitteilung an meine Freunde* (Communication to My Friends)
	Nov. Prose sketches of *Das Rheingold* and *Die Walküre*
2 Dec. Louis-Napoleon's 'coup d'état' Première of Verdi's *Rigoletto* in Venice	

Historical Events	Wagner's Personal History
	1852
	Feb. Meets the Wesendonks
1853	**1853**
de Gobineau's 'Essau sur l'inégalité des races humaines'	Feb. Private edition in Zurich of the 'Ring' poem
Premières in Rome and Venice of Verdi's *Il Trovatore* and *La Traviata*	Sept. 'The Vision of La Spezia'
	Oct. Meets the sixteen-year-old Cosima in Paris
	1854
	Friendship with Mathilde Wesendonk
	Sept. Reading of Schopenhauer
	First thoughts about *Tristan und Isolde*
	1855
	2 Mar. – 30 June Wagner in London
	Summer Attacks of erysipelas
1856	
Heine dies in Paris	
1857	**1857**
Aug. Cosima marries Hans von Bülow	Apr. Wagners move into the Asyl in grounds of Villa Wesendonk

Historical Events	Wagner's Personal History
	June Discontinues composing *Siegfried* in Act II
	Sept. 'Tristan' poem
1858	**1858**
Dec. Birth of Puccini in Lucca	Aug.–Dec. In Venice
	1859
	Mar. Leaves Venice
	6 Aug. Completes score of *Tristan und Isolde*
	Oct. In Paris
1859	
Publication of Darwin's *The Origin of Species*	
1860	**1860**
July Birth of Mahler	Mar. Visits Rossini in Paris
Sept. Death of Schopenhauer	
1861	**1861**
Liszt settles in Rome and becomes Abbé Liszt	13 Mar. Première of the 'Paris' *Tannhäuser*
1862	**1862**
	Feb. Poem of 'Die Meistersinger'

Historical Events	Wagner's Personal History
	Settles in Biebrich
Aug. Birth of Claude Debussy	Parting from Minna
Sept. Bismarck becomes Prussian prime minister	Friendship with Mathilde Maier and with Friederike Meyer

1863

22 May   50th birthday

1864	1864
10 Mar. Accession of Ludwig II of Bavaria	Mar. Flees from Vienna to escape creditors
	3 May Found by Pfistermeister in Stuttgart
	4 May Meets Ludwig II in Munich
	Sept. Resumes composition of *Siegfried*
	Oct. Moves into Brienner-strasse in Munich

1865

10 Apr.   Birth of Isolde von Bülow, first child of Wagner and Cosima

10 June   Première of *Tristan und Isolde*

July   Starts dictating autobiography *Mein Leben* to Cosima

Dec.   Wagner is forced to leave Munich

Historical Events	Wagner's Personal History
1866	1866
	Apr. Moves into Tribschen outside Lucerne
June Outbreak of Austro-Prussian War	
3 July Defeat of Austria at Königgrätz	
1867	1867
Jan. Engagement of Ludwig II to his cousin Sophie	
	Feb. Birth of Eva, second child of Wagner and Cosima
Oct. Ludwig breaks off his engagement	
1868	1868
	21 June Première of *Die Meistersinger* in Munich
Nov. Rossini dies in Paris	8 Nov. Meets Nietzsche in Leipzig
1869	1869
Mar. Berlioz dies in Paris	
	6 June Birth of Siegfried Wagner
	Sept. Munich première of *Das Rheingold*
1870	1870
	June Munich première of *Die Walküre*
13 July The Ems telegram	

Historical Events	Wagner's Personal History
19 July Franco-Prussian War	
	25 Aug. Marriage of Wagner and Cosima
2 Sept. French defeat at Sedan	
	25 Dec. *Siegfried-Idyll*

1871	1871
Jan. German Empire proclaimed at Versailles	Jan. Composition of *Kaisermarsch*
	Feb. Completion of *Siegfried*
	Apr. In Bayreuth

1872

Apr.   Wagners remove from Tribschen to Bayreuth

22 May   Laying of foundation stone for Festspielhaus

1874

Apr.   Move into Wahnfried

21 Nov.   Completion of *Ring*

1876

6–10 Aug.   Ludwig II in Bayreuth for *Ring* rehearsals

13 Aug.   Opening of festival

Sept.–Dec.   Wagners in Italy

1877

30 April–4 June   In London

Historical Events	Wagner's Personal History
	1880
	Nov. Last meeting in Munich with Ludwig II
	1882
	Jan. Completion of *Parsifal* in Palermo
	July 26 Première of *Parsifal* at Bayreuth
	1883
	13 Feb. Death in Venice

Bibliography

WAGNER'S WRITINGS

Gesammelte Schriften und Dichtungen, Leipzig, 1871–83, 10 vols.

Die Musikdramen, ed. Joachim Kaiser, Hoffmann & Campe, 1971.

My Life, authorized translation from German, New York: Dodd, Mead, 1911, 2 vols.

Wagner-Lexikon, ed. Carl Friedrich Glasenapp, Stuttgart, 1883.

WAGNER'S CORRESPONDENCE

Briefe en eine Putzmacherin, Berlin, 1906.

Correspondence of Wagner and Liszt, trans. F. Nueffer, H. Grevel, London, 1888, 2 vols.

König Ludwig II und Richard Wagner Briefwechsel, Karlsruhe, 1936–9, 5 vols.

The Letters of Richard Wagner to Anton Pusinelli, trans. and ed. with critical notes by E. Lenrow, New York: Knopf, 1932.

The Nietzsche-Wagner Correspondence, London: Duckworth, 1922.

Richard to Minna Wagner, Letters to His First Wife, trans. with a preface by W. A. Ellis, New York: Charles Scribners, 1909, 2 vols.

Sämtliche Briefe, ed. Gertrud Strobel, Leipzig, 1967–77, 3 vols. (12 further volumes are planned.)

WAGNER'S DRAMATIC WORKS

Die Feen, 1833.

Das Liebesverbot, oder Die Novize von Palermo, 1834–6.

Rienzi, der letzte der Tribunen, 1838–40.

299

Der fliegende Holländer, 1841.

Tannhäuser, oder Der Sängerkrieg auf der Wartburg, 1841–5.

Lohengrin, 1845–8.

Tristan und Isolde, 1857–9.

Der Ring des Nibelungen. Ein Bühnenfestspiel in drei Tagen und einem Vorabend.
> *Das Rheingold*, 1852–4.
> *Die Walküre*, 1852–6.
> *Siegfried (Der junge Siegfried)*, 1851–71.
> *Götterdämmerung (Siegfrieds Tod)*, 1848–74.

Parsifal, 1877–82.

WAGNER'S INSTRUMENTAL AND VOCAL WORKS

Arrangement von Beethovens IX. Symphonie für Klavier, 1830.

Paukenschlag-Overtüre in B-dur, 1830.

Klaviersonate in B-dur, Opus 1, 1832.

Ouvertüre und Schlussmusik zu 'König Enzio', 1832.

Grosse Konzert-Ouvertüre in C-dur für Orchester, 1832.

Sieben Kompositionen zu Goethes 'Faust', 1832.

Symphonie in C-dur, 1832.

Ouvertüre Polonia. Started 1832, ended 1836.

Neujahrs-Kantate zum 1 Januar 1835.

Christoph Columbus. Ouvertüre für grosses Orchester, 1835.

Ouvertüre 'Rule Britannia', 1837.

Die beiden Grenadiere. Lied. 1839–40.

Eine Faust-Ouvertüre, 1840.

Das Liebesmahl der Apostel, 1843.

Gruss seiner Treuen an Friedrich August den Geliebten, 1844.

Zur feierlichen Heimbringung der sterblichen Ueberreste Carl Maria von Webers. Trauermarsch und Gesang. 1844.

Eine Sonate für das Album der Frau M. W., 1853.

Zwei Albumblätter in C-dur und As-dur, 1861.

Huldigungsmarsch, 1864.

Siegfried-Idyll für kleines Orchester, 1870.

Kaisermarsch fur grosses Festorchester und Volksgesang, 1871.

Albumblatt in Es-dur, 1875.

Grosser Festmarsch zur Eröffnung der 100 jährigen Gedenfeier der Unabhängigkeitserklärung der Vereinigten Staaten 1876 (US centenary march).

BIOGRAPHIES AND CRITICAL STUDIES

Adorno, T., *Versuch uber Wagner*, Berlin, 1952.

Barth, H., et al., *Wagner, A Documentary Study*, New York: Oxford University Press, 1975.

Baudelaire, Charles, 'Richard Wagner et *Tannhäuser* à Paris' (1861), in *The Painter of Modern Life and Other Essays*, trans. and ed. Jonathan Mayne, London: Phaidon Press, 1964.

Blunt, W., *The Dream King*, London: Hamish Hamilton, 1970.

Burrell, Hon. Mrs, *Richard Wagner, His Life and Works 1813–1834*, London, 1898.

Channon, H., *The Ludwigs of Bavaria*, London: Methuen, 1933.

Dahlhaus, Carl, *Richard Wagner's Musikdramen*, Regensburg, 1971.

Dujardin, E., *Revue Wagnérienne*, Paris, 1885–8, 3 vols.

Glasenapp, C. F., *Life of Richard Wagner*, trans. Wm. Ashton Ellis, London: Kegan Paul, 1900–8, 6 vols.

Gutman, Robert W., *Richard Wagner: The Man, His Mind, and His Music*, New York: Harcourt Brace Jovanovich, 1968.

Kapp, J., *Richard Wagner Eine Biographie*, Berlin, 1910.
    The Loves of Richard Wagner, London: W. H. Allen, 1951.

Kindermann, Heinz, *Theater-geschichte Europas*, Salzburg, 1965.

Lichtenberger, H., *Richard Wagner – poète et penseur*, Paris, 1898.

Lippert, W., *Wagner in Exile 1849–1862*, London: Harrap, 1930.

Mayer, Hans, *Richard Wagner in Selbstzengnissen und Bilddokumenten*, Hamburg, 1959.

Neumann, Angelo, *Personal Recollections of Wagner*, trans. by Edith Livemore, New York: Henry Holt, 1908.

Newman, E., *The Life of Richard Wagner*, New York: Knopf, 1933–49, 4 vols.
    Fact and Fiction about Wagner, London: Cassell, 1931.

Pourtales, G. de, *Richard Wagner: the Story of an Artist*, trans. Lewis May, Westport: Greenwood, 1972.

Praeger, F., *Wagner as I Knew Him*, London: Longmans, 1892.

Shaw, Bernard, *The Perfect Wagnerite*, Chicago: Herbert S. Stone, 1899.

Wallace, W., *Richard Wagner as He Lived*, New York: Harper, 1925.

Westernhagen, Curt v., *Wagner*, Zurich, 1968.

Index